Japan

Japan

A New Kind of Superpower?

EDITED BY CRAIG GARBY AND
MARY BROWN BULLOCK

THE WOODROW WILSON CENTER PRESS
Washington, D.C.

THE JOHNS HOPKINS UNIVERSITY PRESS
Baltimore and London

Editorial offices:

The Woodrow Wilson Center Press

370 L'Enfant Promenade, S.W., Suite 704

Washington, D.C. 20024-2518

Telephone 202-287-3000, ext. 218

Order from:

The Johns Hopkins University Press

Hampden Station

Baltimore, Maryland 21211

Telephone 1-800-537-5487

2   4   6   8   9   7   5   3   1

Library of Congress Cataloging-in-Publication Data

Japan : a new kind of superpower? / edited by Craig Garby and
Mary Brown Bullock.

   p.   cm.

Includes bibliographical references and index.

   ISBN 0-943875-62-5 (alk. paper).—ISBN 0-943875-63-3 (alk. paper: pbk.)

   1. Japan—Foreign economic relations.   2. Japan—Foreign
relations—1989–   3. Japan—Economic policy—1989–   4. World
politics—1989–   I. Garby, Craig.   II. Bullock, Mary Brown.

HF1601.J3518   1994   94-25031
337.52—dc20   CIP

Contents

Contents

Tables and Figures

Tables

Figures

Acknowledgments

The editors would like to thank all who participated in the conference, "Japan and the World," which took place at the Woodrow Wilson Center from January 27–28, 1992. The chapters in this volume are drawn from papers presented at the conference, and in their revisions, benefited from the recommendations from commentators and participants.

Funds for the conference and this volume were provided by the Pew Charitable Trusts, the Rockefeller Brothers Fund, the Woodrow Wilson Center Conference Fund, and the Xerox Foundation.

Benjamin Self of the Asia Program and Carolee Belkin Walker and Traci Nagle of the Woodrow Wilson Center Press were of great assistance in the final stages of editing and production.

Japan

Introduction

Japan and the World

CRAIG GARBY and MARY BROWN BULLOCK

THE EARLY 1990s brought momentous change to Japan and the international world order. The collapse of the Soviet empire, the inauguration of the Heisei era, and the defeat of the Liberal Democratic Party signalled a new era both at home and abroad. While a lingering economic recession cast some doubt on the Japanese economic miracle, there remained no question but that Japan is emerging in this post–cold war world as an entirely new type of power: an economic superpower.

A spate of historic anniversaries reminds us that Japan's changing world role has been a hallmark of this century. The fiftieth anniversary of Pearl Harbor was observed in television documentaries, academic conferences, and muted national ceremonies. Less attention, perhaps, may be given to the 1994 centennial of Asia's first modern war in which the small island nation successfully challenged its giant neighbor, China, and emerged as the Pacific's twentieth-century power. Looking ahead, however, it is clear that the fiftieth anniversary of Hiroshima will not go unnoticed. In a region where concerns about nuclear proliferation have intensified, world memory will be sensitized anew to the debates and horrors of the atomic age.

Japan has been to slow to wrestle with the legacies of the kind of power it wielded during World War II. But with the passing of the Showa Emperor, and in the interval between the anniversaries of Pearl Harbor and V-J Day, serious efforts are being made to come to grips with the past in order to forge a new international identity. Wide-reaching domestic polit-

1

ical reform and continuing economic recession have softened Japan's image of invincibility. When Hiroshima becomes the focus of world memorials, the attendant empathy toward Japanese victims may seem less discordant.

During 1992 and 1993 a minuet of state visits and multilateral conferences involving Japan and its erstwhile World War II adversaries symbolized the ascribed role of Japan in any "new world order." Emperor Akihito made a quietly successful diplomatic mission to China, expressing "regret" for the "unfortunate period" in which Japan "inflicted sufferings on the people of China." Prime Minister Morihiro Hosokawa travelled to Kyongju, capital of Korea during the height of the Silla Dynasty, to meet with President Kim Young-sam. Images of Japanese leaders touring cultural sites that emphasize the glorious traditions of China and Korea, coupled with more explicit apologies for wartime atrocities, helped to ease Japan's relations with its nearest neighbors. With regard to Russia and the Northern Islands, however, Japan held firm. It was Boris Yeltsin who finally travelled to Tokyo, but gained little in return. In the most ill-fated international venture of his term, U.S. President George Bush also travelled to Tokyo, accompanied by the chief executive officers of the American automobile industry, only to require assistance from Prime Minister Kiichi Miyazawa when he became ill at a state dinner. Assuaging regional fears, asserting national sovereignty, accommodating an important ally—these are emergent political themes of economic superpower Japan.

Tokyo has yet to become the center of state-to-state relations, and its relatively passive role in the recent Asia-Pacific Economic Cooperation conference in Seattle reveals continuing uncertainty regarding its regional and global roles. Nonetheless, Japan's late-twentieth-century role contrasts with both historic and more recent concepts of Japanese passivism in foreign relations, from Japan being forced to "open" in the nineteenth century to Japan being the recipient of *gaiatsu* (foreign pressure) in recent decades. Speaking at the Woodrow Wilson Center's conference on "Japan and the World" in January 1992, from which this collection of essays evolved, former Senator Howard Baker recalled the famous "opening of Japan":

> In 1845, Commodore James Biddle sailed into Tokyo Bay on a mission to establish contact between the United States and Japan. Commodore Biddle's ship was surrounded by vessels from the Japanese Coastal Guard and he was forced to withdraw without ever setting foot on Japanese soil.
>
> Eight years later, President Millard Fillmore dispatched Commodore Matthew Perry in another attempt. Commodore Perry, escorted

this time by an armed squadron of U.S. Navy ships, came to anchor in Tokyo Bay in July of 1853. His display of military might, though he was under orders not to use force, so impressed the ruling shogun that the shogun readily agreed to accept a letter from the President to the Japanese Emperor proposing the opening of diplomatic and trade relations between Japan and the United States.

Well versed in the ways of oriental culture, Commodore Perry immediately set sail for Macao, returning to Japan seven months later with an even larger squadron of ships to inquire if the Japanese leadership had any response to President Fillmore's letter. Now, the response was entirely positive. In the tiny village of Yokohama, the shogun and the commodore exchanged gifts, Japanese lacquers, bronzes, porcelain and brocade for an American telegraph instrument, a steam locomotive built to one-quarter-scale, a copy of James Audubon's *Birds and Quadrupeds of America* and various farm implements and firearms, as well as a barrel of whiskey.

Amid these tokens of new friendship, the shogun and the commodore signed the Treaty of Kanagawa which allowed the United States to establish a consulate in Japan and to sail vessels into certain Japanese ports for supplies and repairs, and to be guaranteed good treatment of castaways from American whaling ships which had the unhappy tendency to founder with considerable frequency on Japanese shoals.

A more recent equivalent of "gunboat diplomacy" has been the *gaiatsu* applied by Japan's trading partners in efforts to open the Japanese market. In his chapter on Japan's political economy, Kozo Yamamura notes that the era of *gaiatsu* began in the 1960s because Japan's trading partners were already being hurt by the strategic trade policies of Japan.

Inherent in the linked concepts of "opening" and *gaiatsu* is a passive Japan that reacts to global interests only when provoked or intimidated. Historically, however, Japan's response has seldom corresponded faithfully to the stimuli. The Meiji modernizers in Japan "opened" with a vengeance, drawing on the latent strengths of the Tokugawa society and economy, as well as selective Western models, to propel an Asiatic nation to military and economic dominance—hardly Commodore Perry's original intention. And more recently, *gaiatsu* in and of itself has had mixed results. As Yamamura points out, by liberalizing slowly and selectively, Japanese firms and financial institutions have in fact retained maximum competitiveness and ensured access to foreign markets.

Today, "new world order," "global interdependence," and "global responsibility" are catchphrases. Once again Japan is being prodded by the outside world to forsake its insular preoccupation and take on an as yet unspecified global role. Much has been written about Japan's failure to assume global responsibilities commensurate with its economic reach. But what do we really know about Japan's potential global role, politically, economically, or regionally? How influential is the Japanese model? What does the term "economic superpower" really mean?

This collection of essays seeks to explore some of these questions. The perspectives are international, including authors from Japan, the United States, Europe, Southeast Asia, and Latin America. The issue is not how the world hopes to define Japan's international responsibilities but how Japan has already begun to shape its own global role.

In the first section, "The Evolving Dimensions of Japanese Power," the political, economic, and military aspects of the Japanese model are examined. Western analysts have increasingly abandoned the neoclassical economist's view of Japan as simply a successful practitioner of Western capitalism and have begun to perceive Japan as innovating a very different version of capitalist political economy. There has not, however, been wide agreement on the specific characteristics of this new model. Questions arise over the nature of Japanese democracy and whether or not Japan as a global leader will be receptive to the needs and desires of other countries, let alone Japan's own citizens. Analysts disagree about the relationship between Japanese government and industry, and the capacity of Japan to open more fully to the international economy. And many question the ability of Japan, still the junior partner in U.S.-Japanese security arrangements, to develop and project military power while retaining its status as a nonwarring state.

In each of these realms—governance, political economy, and security—Japan exhibits unmistakable evolution. In his chapter "Democracy in Japan," T. J. Pempel concludes that in this century, Japan has moved from an authoritative constitutional government to a government that, although far from perfect, can only be labeled democratic. The recent defeat of the Liberal Democratic Party (LDP) by the ballot box and restructuring of the Japanese electoral system further substantiates his thesis.

Pempel writes that the Meiji Constitution, which prevailed in Japan from late in the nineteenth century until the middle of this century, was not designed with democracy as an underlying principle or a primary goal; rather, it was designed to facilitate national cohesion and centralized authority. Japan's circumscription of democratic rights during that period was not unique, however, as even leading Western nations concurrently denied democratic privileges to segments of their respective societies. Furthermore, Pempel asserts, Japanese institutions allowed for increased democratization of the political system over time. The democratic system established in postwar Japan thus had some roots in earlier times and did not represent a total break with Japanese history.

During the Occupation, Americans strove to establish the political, economic, and social conditions that would transform Japan into a nonwarring democracy. Pempel examines constitutional rights, economic and social discrimination, the education system, and state intrusion into the nonpolitical sphere in contemporary Japan. He also analyzes civil society in Japan, including the media, interest groups, and political parties. Finally, he addresses the powers of Japanese big business, the bureaucracy, and the historic role of the LDP. He concludes that, despite many shortcomings, Japanese democracy now possesses most of the features normally associated with the Western democracies; thus, Japan is empirically close to the democracies of Western Europe, North America, and Australasia.

In his chapter "The Deliberate Emergence of a Free Trader: The Japanese Political Economy in Transition," Yamamura finds that Japan is in the process of changing from a relatively closed, unified practitioner of strategic trade to a more open, multidimensional exponent of free trade—with a twist. Japan's largest firms and financial institutions, fearful of losing access to foreign markets, are liberalizing *selectively*.

Yamamura examines the economic policies formulated by business, the bureaucracy, and the LDP, a collection that he terms the "power group." In the 1950s and 1960s, this group made full use of the institutions it created or adapted from its prewar predecessors and pursued the economic policy of "catching up" with the West. Although Japan was not a strong state, the power group exerted its influence extensively in civil society. A myriad of policies, writes Yamamura, made Japan an effective practitioner of strategic trade policy, with all of the implications for its trading partners.

Yamamura notes that by the late 1960s, however, the political consensus for rapid growth had eroded. Catch-up economic growth came to an end in one industry after another. Yamamura examines the LDP politicians' growing dependence on big business support, with the declining influence wielded by the bureaucracy over business and the *gaiatsu* applied by Japan's foreign trading partners.

Yamamura argues that the largest firms and financial institutions, fearing they would be denied access to foreign markets and technology, significantly changed Japanese economic institutions by the 1980s. Capital markets began to be liberalized, and numerous trade-impeding inspections, certifications, and other requirements began to be eliminated. But these newly converted free traders, Yamamura writes, exercise their power to liberalize economic institutions selectively, thus severely limiting the pace of change in many areas. They carefully weigh their dependence on foreign markets and technology against their desires to retain the institutions that made them so efficient.

Thus, Yamamura's model of Japanese political economy is neither that of the neoclassical economist, in which Japanese economic institutions change in response to market forces and the needs of the electorate, nor that of the revisionist, in which Japan's unique economic and political institutions conspire to increase Japan's economic power. Instead, Yamamura argues that the evolving Japanese political economy now has elements of both—it is a "selective free trader." Furthermore, Yamamura maintains that this Japan, a nation that increasingly exerts its financial, technological, and managerial powers globally, is a new kind of superpower.

Peter J. Katzenstein and Nobuo Okawara, in "Japanese Security Issues," examine a more traditional aspect of Japan as a superpower: its national security status. Japan, after having innovated a pragmatic concept for "comprehensive security," is found to be evolving gradually into a military power and having difficulty reconciling this with its deeply felt status as a nonwarring democracy.

Japan's military policies in the postwar era can be characterized by extreme restraint and caution. The renunciation-of-war chapter of Japan's new constitution promulgated in 1947 and the Mutual Cooperation and Security Treaty of 1960 have strongly influenced the structure and roles of Japan's postwar military. Article 9 of the constitution states:

> Aspiring sincerely to an international peace based on justice and order, the Japanese people forever renounce war as a sovereign right of the nation and the threat or use of force as a means of settling international disputes.
>
> In order to accomplish the aim of the preceding paragraph, land, sea, and air forces, as well as other war potential, will never be maintained. The right of belligerency of the state will not be recognized.

The U.S.-Japanese Mutual Cooperation and Security Treaty of 1960, emphasizing principles of democracy, individual liberty, and the rule of law, as well as economic cooperation, underscored Japan's nonwarring status. Katzenstein and Okawara write that Tokyo literally considered this a treaty of mutual security and cooperation, not an alliance. One goal of Japan's postwar security policy, they continue, was to prevent Japan from being drawn into the global affairs of the United States and the defense of the Western Pacific. And the American nuclear umbrella created conditions that facilitated Japan's economic expansion.

At the same time, Japan innovated the concept of "comprehensive security," which defines national security by the economic as well as the military dimensions of security. Katzenstein and Okawara argue that this concept provided a rationale to keep defense spending under control during a period in which the Americans were applying pressure for increased Japanese military spending. The policies also were popular with the Japanese public, which vehemently opposed the remilitarization of Japan.

Between the 1960s and the 1980s, however, defense links between the United States and Japan gradually grew, so that Japan's defensive military posture changed significantly. Indeed, Katzenstein and Okawara contend that the security links have grown so much that the U.S.-Japan relationship now constitutes a de facto military alliance.

Katzenstein and Okawara also examine the changes coming in Japan's willingness to send its Self Defense Forces overseas to participate in U.N. peacekeeping operations. Japan has followed deliberate policies of extreme caution and restraint in this area, fearing evoking memories of Japanese military aggression, but with the sending of minesweepers to the Persian Gulf and peacekeeping forces to Cambodia and elsewhere, Japan's stance has changed.

Katzenstein and Okawara address Japan's rapid move to the frontiers of high technology, which makes Japan a potentially major military power. And the erosion of the informal ban of the Ministry of International Trade and Industry on the export of dual-use technologies in recent years, they note, further underscores the potential military prominence of Japan in the coming decades. In sum, Katzenstein and Okawara find that the incremental policy changes adopted by Japan and the technological nature of Japan's weapons now present a base from which a national military option could be pursued, unlikely as that may be.

Thus, this section suggests that Japan is indeed a superpower, but one that differs from superpowers of old. Japan's greatest strength lies in its continuing development of innovative financial, managerial, and technological systems. Japan's concept of "comprehensive security" and its refusal to separate economic from military considerations in security establish a remarkably efficient and pragmatic model of a superpower.

However, Japan's assumption of greater international responsibilities and leadership will not occur without difficulties. As Pempel points out, Japanese democracy is not a socially liberal democracy. From ethnic, linguistic, religious, and cultural perspectives, Japan is not a pluralistic country; hence, the capacity of Japanese institutions to contend with social pluralism has not developed to the same extent as in other democracies. The jury is out on the consequences.

In the second section, "Japan in a Multipolar World," Japan's role and status in regional economic bloc formation are examined. Rather than beginning an analysis of Japan in the world with a discussion of U.S.-Japanese relations, which could be considered the independent variable, this section addresses Japan's relationships with Europe, the Americas, and Asia, the dependent variables that change as the U.S.-Japanese relationship changes. In this manner, new light can be shed on Japan and the U.S.-Japanese relationship, and both can be seen in broadened contexts. What emerges is striking: Japan's internationalization, or its "insiderization" process, is extensive; the perception of Japan as a relevant new paradigm is growing; and regional uncertainties concerning Japan remain.

In his chapter "Japan and E.C. '92," Henri-Claude de Bettignies reveals that while the Europeans have been preoccupied with the painful process of building a Common Market, the Japanese presence in Europe has grown much more rapidly than the European presence in Japan. De Bettignies compares the current European-Japanese situation with that of Europe and America thirty years ago, emphasizing that despite initial panic in the face of the "American challenge," Europe adapted to and learned from the United States. The analogy is not perfect, however, for he notes that Japan's market today is more closed than that of America thirty years ago. De Bettignies examines the factors behind Japan's extensive investment in Great Britain and its growing investment in Germany, France, and the rest of Europe.

Carlos J. Moneta, in "Japan and the North American Free Trade Agreement," also points out the importance of Japan's internationalization. He observes, however, that in recent years Latin American exports to Japan have been losing ground to those of the newly industrialized Asian countries. Furthermore, he writes that even though Southeast Asian nations have been exporting more and more manufactured goods to Japan, Latin America still exports largely primary products. The successful passage of the North American Free Trade Agreement (NAFTA) in late 1993 may further weaken the Japanese–Latin American connection.

Lee Poh-ping, in "Japan and the Asia-Pacific Region: A Southeast Asian Perspective," reveals that Japan now trades more with Asia than with the United States and that this increase in trade has Asia clamoring for Japan to open its market further. Indeed, he writes that a number of Asia-Pacific nations are urging Japan to become an Asian leader, developing the region on one level while representing Asia in forums such as the Group of Seven on another. Japan's Asian leadership, however, will be complicated by the attitudes of China, which considers Japan more a rival for influence than a leader.

De Bettignies also observes an acceleration of Japan's "insiderization" process, whereby Japanese management maintains direct contact in regions throughout the world in order to obtain immediate market information from vendors, suppliers, users, and consumers. And Moneta writes that changes in foreign direct investment trends and in transnational corporation strategies indicate that Japan is seeking a role as "internal actor" in each of the other world economic centers by establishing a network of productive enterprises, integrated at the regional level and increasingly independent of the parent companies.

Several countries now actively emulate the Japanese model. Lee argues that Japan studiously avoided spreading an ideology of its own, following the disaster of its Greater East Asia Co-Prosperity Sphere but that, nonetheless, Japan's stunning developmental success served as a model for Southeast Asian nations in particular to imitate. And de Bettignies writes that Europe too sees Japan as the new champion exemplifying a radically different paradigm, a different mindscape. He notes that the difficult access to the Japanese market, the low levels of manufactured goods imported, the collusive behavior of economic and political actors in Japan, and the subtle but effective invisible hand of the system convince many Europeans that Japanese capitalism is a peculiar brand of developmental state capitalism in which the invisible hand of the market is rigged. Yet Japan's performance forces us to question the Western model, he asserts, because the Japanese system seems to work better than the West's.

Japan's very success also is arousing regional uncertainties concerning Japan. De Bettignies observes that Europeans are worried about the erosion of U.S. global leadership and wonder whether Japan will be able to lead while the United States confronts its domestic problems, an inward-looking Europe attempts to build a post-1992 identity, and the former Soviet Union struggles in disarray. He asks: "Can Japan play the role played by the United States in the 1960s? Has Japan a 'mission,' an 'ideal,' to promote?" Lee writes that the uncertainties over Japan in Asia, although not uniform from country to country, tend to lie in the military sphere rather than in the economic sphere. He notes that memories of Japanese aggressions in World War II matter little now in economic relations, although in security cooperation, such memories do have an impact. Moneta, writing before NAFTA, concludes that Latin American countries, rather than feeling uncertain, see in Japan the opportunity both to offset the predominant U.S. presence and to diversify economic ties, obtain investments, acquire technologies, and gain access to new markets.

In the final section, "Japan in Multilateral Settings," Japan's evolving roles in the international monetary regime, international aid, and the United Nations are examined. Widespread controversy still surrounds the degree to which Japan has assumed global responsibilities. How involved is Japan in accepting global leadership? What is Japan's vision of its own international role? Typical of the conflicting views are the final three chapters in this book. Koichi Hamada, in "Japan's Prospective Role in the International Monetary Regime," presents Japan in the institutionally mechanistic setting of international monetary policy and notes that Japan is gradually assuming greater responsibilities within the confines of the present system. Susan J. Pharr, in "Japanese Aid in the New World Order," presents a pragmatic and increasingly assertive Japan that is pushing an innovative model of developmental capitalism in its aid policies. Robert M. Immerman, in "Japan in the United Nations," questions the explicitly political aspects of Japan's quest for international leadership and criticizes Japan's motives.

What emerges from these three chapters is the differing degree of confidence and assertiveness with which Japan engages these international arenas. Hamada suggests that in international monetary issues, Japan's powerful position is not yet fully mature, that Japan is still growing and filling its position within the current regime. Hamada, examining the openness of Japan's financial markets, the international use of the yen, the world economy's need for Japanese funds, and the potential role of Japan in a new international monetary regime, describes a cautious but quietly influential Japan working within the rules of the present monetary system.

Hamada points out that the Ministry of Finance is deregulating and internationalizing the qualitatively immature Japanese financial market but that it is proceeding slowly in an effort to avoid a U.S.-style savings and loan debacle. He asserts that Japan has not yet fostered international entrepreneurship in the finance industry, although this appears close at hand.

And he argues that although Japan is one of the most influential countries in economic institutions such as the International Monetary Fund, questions remain concerning Japanese political and, more important, intellectual leadership.

In the realm of international aid, Pharr finds Japan adopting an assertive stance and maintains that Japan's economic leadership in the Third World will be an important foreign policy reality in the 1990s. Indeed, Japan currently vies with the United States as the largest donor of aid to the developing world. However, Pharr reveals that Japanese aid assumes a form different from that of other donor countries. Japan continues to support economic infrastructure building in developing countries, despite strong criticism from donor countries that have long pushed other types of aid. Japan emphasizes that developing countries often request such assistance, that Japan possesses in abundance the requisite skills for providing such infrastructure building, and that even the World Bank has stressed the importance of economic infrastructure for development.

One model of Japanese aid incorporates a vision of an economically integrated Asia in which countries at all stages of development become interlinked through patterns of aid, trade, and investment. Japan, as the most developed Asian nation, would be at the top of the pyramid. Japan would extend tailored portfolios of aid to developing Asian countries, which, as they successfully developed, would then become donors themselves.

Pharr concludes that Japan is assuming a mantle of leadership in emergent international development issues. Japan's Miyazawa Plan, which later became the Brady Plan, takes the initiative in dealing with the Third World debt crisis. Japan is beginning to advocate policies linking development with international environmental concerns. And Japan is discussing linking aid to human rights and arms control.

In contrast to Pharr's view that Japanese aid leadership is rational and responsible and has taken into account the concerns of the international community, Immerman argues that Japan's motives for U.N. leadership are suspect. He contends that the professionals in Japan's Ministry of Foreign Affairs have been eclipsed by the ruling elites of the political and business communities and that incremental assumption of greater international political and economic responsibilities has been replaced by an emphasis on acquiring greater prestige and status.

Immerman asserts that even though a "U.N.-centered foreign policy" has been accepted by all segments of the political spectrum, the ideals of the United Nations have remained alien to the Japanese. Japan has sought nothing more than to pay its U.N. bills, pay lip service to the organization's ideals, and avoid being singled out for criticism by others, according to Immerman.

Immerman argues that the inability of the professionals at the Ministry of Foreign Affairs to provide leadership during the Gulf War brought political and business elites to the fore and that these communities have stressed prestige for Japan rather than policy direction for the international community. According to Immerman, this explains Japan's actively seeking the appointment of Sadako Ogata as high commissioner on refugees, Japan's vigorously campaigning for an unprecedented seventh consecutive term on the Security Council, Japan's lobbying for Yasushi Akashi's appointment as special representative in Cambodia, and Japan's pressing for a permanent position on the Security Council, while remaining passive on such substantive issues as the Gulf War, the breakup of Yugoslavia, and crises in sub-Saharan Africa.

The collapse of the LDP and the emergence of a new domestic political coalition may in time bring change to Japan's role in multilateral organizations. One early example was Prime Minister Morihiro Hosokawa's retreat from the previous administration's demand for a permanent seat on the U.N. Security Council.

Regardless of the debates concerning the degree to which Japan has accepted international leadership responsibilities, the authors of the three parts of this book agree that Japan will be a twenty-first-century power. As Japan continues to spill onto the world stage, it will continue to shake up former axioms and theorems in political economy and foreign affairs. Already, for example, Japan has begun forcing recognition of an alternative model of economic development at such institutions as the World Bank. Japan maintains that economists in these international organizations, toeing the line of laissez-faire ideology, have overlooked the benefits of Japanese-style industrial policies to promote economic development abroad. By forcing the issue now, Japan is in effect institutionalizing and exporting an alternative style of capitalism to the rest of the world. And Japanese innovation is bound to influence the international community in numerous other areas as well.

In the concluding chapter, "Japan—A Twenty-first-Century Power?" Paul Kennedy ponders which attributes great powers will possess in the next century. Transnational forces bearing down on global society—the population explosion, environmental crises, technology-driven changes in production, and revolutions in communications and finance—will create "winners" and "losers" among nations, and the old superpower combination of military, technological, financial, and cultural strengths may no longer determine a country's success. Kennedy compares how Japan, the United States, and other nations will perform in the face of these new global challenges and finds that Japan is better positioned than the rest.

Great world powers, from ancient through modern times, have in some measure transformed their era and the very definition of power. Japan's astonishing twentieth-century evolution—politically and economically, regionally and internationally—is changing our concept of "superpower." And, if this collection of essays is correct, the patterns of Japan's twenty-first-century engagement with the world are already clear.

Part I

The Evolving Dimensions of Japanese Power

Chapter 1

Democracy in Japan

T. J. PEMPEL

Introduction

THE QUESTION OF Japanese democracy poses a conundrum to many in the West, especially to Americans. On the one hand, Japan has all of the formal institutions Americans associate with democracy. On the other hand, the political news coming out of Japan on a regular basis makes one wonder if democracy exists in practice. Japan has several political parties competing in most national elections, yet one, the Liberal Democratic Party, won at least twice as many seats as any other in all elections from its formation in 1955 until it split and was replaced by a coalition government in July 1993. The Japanese electoral system, we can note, is biased. Corruption scandals haunt Japanese politics on a recurring basis. Many would contend that the Japanese bureaucracy really "runs things," whereas the elected politicians, and the parliament in particular, are comparatively weaker players in the overall system. "Behind the scenes manipulation"—such as that depicted in Michael Crichton's *Rising Sun*[1] or in Karel van Wolferen's *The Enigma of Japanese Power*[2]—is taken as a given when describing "the Japanese system," and such manipulation is perforce seen as antidemocratic. This picture is given added reality from the waves of influence-peddling scandals involving top officials. And perhaps most fundamentally, many Westerners feel that somehow or other, the Japanese people—both citizen and politician—ultimately lack a commitment to the

17

values that are associated with democracy. People like ex-Prime Minister Yasuhiro Nakasone or former Speaker of the House Yoshio Sakurauchi, when they talk disdainfully of American ethnic pluralism and how it interferes with the work ethic, are reflecting a deep Japanese suspicion of social liberalism and individual diversity. The Japanese, from such a perspective, are not democratic inside; democracy may be the *tatemae* (surface), but it certainly is not the *honne* (reality). Japan may have the formal institutions of democracy, but these are, for many, simply empty shells. This chapter will attempt to explore the broad question of Japanese democracy in a comparative perspective in an effort to gain a more sensitive appreciation of how one might assess the question of "democracy in Japan."

Background

Democracy is a term that carries heavy positive connotations. As a result, most countries in the world, despite their widely differing political, social, and economic systems, use it in some form or another to describe themselves. "People's democracies," "revolutionary democracies," "capitalist democracies," "democratic republics," "liberal democracies," "representative democracies," and "federal democracies" are but a few of the descriptions one could cite as evidence of the popularity of the term *democracy* and of the widespread differences in the types of political systems to which it is applied.

To bypass a broad theoretical debate on the relative merits of these many competing claims for the label of democracy, we can note three things. First, as the term *democracy* is commonly used by Western social scientists, it usually involves the right of citizens to determine their form of government and to choose those who will constitute that government. It also requires that government be responsive to a greater or lesser extent to the preferences of citizens. And finally, it requires that citizens' preferences be weighted relatively equally.

By such empirical and comparative standards, contemporary Japan stands comfortably with the so-called advanced industrialized democracies of Western Europe, North America, and Australasia. This was not the case before the end of World War II, but since then, Japan's political system has taken on most of the features normally associated with the Western democracies, and it is in that company that Japan now finds itself. Empirically

Japan is structurally similar to the democracies of Western Europe and North America.

At the same time, democracy in Japan, as in these other countries, is far from the purest form of absolute democracy one might imagine. Even if Japan is "democratic," there is room for increased democratization. Japan is far from the embodiment of perfect democratic ideals.

Historical Legacies

Tokugawa Japan provided many strengths on which the modern Japanese nation-state could draw as modernization and industrialization began. But democracy was neither a goal nor an outcome of the Tokugawa system or of the Meiji system that followed. Under the Meiji Constitution, which prevailed in Japan from 1889 until 1947, democracy was also neither the principal goal nor an underlying axiom of the Japanese political system. Rather, the constitution was designed to facilitate national cohesion and centralized authority. Rapid changes in Japanese society were deemed necessary by Japan's modernizing elite; only such changes, it was believed, would allow Japan to industrialize and modernize quickly and thus protect Japanese sovereignty from the imperial Western powers. A strong central authority was seen as necessary to such ends; as a result the constitution's drafters designed political institutions that would ensure a strong central government capable of acting purposefully and with minimal opposition, not institutions that would create democratic controls over the nation's rulers.

The constitution was modeled on that of Otto von Bismarck's Prussia. It was the emperor's "gift" to his people; it was neither a popularly derived nor a representatively ratified document. Under it, his authority, as articulated through behind-the-scenes advisers to the throne, was supreme. The two-house parliament included one that was purely appointive and based largely on heredity and service to the state. Powers of the elected House of Representatives, the only proto-democratic body, were severely circumscribed. Most important, elected officials had no guaranteed right to determine the composition of the executive branch of government. Instead, the cabinet and the prime minister were chosen by the emperor and his advisers.

Although electoral strength in the lower house ultimately became an important factor in the choice of governments during the 1920s, votes were always but one of many factors relevant to the selection of governments.

This point was made most obvious during the 1930s when the army, constitutionally exempt from civilian and cabinet control, became the major force in cabinet selection and went on to institute the authoritarian regime that prevailed in Japan from then until the end of World War II.

Suffrage was sharply limited to males of high economic status until universal male suffrage was introduced in 1925; women did not win the right to vote until 1947. Local governmental leaders, including prefectural governors, were appointed, not elected. State Shinto circumscribed religious and political freedoms. A tight web of laws restricted the rights of citizens to organize labor unions, political parties, and interest groups; the media was subject to strict censorship; and the police, the military, and right-wing terrorist groups subverted the civil liberties of citizens in numerous ways. Citizens' duties to the state far outweighed the constitutional and legal guarantees of citizens' rights.

Comparative Perspective

Despite all of the valid criticisms that could be leveled at the authoritarian character of prewar Japan, two points are important from a comparative perspective. First, despite all of the circumscriptions, the prewar Japanese political system contained the potential to become more democratic, and indeed it did so with time. Popular votes, political parties, the parliament, and citizens' rights all increased in political consideration by the 1920s. Such aspects of democracy had come to be far more relevant by that point than they had been in the late nineteenth century. Countergovernmental organizations such as labor unions also succeeded in gaining greater autonomy and influence by the 1920s. Antigovernmental parties, including Marxian-based parties, were able to organize, and they achieved increased popular support during the 1920s and 1930s despite governmental and police efforts at suppression. Some Japanese newspapers, and many Japanese intellectuals, struggled to achieve commendable records of autonomy, even during the war.

Second, during the late nineteenth and early twentieth centuries, the Japanese political system was by no means unique in its circumscription of democratic rights and privileges. Other countries may have been more democratic in many ways, but it is worth remembering that in the United States, for example, slavery was legal until 1862, and blacks faced severe and explicitly legal barriers to equality in many regions of the country at least until the passage of the Civil Rights Act of 1965. Catholics, Jews, and agnostics could not become members of the British parliament until well into the nineteenth century; the House of Peers, with its undemocratic privileges for the British nobility, was a powerful impediment to democratic government until the reforms of 1911. Universal male suffrage was severely restricted in Britain until 1884 and in much of the rest of Europe until after World War I; women did not get the right to vote in the United States until 1920, in Britain until 1929, in France until 1945, and in Switzerland until the 1970s. Union organizers had to confront hostile police, courts, and private security forces in the United States. and most of Europe until well into the 1920s and later in many instances.

Such comparisons do not negate the very real institutional barriers to democracy that existed in the prewar Japanese political system. Nor do they imply that democracy was meaningless in these other countries until some liberating date in the 1920s or 1940s. Rather, they suggest that although Japanese institutions were less than fully democratic, they still allowed for increased democratization of the political system over time. Moreover, to the extent that democratization has involved anything like an evolutionary process in various countries, Japan could be said to have trailed many other countries, but by not more than a few decades.

As a consequence, the postwar democratic system in Japan has undeniable roots in these earlier times, and the introduction of more democratic processes and institutions did not involve a totally radical break with the past.

Contemporary Japanese Democracy

Political Restructuring under the U.S. Occupation

When the American military forces occupied Japan following that country's surrender in 1945, they sought to establish the political, social, and economic conditions they believed would transform Japan into a nonwarring democracy. During the six and one-half years of the Occupation, numerous changes were carried out to achieve these ends.

The most important change was the comprehensive restructuring of the political system to ensure democracy. A new constitution, written by the Americans, replaced the Meiji Constitution. Under this new document, popular sovereignty replaced imperial fiat. A wide assortment of personal and political rights were guaranteed to all citizens. Both houses of parliament were made completely subject to popular elections; parliament became "the highest organ of state power." Cabinets were required to be approved by parliament, and the prime minister and at least half of the cabinet members had to be elected parliamentarians. Local governments, down to the town and village levels, were also made elective. The civil and criminal codes were drastically overhauled to make day-to-day laws compatible with the democratic principles of the constitution. In the same spirit, numerous social and economic changes were also introduced.

Citizens and Rights

Japan's constitution provides one of the world's most extensive catalogues of guaranteed citizens' rights anywhere in the world. These in turn form the basis for the day-to-day freedoms most of us associate with democracy. Among them are the right to equality under law and the absence of discrimination on the basis of race, creed, sex, social status, or family status (Art. 14); the right of freedom of conscience (Art. 19); religious freedom (Art. 20); freedom of residence and occupation (Art. 22); academic freedom (Art. 23); the right to a minimum standard of wholesome and cultured living (Art. 25); the right to an equal education (Art. 26); the right of workers to organize and bargain collectively (Art. 28); and freedom from search and seizure without specific warrants (Art. 35).

A number of specific political assurances supplement these general rights. Among the most noteworthy are the right to choose public officials through universal suffrage based on the secret ballot (Art. 15); the right to petition for political changes (Art. 16); the rights of free speech, press, and expression (Art. 21); the right of access to the courts (Art. 32); the right to hear charges on arrest and to have legal counsel (Art. 34); the right to a speedy trial (Art. 37); and freedom from testifying against oneself (Art. 38).

On balance, these are tangible and meaningful guarantees, not simply paper promises. At the same time, even a cursory familiarity with Japanese society and daily practices will reveal many specific instances in which concrete realities fall short of the stated constitutional ideal. Three broad aspects with particularly political implications can be noted: economic and social discrimination; education; and the intrusion of the Japanese state.

Economic and Social Discrimination

Citizen equality in Japan is high. Economic and social discrimination is probably no less (though probably no more) significant in Japan than in the other industrialized democracies. There are areas where it is somewhat different and many areas where it is comparatively interesting. Class counts in Japan, as in all capitalist countries, but in Japan it is surely far less significant than in Britain, for example, or France. Statistical comparisons of economic equality invariably show Japan to be more economically egalitarian than most other industrialized countries, including the United States, France, England, and Germany. In addition, a widely cited claim notes that 90 percent of Japan's citizens identify themselves as "middle class." Unemployment tends to be much lower in Japan than in most other democracies. Health care, low and declining crime rates, life expectancy, and the dispersion of consumer durables all suggest that the differences between "haves" and "have nots," though by no means absent in Japan, are far less pervasive than in many other industrialized democracies.

Yet in areas such as jobs, housing, education, marriage opportunities, and general social interaction, there is widespread and accepted discrimination against several minority groups: the offspring of Japan's traditional untouchable caste, the *burakumin*; descendants of Korean or Chinese immigrants to Japan; many other (particularly nonwhite) foreigners; the remnants of the Ainu tribes in the northern island of Hokkaido; the physically disabled; and others. Most such discrimination lacks a legal basis but is nonetheless pervasive. Little of it is ever subject to legal redress. Yet virtually all of these minorities are numerically minuscule, making the problem of discrimination in Japan of a different political magnitude than in many other industrialized countries, except for the comparably baleful effects on the individuals discriminated against.

Also worthy of note is the discrimination against women in Japan, particularly in jobs and education. Despite the constitutional provision guaranteeing sexual equality, and despite a May 1985 Equal Employment Opportunity Law, Japanese women still earn less than one-half the salaries of their male counterparts; vastly greater numbers attend only junior colleges whereas their male peers attend four-year universities; affordable child care is difficult to come by; and women are most frequently the first to be laid off during economic downturns. These and various other forms of discrimination are widespread.

Economic class divisions became more acute in the late 1980s and early 1990s as a consequence of the speculation-fueled explosion in land and housing prices. Those fortunate enough to own land or housing suddenly found themselves quite wealthy, whereas those without such equity were typically incapable of entering the market even if they were willing to consider two- or three-generation mortgages. The deflation policies of the government during 1992–93 took much of the air out of Japan's "economic bubble," but these policies did little to reduce the sharp gap between homeowners and nonhomeowners.

Education

For the formal rights of citizenship to be meaningful, a nation's citizens must have the educational and informational bases from which to make informed political decisions. Japan has one of the most extensive educational systems in the industrialized world, with 40 percent of those between the ages of eighteen and twenty-two attending institutions of higher education, compared with 45–52 percent in the United States, 26 percent in both France and Germany, and about 21 percent in Britain. Moreover, Japan's education is meaningful: there are few dropouts; Japanese students invariably outperform most of their foreign counterparts in international test competitions; and literacy is virtually 100 percent.

At the same time, many valid criticisms can be leveled at the Japanese school system. First, there is widespread emphasis on conformity over individuality. This is manifest in rigid dress codes, tight behavioral standards, the emphasis on rote memorization of facts, and the importance given to single, standardized tests. Second, for much of the period since the 1950s, the government has attempted to reintroduce moral education into the curriculum, in an effort to ensure greater nationalism and/or respect for (predemocratic) Japanese traditions. Third, the government has similarly engaged in what many have criticized as the rewriting of Japanese history, censoring, in particular, negative interpretations of Japan's foreign policy activities during the prewar period. For many, both within Japan and throughout Asia, these latter two actions revive the specter of prewar nationalist indoctrination or, at the extremes, "a return to fascism" or to right-wing extremism. Although a number of right-wing groups are politically active in Japan, most have limited memberships. Their *formal* influence in government and the economy is slight, and at present there seems little danger of their gaining anything like the institutionalized power such groups held during the prewar period.

These problems are at the heart of any comparative study of the relationship between education and democracy, raising the question of when education ends and indoctrination begins. One would be hard-pressed to find any other democracy that did not attempt to socialize its younger citizens with patriotism, loyalty, and a rather one-sided version of its national history. Thus, Japan is by no means alone in having to confront this issue, but clearly today's Japan is by all measures vastly different from its prewar predecessor.

State Intrusion and the Nonpolitical Sphere

An important but often overlooked component of democracy is that the citizen should be able to have a private life free from mobilization campaigns, the requirement to participate in state-run religious services, police surveillance, forced service to state projects, and the like. In Japan, the government collects taxes; all citizens must be registered; several radio and television stations are under government auspices; virtually all government and semigovernmental agencies engage in public relations activities designed to convince the citizen of the meritorious nature of their work; and strict laws govern various aspects of social behavior, from drunken driving to safety standards for drugs and toys to inheritance rights. Customs clearance, nosy officials, and seemingly omnipresent police officers make it clear that the Japanese state is a factor in citizens' daily life. But on balance, most Japanese citizens are free on a day-to-day basis to escape from politics and the state and to have families, pursue hobbies, engage in sports, purchase a variety of available food and clothing, work at their jobs, and socialize with friends without government oversight. In short, a relatively clear demarcation exists between "public" and "private," allowing the citizen a wide sphere of depoliticized activity. Although the committed democrat could argue for changes at the margins of many of the intrusions by the Japanese state, most aspects of Japanese private life are not vastly different from those in other countries. Again, on balance, the privacy of the citizen in Japan accords well with the maintenance of a democratic political culture.

Between Citizen and State

If one of the first requisites of democracy involves the rights of the citizen, a second is surely the need for mechanisms that permit citizens' preferences to be articulated and translated into political choices. Three such mechanisms require comment: the media; interest groups; and the system of elections and political parties.

Media

Politically independent, competitive, and widely available mass media are critical in providing citizens with access to information on the basis of which they can form reasoned opinions on political matters. Contemporary Japan has one of the world's highest rates of newspaper readership, with four national dailies blanketing the country twice a day, plus uncountable local and specialized papers. Books and magazines appealing to a wide range of tastes are available and sell widely. Total publications greatly outnumber those in most European countries on an absolute basis; on a per capita basis, Japan is on a par with most of these countries. Radios and televisions are widely available to most families. Foreign literary works, journals, and other forms of information and criticism are also broadly available. In short, the Japanese citizen is, if anything, saturated with information.

Still, many have observed a disturbingly conformist quality to Japan's major newspapers and journals. Before the January 1993 betrothal of Crown Prince Naruhito, for example, all the major Japanese media agreed that, in deference to the royal family, they would not pursue stories about potential brides for the crown prince. In general, there is a great deal of media deference to those in power. Furthermore, as a whole the press, radio, television, and journals in Japan are far more heavily devoted to apathy-inducing programming than to sharp and critical analysis. Yet editorials are frequently critical of government or official actions; numerous diverse sources of information find their way into the press; scathing criticism is readily available outside the mainstream press; and the newspapers have been at the forefront of pursuing government corruption such as the Lockheed, Recruit, and Sagawa Kyūbin scandals.

Interest Groups

A second important democratic component linking citizens to government is the formation of interest groups. Again, the Japanese situation seems vigorously democratic, since virtually any social interest one might imagine seems to be organized in Japan. Many, of course, are vastly more influential than others. But typically, most organize widely, lobby lustily, endorse or withhold endorsement of political candidates, and pursue their political or nonpolitical ends as they see fit. Petition drives, contributions, informational meetings, boycotts, leafletting, marches, sit-downs, and direct confrontations with officials are but a few of the wide range of activities carried out by the more politically active of these groups. Often criticized for the alleged selfishness they display, these interest groups are also testimony to the relative freedom of association in Japan and to the vigor with which that freedom is exercised.

Elections and Political Parties

All Japanese citizens over the age of twenty are eligible to vote. There is no literacy requirement or poll tax; registration is relatively easy; and turnout in most elections is high by international standards, typically involving two-thirds to three-quarters of the eligible voters, even in local elections.

In addition, citizens have a relatively wide range of choices among candidates, at least above the municipal level, where elections are often uncontested. Over the postwar period, Japan has had from a minimum of three to at least seven major political parties contesting for national office. These range from the relatively conservative Liberal Democratic Party (LDP), which is probusiness, proagricultural, and pro–United States, through moderate and more radical Socialist parties, such as the Social Democratic Party of Japan (SDPJ)—formerly the Japan Socialist Party (JSP)—and the Democratic Socialist Party (DSP), to the Japan Communist Party (JCP), which is legal, and the Clean Government Party (CGP), which is affiliated with a large Buddhist religious group. In 1993 a major splintering of the LDP created even more parties. In addition individuals often campaign successfully as independents or without party affiliation. Declaring one's candidacy is a relatively simple matter facing few legal barriers, even though election itself is by no means without barriers.

Two points deserve special elaboration here. First, Japanese voters have a wide range of choices among candidates, parties, and political philosophies. In addition to candidates who represent strongly nationalistic and right-of-center positions, Japan has a strong Marxian tradition. In this sense, the party spectrum in Japan is analogous to that in much of continental Europe. Certainly, the Japanese electoral and party systems provide a greater range of choices than is available in single-member district systems and/or two- or three-party systems such as those in Britain, Australia, Canada, Germany, or the United States.

Yet all electoral systems have their peculiar biases, and the Japanese case favors both the larger and the smaller parties to a slight extent; the middle-

sized parties tend to get a lower proportion of total seats than the proportion of their total vote would suggest. But these discrepancies are relatively
small. In addition, Japan has its share of election frauds, but until the
scandals of the early 1990s, these have rarely been out of line with frauds
in many other industrialized countries. Where Japan does stand out is in
the extensive gerrymandering of its districts to overrepresent rural and
semirural areas at the expense of urban areas. (Yet as anyone who has looked
at the redistricting of the state of North Carolina in 1992 can attest, the
drawing of bizarre lines for electoral districts is hardly a uniquely Japanese
phenomenon.)

At the same time, the peculiarities of the Japanese electoral system have
made it very difficult to vote *against* a party, since in the lower house of
parliament, at least until 1993, several parliamentarians have been returned
from each district but a voter could vote for only one candidate. Thus,
unlike in Britain or the United States, where a successful candidate typically
receives about 50 percent of the total vote cast or more, in Japan most
winners needed only 15–20 percent of the vote. Small groups of well-
organized supporters for any candidate could ensure his/her election, often
with a very small percent of the total vote in a constituency. And it has
been exceptionally difficult, in moments of public animosity to government
actions, to "throw the rascals out," at least when the "rascals" were seen to
be the ruling party itself. As a consequence of the same phenomenon, it
has also been difficult to see any direct impact of national issues on local
voting. As a result, several distinctly antidemocratic biases can be detected
in the mixture of the party and electoral systems in Japan, but again,
although these suggest important areas of criticism, they by no means
invalidate the broader claims to a democratic system that translates citizen
preferences into governments.

This problem and, more important, recent revelations about the high
costs of elections in Japan, with the consequent temptation of politicians
to raise vast sums of campaign money illegally, have catalyzed a drive toward
national reform of the electoral system. The key element would involve an
elimination of Japan's multimember, single-ballot system. Yet, most studies
show that a shift to a single-member district system, such as is used in the
United States or Britain, and which was long favored by the LDP, would
virtually eliminate several of Japan's smaller parties from parliament. The
Hosokawa government managed, after intense political struggle, to get an
agreement through the lower house on a mixture of the single-member
district system plus a national system of proportional representation.

thereby cutting the costs of election but retaining a relatively diverse spectrum of political representation. Although the final form of the new electoral system remains unsettled, it is clear that whatever system emerges will involve widespread compromise along a broad spectrum of political parties and competing interests; in short, the very essence of a democratic process.

Institutions of Governance

In the broadest sense, Japanese institutions of government parallel those of many other parliamentary governments. The cabinet is chosen by the parliament, which is subject to regular and free elections. So long as a cabinet enjoys the confidence of a majority of the parliamentary members, it can remain in power. On the other hand, unlike presidential systems, which require periodic elections of the chief executive, in parliamentary systems, once that confidence is lost, the cabinet can be forced to resign immediately through a vote of no-confidence. Japanese prefectural and city governments lack the specific powers often found in federal political systems, such as those of Germany, Canada, Australia, or the United States. But they have most or more of the powers found in centralized systems, such as those of Sweden, France, or Britain.

In these respects, Japanese political institutions are not dramatically different from those in most other political democracies. At the same time, a discussion of formal institutions leaves unanswered at least two questions. First, just how much actual power do elected officials have? If those subject to popular control are not in fact the political system's real decision makers, then surely democracy is circumvented. And second, once in power, just how responsive are policymakers to public control?

Power of Elected Officials

Despite its constitutional guarantee as the "highest organ of state power," the Japanese parliament is not widely accepted as such by many academics and critics. Certainly, it is not the actual lawmaking body that the U.S. Congress represents, although Congress is much more the exception than the rule among democracies. Still, the parliament in Japan has been principally a ratifier of decisions made elsewhere. At least three major candidates for the "elsewhere" can be cited: big business, the bureaucracy, and until its fall from power in 1993, the Liberal Democratic Party.

Big Business

Those who argue that big business wields the real power in Japan point to a variety of specifics, most of them linked in one way or another to variants of Marxian economic analysis. In the standard dichotomy between business and labor, the latter certainly holds very little real power in Japan and is vastly weaker politically and economically than organized labor in virtually any other industrialized democracy. Japan is also the site of some of the largest corporations and banks in the world. Nor is there any question that public policy has been good to big business in Japan over the past three decades while Japanese consumers and owners of smaller shops have often borne disproportionate costs for Japan's macroeconomic successes.

At the same time, a number of government actions involving environmental cleanups, tax revisions, liberalization of imports, changes in the retirement age, and financial and stock market liberalization have become law despite strong opposition from important voices in Japanese big business. More important, perhaps, the influence of Japanese big business has rarely been shown to be significantly greater than that of big business or finance in other industrialized democracies. Much of the criticism leveled against the allegedly undemocratic powers of Japanese big business is in fact a broad-scale criticism, equally applicable—or not—to virtually all capitalist countries. The recent savings and loan debacle in the United States, the scandalous character of recent Swedish arms sales, or the massive influence buying by businesses in Italy makes this clear.

Bureaucracy

The debate over the relative power of the elected Japanese parliament versus that of the nonelective bureaucracy has gone on for several decades and bears a similarity to the debates on related questions of power in other democracies. There is very little question that most laws are drawn up by senior civil servants, not legislators. And the national bureaucracy conducts most of the preliminary investigations and fact-finding before any legislation is written. Great discretion is left to bureaucrats to implement very broadly crafted laws. Many former bureaucrats retire to take up political careers, often in the LDP; one in four LDP parliamentarians has a bureaucratic background. Elected officials hold only the top two posts in each government agency, and usually they are in and out of office quickly, leaving the bulk of the day-to-day activities in the hands of the more permanent civil service. Most of these criticisms, in one form or another, can be mustered to debate the same issue in other parliamentary democracies, although a good deal of comparative evidence indicates that the Japanese bureaucracy is more influential in these matters than are bureaucracies in other countries.

At the same time it is important to note that the bureaucracy was for thirty-eight years (1955–93) practically speaking, under the political controls of the parliament and the long-ruling Liberal Democratic Party. Even if many bureaucratic agencies appear to be acting autonomously, it is rarely suggested that they are acting *against* the political wishes of the parliamentary majority. Thus, if the bureaucracy in Japan is powerful, as indeed most evidence suggests, its power remains broadly subject to the preferences set by the parliamentary majority. Whether the relative balance between bureaucracy and parliament will remain the same in the post-LDP era remains to be seen.

Liberal Democratic Party

Finally, many have suggested that real decision making in Japan took place within the long-ruling Liberal Democratic Party (in power from 1955 until 1993) and that only after the party had reached some form of agreement did the parliament as a body become meaningfully involved in legislation. Again the evidence is strong to suggest this is true. Very rarely did a bill that had been approved by the LDP get turned down in parliament, largely because party discipline in that body was virtually ironclad. Yet how to interpret this with regard to Japanese democracy is a somewhat different matter.

Three points are worth mentioning. First, the LDP was returned to office as the majority party from 1955 to 1993. Usually it received more than twice as many votes as its nearest competitor. As such, it had a certain democratically legitimated claim to rule. Hammering out a consensus among its members before approaching parliament did not itself thwart democracy.

Second, strong cultural and procedural norms in Japan operate against what the Japanese usually refer to as the "tyranny of the majority." Although the LDP used its majority to ram through controversial legislation on a number of occasions, cross-party consensus building was far more frequent. Usually the LDP tried to ensure support for its proposals by at least one and often more opposition parties, and few government bills passed with only LDP support. This necessitated compromises by the LDP. Indeed, many parliaments were effectively shut down when opposition party members refused to attend sessions until some compromises were worked out with the ruling party. Thus in 1992, boycotts of the Diet by opposition parties effectively stymied the entire legislative process until some such compromise was reached. Moreover, when the LDP failed, as it did in 1989, to win an electoral majority in the upper house elections, the government was also forced to make compromises with various of the smaller opposition parties. The institutional arrangements of parliamentary democracy could not be dispensed with.

Finally, this power of the opposition seems also to be a function of the electoral fortunes of the parties and "public opinion." Thus, compromises were most frequent when the parliamentary majorities of the LDP were slimmest and when issues were generating the most heat in the press and among the citizenry. The Nara by-election in early 1992 was only one recent indication of how quickly electoral results translate into governmental panic (and political responsiveness). Clearly the July 1993 split in the LDP and the installation of a coalition government demonstrates the outer limits and temporality of LDP power and again suggests the vibrancy of Japanese electoral democracy. In short, again there seem to be many democratic checks on what might otherwise appear to be a terribly unparliamentary system of governance.

Government Responsiveness beyond Elections

The question was raised above as to just how responsive Japan's apparently democratic institutions are to changing public preferences. And we saw that in fact the government must be sensitive to media concerns, to opposition demands, and to interest-group pressures. However, the extent to which the Japanese government is responsive to citizen pressures outside of regular elections can perhaps best be captured by the effectiveness of the various citizens' movements that developed around such issues as pollution, consumerism, and taxation. For the most part, these movements sprang up when existing institutions—such as bureaucratic agencies, local governments, political parties, or interest groups—failed to deal adequately with issues of concern to large numbers of citizens. Using public protest, the court system, the powers of nonestablished authorities, the media, and other sources, these movements effectively forced an otherwise nonreceptive government to act on their demands. Such protests do not always work; but the success of several of the more famous speaks volumes in favor of the ability of Japanese citizens to extract responsiveness from an otherwise recalcitrant system. Indeed, as I have argued in my work on Japan's "creative conservatism,"[3] such responsiveness was a key to the LDP's longevity.

Conclusion

The above analysis suggests that despite many shortcomings, Japanese democracy is, in most important respects, on a rough par with industrialized democracies in Western Europe, North America, and Australasia. It certainly has as much right as any of them to lay legitimate claim to the term *democracy*.

At the same time, as is equally true of the rest of the democratic group, Japan's democracy is far from perfect. There are many areas where Japanese practices fall short of democratic ideals. Most notably, Japan is not a pluralistic country; the ethnic, linguistic, religious, and cultural differences that seem so endemic to most other democracies are largely lacking in Japan. Japan's democratic institutions do not have to contend with high levels of social pluralism; hence, their capacity to do so is often less frequently subject to severe tests than have been the institutions of many other democracies. Japanese democracy is not a socially liberal democracy. Nonetheless, if Japanese democracy is to be viewed in ways that do justice to the complexity of the concept of democracy, then it is important to recognize that Japan belongs in the same broad category as the other countries typically labeled as industrialized democracies. At the same time, like the others in the group, it falls short of the perhaps inaccessible goal of democratic perfection. The areas in which Japan could become more democratic remain many indeed.

In its present guise, Japanese democracy has not been highly conducive to Japan's taking an increased leadership role in world affairs. The very power of Japan's citizens has frequently served as a brake against Japanese governmental efforts to act more firmly and independently in favor of, among other things, increasing the economic liberalization of trade and investment, dispatching Japanese troops abroad for U.N. peacekeeping missions, or sharing military technologies with the United States. In many such instances, a well-organized minority has been in the forefront of slowing down Japanese governmental leadership efforts. Presumably, for example, the majority of Japan's consumers (and many Japanese businesses) would greatly benefit from an increased liberalization of Japan's economy and greater access to Western agricultural and manufactured goods. At the same time, most public opinion polls show that a strong majority of Japanese citizens are deeply opposed to the use of Japanese military troops abroad. Thus, the recent American (and often European) clamoring for an increased world activism by Japan must confront a discomforting reality, namely that the very depth of Japanese democracy may be one of the more significant impediments to that country's moving toward such an expanded world leadership role.

Notes

1. Michael Crichton, *Rising Sun* (New York: Knopf, 1992).

2. Karel van Wolferen, *The Enigma of Japanese Power: People and Politics in a Stateless Nation* (New York: Alfred A. Knopf, 1989).

3. T. J. Pempel, *Policy and Politics in Japan: Creative Conservatism* (Philadelphia: Temple University Press, 1982).

Chapter 2

The Deliberate Emergence of a Free Trader: The Japanese Political Economy in Transition

KOZO YAMAMURA

ARE THE ESSENTIAL characteristics of the Japanese political economy unique, thus requiring a new concept of "superpower"? How will this superpower fit into the evolving new world order? To ponder these questions is to ask other questions: What are the characteristics of the Japanese political economy? Are they changing today? How are they likely to change in the coming decades, affecting the performance of the Japanese political economy and its role in the world?

These questions have for some time been cynosures of scholars, journalists, and others interested in Japan. As a result, numerous books and articles have been published offering possible answers.[1] Nonetheless, the questions remain important; political and economic realities continue to change both swiftly and in many dimensions, both in the world and in Japan.

In addressing these issues, I will first define the term *political economy* as used in this chapter. I will then describe the initial conditions of the Japanese political economy, or the conditions during the rapid growth period of the 1950s and 1960s. Japan's political economy today is shaped by the transformation of the political and economic incentives structure already existing by the 1950s and 1960s. Third, I will describe the coun-

teracting forces and developments that are retarding the pace of transformation of the initial conditions. Fourth, I will argue that despite these
counteracting forces, the Japanese political economy is changing. The
changes are being guided by the needs and desires of the new free traders,
the internationally competitive manufacturing firms and major financial
institutions that hope to retain access to global markets. The pace of
change, however, will remain slow; the free traders desire to retain select
practices from the initial conditions period, practices that enable them to
increase their ability to export and invest abroad. Last, I will offer answers
to the questions asked at the outset of this essay.

The Political Economy

By *political economy*, I mean the political and economic institutions that
determine the structure of incentives shaping political and economic interactions. Institutions are defined broadly to include laws, policies, norms
of behavior, and institutions in the ordinary sense of the term—all of which
determine the characteristics, behavior, and performance of the polity and
economy. Institutions change, reflecting individual and collective beliefs,
preferences, and strategies, which themselves change by evolving social,
economic, and political conditions. All political and economic institutions
necessarily interact and interdependently create constraints and incentives
affecting the behavior of individuals and groups. This chapter employs a
definition of political economy derived from the analytic insights of "positive political economy,"[2] a theoretical body that "emphasizes both economic behavior in political processes and political behavior in the marketplace." Positive political economy "uses an economic approach—
constrained maximizing and strategic behavior of self-interested agents—
to explain the origins and maintenance of political institutions" and
"stresses the political context in which market phenomena take place."[3]

Initial Conditions

Compared with the political economies of most industrialized democracies, Japan's political economy in the 1950s and 1960s had a more easily
defined and more readily identifiable "power group," consisting of the
ruling party, the dominant economic interest groups providing political

support to the ruling party, and the bureaucracy. This power group exerted much influence in determining the character of political and economic institutions. And these institutions were substantively more interdependent, that is, the political and economic incentive structures of individuals and groups were more closely intertwined.[4]

The power group as a whole or each of the constituent subgroups alone was able to act as an effective "discriminating monopolist," able to charge different "prices" according to the conditions of each "market," in maximizing its ability to retain political bureaucratic power or to realize economic gains.[5] Discrimination was based on the contributions that various interest groups and individuals made in enabling each subconstituent of the power group to increase political or bureaucratic power or achieve desired economic goals. The power group, acting as a discriminating monopolist and making full use of the institutions it created (or adapted from its prewar predecessors), pursued the economic policy of "catching up" with the West as rapidly as possible.

This course would enable large manufacturing firms to achieve "dynamic technological efficiency," the greater productive efficiency achieved by adopting successively more advanced technology to produce increasingly higher-value-added products. Put differently, this strategy maximizes "adaptive efficiency" over time rather than attempting to achieve "allocative efficiency" at all times.[6]

Dynamic technological efficiency is achieved with the aid of "J-efficiency" (Japan efficiency), the efficiency that large Japanese manufacturing firms are able to achieve because of both institutional characteristics and government policies.[7] The most important institutional characteristics are the structure of governance of large firms (the weakness of stockholders' power, allowing management and employees to "dually control" firms)[8] and the long-term, intensive, multifaceted interfirm relations maintained typically by belonging to a *keiretsu*, or industrial grouping.[9] The policies and practices used to cultivate J-efficiency include direct and indirect subsidies, preferential access to capital at the lowest possible costs, lax enforcement of and de facto exemption from the Antimonopoly Act, and numerous other industry-specific and trade-related laws, all of which provided subsidies to Japanese companies and restricted foreign firms' access to Japanese markets.[10]

Throughout the rapid growth period, the power group maintained a structure of interdependent political and economic incentives that was decidedly "adversarial." That is to say, the effect of all the policies and practices—especially those impeding trade and foreign investments in Japan, including "administrative guidance" by various ministries—was to make Japan an effective practitioner of strategic trade policy, with all its implications. Practitioners of strategic trade maintain institutions, unilaterally and "asymmetrically" (i.e., without retaliation), to increase their own national income at the expense of their trading partners. And, as analytic works on strategic trade policy show, the principal effects on foreign firms are to deny them market access and force them to exit from, or abandon plans to enter, the targeted industries.[11]

Although Japan was not a "strong state" in the sense that political scientists define the term, the power group, as a whole or in varying combinations of its constituent subgroups, exerted its influence both extensively and intensively in civil society. Japan has a "group-oriented" and "network" society in which the social behavior of individuals is best explained by "exchange relations," where roughly equal-value favors and gifts are exchanged to maintain lasting intragroup and interpersonal relations. These social characteristics helped to reduce the political and economic costs of pursuing dynamic technological efficiency and enabled the power group to adopt strategic trade policy.[12]

Transformation

By the late 1960s, the political economy of Japan in the rapid growth period was confronted by increasingly strong forces demanding changes in the by-then firmly embedded incentive structure of the period. Since much has been written about these forces, let me here summarize only the most important among them.

1. The political consensus for rapid growth eroded. The performance of the Liberal Democratic Party (LDP) at the polls began to decline in the mid-1960s, bringing about a decade of *hokaku hakuchū* (literally, "the close matching of [the powers of] the conservatives vs. the progressives [opposition parties]") from 1969 to 1979.[13] Even with its efforts to be a catchall party by allocating increasingly larger amounts of tax revenue for social welfare and moderating many of the most unabashedly proindustry policies, the LDP's hold on power was challenged.[14] Indeed, although the LDP's share of votes in the lower house elections did rebound in the early 1980s, the political and economic incentive structure of the power group could no longer be maintained unaltered, as it once was for political, bureaucratic, and economic interests.

2. By the 1970s, the economic growth rate began to fall to less than half that of the rapid growth period as catch-up economic growth came to an end in one industry after another and Japan experienced the "Oil Shock" of 1973. The declining growth rate was the first of several changes that steadily weakened the cohesion of the power group. In addition, large manufacturing firms acquired technological prowess and required less capital, becoming less dependent on the LDP and the bureaucracy. And the LDP and the bureaucracy came to have fewer "favors" and less "guidance" to offer.

Post-catch-up LDP politicians, in efforts to obtain financial support from large firms and financial institutions, increasingly joined *zoku* (literally, "tribes")—the politically influential Diet and/or LDP policy committees dealing with specific legislative areas such as agriculture, health, construction, and high tech. Belonging to a *zoku* enabled Diet members to exchange the influence they gained for financial contributions from the firms and/or financial institutions whose interests were affected by the policy decisions of that *zoku*.[15]

The relative position of bureaucrats in the power group only declined: industry needed them less, and Diet members in *zoku* gained the specialized knowledge of policy areas and legislative expertise that bureaucrats had once virtually monopolized. Furthermore, bureaucrats had diminishing resources—both budgetary and "guidance"—to distribute. And the bureaucrats had to expend increasing amounts of energy in interministerial rivalries. The process of *seikō kantei* (the rise of politicians' power and the decline of the bureaucrats') continued.

3. The era of *gaiatsu* (foreign pressure) began in the 1960s, as Japan's strategic trade policies hurt foreign trading partners. The intensity of *gaiatsu* on Japan—whose high economic performance was being maintained by free-riding both on the U.S. nuclear umbrella and on the free-trade regime for which Japan bore almost no maintenance cost—increased as Japan continued to export more products that outcompeted those of foreign firms in home markets. As many works have examined, both political and economic pressures continued to intensify throughout the 1970s and 1980s, ranging from Voluntary Export Restraints (VERs) and Market-Oriented Sector-Selective (MOSS) discussions to Super 301 and the most recent Structural Impediments Initiative (SII) negotiations.[16]

4. Society was not immune to change. As the rapid growth period ended, the group-orientedness and network characteristics were becoming less effective in muting an increasing number of citizens' dissatisfaction with the pursuit of dynamic technological efficiency and strategic inter-

national trade. More and more voters, now living in cities and less group-oriented, became less willing to accept the costs of rapid growth. They demanded that the power group reduce environmental pollution, high prices on manufactured and imported goods, lengths of commutes from their "rabbit hutches," and other costs of rapid growth. Ultimately, this brought about the LDP's loosening grip on power and the decade of *hokaku hakuchū*.

Changes in the political and economic institutions, however, came slowly. The LDP continued to retain a majority in the lower house and even increased its seats in the 1980s, as noted. Government continued to employ proindustry policies, including creating several high-tech joint research programs in computers and semiconductors led by the Ministry of International Trade and Industry (MITI), enacting Antitrust Law revisions that are more cosmetic than real, and shelving the product liability law.[17] Ministries continued to issue large amounts of administrative guidance, although increasingly to protect their own bureaucratic turf rather than to help firms achieve higher economic performance. And many promises made to Japan's trading partners to eliminate or reduce trade-impeding institutions were only partially kept or not kept at all.[18]

Changes in the institutions proceeded slowly because the forces for change, described above, were blunted. Despite strong criticism of many LDP policies benefiting industry and financial institutions in the 1980s—weak environmental policies, policies that let the prices of imported goods remain high despite the rapid appreciation of the yen, and policies that let land prices soar—the LDP continued to retain a comfortable majority in the lower house. This was in part because of the catchall policies of the LDP but, more important, because a majority of voters—the new middle mass—feared they would lose their "quasi-social entitlements" if they voted for the opposition parties.[19]

Many voters, even those against whom LDP policies discriminated, continued to vote for the LDP because they did not have a "correct model," or a model by which they could see the effects of an LDP policy on their own welfare and isolate the effects of the preferred policies from those of policies they opposed.[20] This situation, which benefited the LDP at the polls, also benefited the institutions aiding large Japanese firms in their pursuit of dynamic technological efficiency. Calculating the gains voters enjoyed over time because of what J-efficient large firms achieved, minus the costs these firms imposed on the voters, was no easy task.

Gaiatsu also failed to have the effects Japan's trade partners sought because more and more Japanese learned—through mass media, scholars, and explanations offered by those whose interests were more directly affected on both sides of the Pacific—that much of the foreign criticism of Japanese economic institutions was of dubious validity or was self-serving. *Gaiatsu* accomplished less because it failed to give due credit to the hard work and managerial skills of Japanese firms and because it ignored the effect of the huge and increasing American budget deficit in the trade balance between Japan and the United States.

To be sure, Japanese society changed in many ways in the 1970s and 1980s. But, relatively speaking, the government and ministries still retained more respect than did their counterparts in other industrial nations. And the large firms and financial institutions—with names such as Mitsui, Mitsubishi, Sumitomo, Sony, and Matsushita—continued to enjoy social clout. Although few would deny that in the last few decades, Tokyo has become more like London and New York in appearance and that more of Japan's youth have eagerly emulated their counterparts in the West, much of the change occurring in Japanese society was more apparent than fundamental. Thus, the power group could still rely on the norms of social behavior and traditional values to reduce the political and economic costs of maintaining the essential institutions it created.

Despite these forces that retarded the transformation of political and economic institutions, a significant change did take place, especially in the 1980s. The largest firms and financial institutions exporting manufactured products and capital increasingly needed to ensure their continued access to foreign markets and technology. Thus, they exercised their considerable political and economic power to liberalize economic institutions, that is, open Japanese markets to foreign investment and products. In other words, the large firms and financial institutions have become free traders willing to exert their political and economic power to change institutions in the interest of maintaining high economic performance in the global markets.

A close examination of the transformation, however, reveals that these new free traders exercise their power to liberalize economic institutions selectively, thus limiting the pace of change. They are selective free traders because they weigh their needs to ensure access to foreign markets and technology against their desire to retain, as much as possible, the institutions that enable them to continue to possess J-efficiency.

Throughout the 1980s political institutions not directly subject to requirements similar to those of the exporters of manufactured goods and capital have changed little. The LDP Diet members had a more inward-looking incentive structure; their principal motivation was to retain political office by maintaining institutions (practices and behavior) that have proven effective to date. Of course, the LDP responded somewhat to the desires of the large firms and financial institutions to liberalize economic institutions because the party as a whole, each of its factions, and individual Diet members were all dependent on the financial contributions of the large firms and financial institutions.

Bureaucrats, in contrast, changed their behavior in response to the interests of their "clients," the industries they are regulating. And those bureaucrats whose incentive structures are most closely intertwined with the desires of the multinationals and large banks have changed more than those whose clients' interests are domestic. Thus, MITI was the first to change, whereas the Ministry of Agriculture, Forestry, and Fisheries fought desperately to the last to protect rice farmers and the Ministry of Construction even today jealously guards its authority to approve approximately ten thousand different types of permits.[21]

In response both to the desires of the dominant exporters of manufactured products and capital and to *gaiatsu*, Japan's economic policy is being transformed. One of the most significant changes that has occurred, principally because of the desire of the largest firms and financial institutions but also because of *gaiatsu*, is the steady liberalization and internationalization of the capital market. The government began a process of eliminating one restriction after another in the 1970s, culminating in 1980 with a fundamental change from "restriction in principle" to "free in principle."[22] As a result, capital today flows into and out of Japan with restrictions that are minor when compared with those of the 1970s.

Japan also made many changes demanded by trading partners in the 1970s and 1980s. The Japanese government eliminated numerous trade-impeding inspections, certifications, and other requirements and reduced the average tariff rate to one of the lowest among industrialized nations. The Japanese substantially liberalized import restrictions on oranges and beef. The government significantly revised the Large Store Law *(Daiten-hō)* in 1990, depriving small and medium-sized retailers of protection against competition from department and chain stores. These changes liberalizing trade could occur because multinational firms, the largest financial institutions, Keidanren, and other major economic organizations became eager to diffuse trade friction and became willing to exert their considerable power over the LDP cabinets and party leaders. And these economic organizations are exerting power today, forcing LDP politicians to "sacrifice" rice farmers despite vociferous opposition from Diet members dependent on farm votes.

Despite their obvious desire to act as an engine of liberalization, the large manufacturing firms and finance institutions are not wholehearted free traders because they are unwilling to lose those institutions that enable them to achieve J-efficiency. To cite several examples, enterprise groups (horizontal *keiretsu*) continue to retain those components that directly and indirectly limit foreign firms' access to Japanese markets. Thus, despite many significant changes in the relationship between the large banks and the firms in enterprise groups—including a reduced need for capital and the internationalization of finance—the main banks continue to be important as the "coordinators" of each enterprise group. Presidents' clubs in each enterprise group still hold monthly meetings. Furthermore, although cross-shareholding among member firms has declined since the 1970s, it is still common practice. And intra-*keiretsu* trading and joint ventures of all types continue to play significant roles in all enterprise groups.[23]

No less significantly, these free traders continue to oppose more vigorous enforcement of the Antitrust Law, drafting of stronger environmental laws, and adoption of product liability laws similar to those in the United States and West Europe. They do not want replacement of the Ministry of Finance's friendly supervision of the securities industry by an independent agency such as the Securities and Exchange Commission, nor do they want enactment of labor laws with legal sanctions to reduce gender discrimination in the workplace.[24]

Until the 1993 elections, political institutions had changed little, as attested by the observation that "the economy is first rate, politics third rate," a comment frequently made by Japanese journalists. In virtually all cases, Japan's prime ministers continued to be selected and replaced behind closed doors through the dynamics of LDP factional politics. Thus a coalition of factions led by the Takeshita faction, the largest, could unceremoniously "dump" the popular Toshiki Kaifu and replace him with Kiichi Miyazawa, the leader of a smaller faction, after not finding a suitable candidate of its own. As with prime ministers, the composition of cabinets was largely dictated by factional politics. Compatability of policy preferences between cabinet members and the prime minister hardly matters in forming a cabinet, obviously still true in the post-LDP coalition government.

Japanese politics continued to be "money driven." Needing large amounts of cash for reelection campaigns and for the huge expenditures necessary to maintain the well-oiled political machinery in their districts, LDP politicians (who have no other sources of income, unlike the Socialist and Communist Diet members) scrambled to become members of as many powerful *zoku* as possible. They also were prone to become "gray" or even "black," tainted by one of the frequent scandals or unfortunate enough to be convicted.

However, being a "gray" or "black" politician was far from fatal to an LDP politician's career. These tainted or even convicted LDP Diet members are not barred from holding cabinet or major party posts. In fact, Miyazawa himself had to resign in 1988 as minister of finance and as vice president of the party because he had become "gray" by his involvement in the Recruit Scandal, but that did not prevent him from later becoming prime minister. And Miyazawa appointed a "gray" Diet member to his cabinet and a "black" Diet member to a high party post. This illustrates the extent to which political corruption was tolerated in Japan and why oft-attempted public gestures to "purify" politics failed.[25] One reason for Kaifu's fall from power was his eagerness to enact a campaign finance law that would have been more effective than its predecessor, known for being a sieve law (*zaruhō*, a Japanese colloquial counterpart to "Swiss cheese").

Among many other unique political realities of Japan, the following two are most revealing. First, nearly 40 percent of LDP Diet members are sons or sons-in-law (the so-called *nisei giin*, second-generation Diet members) or other close relatives of former Diet members.[26] *Nisei giin* come from "inherited" districts, where those who wield political power in the electoral districts attempt to extend personal relationships established with Diet members even after they retire. These relationships, cemented by years of large campaign contributions in return for "pork," can best be preserved through election of family members of the retiring Diet members. Second, until the political reforms of 1993 called for major electoral changes, the constitutional provision guaranteeing one man/one vote was still violated (in favor of LDP candidates). Until these changes became reality and despite several court challenges in the past three decades, the weight of votes differed by electoral district by as much as 3.4 to 1. Figures from the 1991 census show that in the 130 multimember lower house, several metropolitan districts of 350,000 to 460,000 voters are represented by one Diet member, whereas in two dozen or so rural districts—which ordinarily cast much higher percentages of votes for LDP candidates—only 135,000 to 175,000 voters claim one Diet seat.[27]

The bureaucracy has changed its behavior not because of pressure from the LDP but rather in response to the changing needs and incentive structure of Japan's dominant exporters of manufactured products and capital.

Beginning in the early 1970s, MITI gradually became an "internationalist." MITI's primary concerns evolved from nurturing industries attempting to become internationally competitive to coping with steadily increasing trade friction threatening to limit Japan's large manufacturing firms' and financial institutions' access to foreign markets. To be sure, changing old habits is difficult, and MITI still promoted high-tech industries throughout the 1980s. But at the same time, the ministry became willing publicly to accuse the Ministry of Agriculture, Forestry, and Fisheries of protecting Japanese agriculture to the detriment of national interest. The Ministry of Finance (MOF) followed MITI's example. As the behavior of Japan's financial institutions changed to benefit more from liberalization and internationalization, MOF's behavior changed to bring about, albeit grudgingly, the increasing liberalization of the capital market. Inevitably, MOF's power was greatly reduced by the end of the 1980s.

Until recently, scholars of the Japanese political economy have maintained that change in the Japanese system was virtually impossible. The following quote illustrates this perception:

> Since there was no changeover of political power, it was practically impossible to demolish vested interests from whoever had obtained political rents. In other words, the current Japanese political system is an intricate nexus of vested interests, shared by political groups, major party politicians, and government bureaucrats. This system made the political cost of changing existing policies extremely high. Except on rare occasions (such as the recent tax revision), only those pressures applied by strong foreign governments seemed to be effective in making drastic policy changes.[28]

This view now needs amendment. The "intricate nexus of vested interests" that is "practically impossible to demolish" can be changed and indeed is changing slowly as a powerful political group—the dominant exporters of manufactured products and capital—finds it desirable to change policies and practices for its own sake. And the changes are not solely attributable to *gaiatsu*.

Continuing Change

Two views of Japanese political economy are prevalent. One argues that Japan's political and economic institutions are unique in that those who exert power over these institutions share the goal of increasing national economic power and agree on means to pursue it. This view also holds that the institutions have been and are likely to remain resistant to change. Many hold this view, although few express it as crudely as did the former prime minister of France.[29]

The other view maintains that Japanese economic institutions—economic policy and the behavior of firms—differ little from those found in other industrialized nations. The institutions change in response to political demands and the needs of the electorate and to market forces and macroeconomic variables. That is, Japan's economic policy and the behavior of Japanese firms can be explained by the universalistic theories that apply to other industrialized political economies. Leading proponents of this view of Japanese economic institutions are neoclassical economists whose analyses, as a rule, assume away the roles institutions play in an economy.[30]

I support neither of these views. Instead, I find that the Japanese political economy, led by a power group once united in pursuing dynamic technological efficiency, has changed in many significant ways during the past two decades and will continue to do so. Changes occurred and will continue because Japan's new free traders will lead the way in response to domestic and international market forces and macroeconomic changes. They are eager to diffuse trade conflicts lest they be denied access to the markets of Japan's trading partners. The defeat of the LDP, the advent of a reformist coalition, and continuing economic recession define a new, but still evolving, context. The pace of change, however, may still be slow for a number of reasons: the free traders wish to continue to benefit from policies and practices enabling them to maintain their J-efficiency; voters lack a "correct" model; the middle mass desires to retain "quasi-entitlements"; and foreign pressure has lost credibility.

For Japan's trading partners, the slowness of change remains a continuing reason for trade friction. To be sure, many of the institutions that enabled Japanese firms to pursue dynamic technological efficiency with J-efficiency have been changed and will continue to be changed. But the remnants of these institutions and, more important, the effects of what these institutions achieved in the past have remained, long after Japanese firms grew competitive. This is demonstrated by the still-limited intra-industry trade (import of manufactured products) in Japan, which accounts for Japan's large trade surplus even while the yen has risen in value. Those who argue that the amounts of Japan's intra-industry trade and the trade surplus can be fully explained by the geographic location and competitiveness of Japanese industries are as oblivious to reality as those who maintain that the difference in the volume of sales of Japanese automobiles in the United States and of U.S. automobiles in Japan can be fully explained by the "unfairness" of Japan's trade policy and practices.[31]

Is Japan a new kind of "superpower"? The answer must be yes. In the post–cold war period, a nation with super economic power can increasingly exert its financial, technological, and managerial powers in all parts of the globe, including in the most industrialized nations. Indeed, whereas the two "old" superpowers are reduced in circumstances—one having become the world's largest debtor, plagued with its own economic and social ills, and the other disintegrated and dependent on the economic aid of its former adversaries—Japan as a new kind of superpower continues to "occupy" many parts of the world. Japan has built factories, established networks, and aquired stocks, bonds, and commercial properties in the United States, Asia, Europe, and elsewhere. What prewar Japan, aspiring to be one of the "old" superpowers, could not accomplish with its imperial forces a half-century ago, postwar Japan as a "new" superpower has accomplished with far more ease in the past two decades.

How will such a Japan "fit" into the world in the coming decades? The answer depends on how quickly Japan can overcome the "slowness" with which it is transforming its political institutions and how well Japan's major trading partners will be able to deal with Japan's economic success. As Sony chairman Akio Morita expressed eloquently in a recent article, in order to overcome the "slowness," the Japanese need to understand that their firms must abandon the strategy of "maximum sales at low profit" (*hakuri tabai*), which they have pursued through investing as much as possible in capacity and research and development. Morita explains that Japanese firms have been able to pursue this strategy successfully and increase their global market shares because they are, in comparison with Western firms, paying an appreciably smaller proportion of total revenue to their employees and making their employees work substantially more hours per year, distributing less profits to shareholders, benefiting from a wide range of "industrial policies," and maintaining various other uniquely Japanese practices. Morita is convinced that a strategy based on these practices, not acceptable under rules of competition in the West, must now be abandoned if Japan wishes to "do away with the mistrust of the West and create a truly prosperous Japan."[32] In effect, he argues that the days when Japan benefited from efforts to achieve dynamic technological effi-

ciency with firms possessing J-efficiency are long gone and that the international costs of not dismantling the political and economic institutions
are increasing rapidly.[33]

The pace of the transformation of Japan's political and economic institution also can be quickened when more become aware of what Masaaki
Homma of Osaka University calls "the pathology of Japanese-type economy." Homma stated:

> With a blueprint of its own, the government has led the economy,
> doing its best both at home and abroad to create conditions most
> conducive to the activity of firms. The system of vertical division in
> which each ministry and agency took full responsibility even down
> to minute details was established to create a unified and coordinated
> system based on their power to approve, inform, grant permission,
> and guide. Markets, under the guidance of ministries and agencies,
> came to be divided and were each guided separately. Guidance was
> provided not in the interest of consumers but to deal with the prob-
> lems faced by an industry or between industries.
>
> Within this framework, firms continued as best they could to
> increase productivity and international competitiveness. The enter-
> prise system based on implicit contracts between firms and between
> a firm and its employees was established.
>
> The political world also functioned reflecting this economic sys-
> tem based on vertical division. *Zoku* Diet members representing the
> interests of each industry appeared and they exerted all the influence
> they could muster in making policies, passing laws, and allocating
> the budget for the interests of the industries they represented.
>
> This Japanese-type economic system that came to be firmly estab-
> lished in the postwar period achieved unparalleled performance in
> making "things" and selling them abroad. This benefited the Japa-
> nese. However, the fact is that this system has become a target of
> much criticism from both Japanese themselves and foreigners and is
> today facing a major transformation.[34]

For Japan to be able to better "fit" into the world, those trading partners
wanting to reduce economic conflicts with Japan must embark on two
serious undertakings. One is to put their own economic houses in order,
that is, manage their macroeconomies better (for the United States, this
would entail reducing budget deficits, increasing savings, and taking all
measures necessary to increase the international competitiveness of firms).
If the United States decides to follow the recommendations made in the
First Annual Report to the President and Congress, issued in March 1992 by

the Competitiveness Policy Council, to "enhance its position as an exporter of products based on high levels of skill and high value added, i.e., manufactures that can support high wages" and to "establish a new mechanism for government and industry to work together to promote the development of generic pre-competitive technologies that are not being financed by the private sector,"[35] it will also go a long way toward making American industries more competitive in the world market.

Japan's political economy is changing, even if only deliberately, led by its new free traders. The process can be hastened only if Japan's major trading partners, especially the United States, regain competitiveness in the world market to ward off the temptation of protectionism. Protectionism by Japan's trading partners will simply make it much more difficult for the views of the Sony chairman and other new free traders to be heard, further slowing the process of Japan's emergence as a free trader that can better "fit" into the global community.

Notes

1. Most of the numerous works on Japanese political economy suffer from the following shortcomings in various combinations: (1) relying on a small number of unrepresentative or extreme examples or on much systematically selected, biased "evidence" (frequently consisting of anecdotes and mass media reports); (2) basing analyses on half-truths, exaggerations, and misconceptions; (3) refusing to recognize that Japan's political and economic institutions have changed during the past thirty years; (4) failing to examine (or being ignorant of) history (behavior and policies of the past affecting or determining the same of today); and (5) offering analyses that suffer from disciplinary myopia, so that political scientists focus their attention only on political institutions, the policy-making process, and policies but fail to examine effects of market forces and macroeconomic policies and changes (even when they are self-consciously analyzing the "political economy" of Japan), causing economists to see the Japanese political economy through thick neoclassical lenses and causing both political scientists and economists to ignore the effects of culture, values, and social norms on the behavior and institutions of Japan's political economy.

2. The three works most useful in gaining an understanding of positive political economy are the following, all published by Cambridge University Press in 1990: James E. Alt and Kenneth A. Shepsle, eds., *Perspectives on Positive Political Economy*; Thrainn Eggerston, *Economic Behavior and Institutions*; and Douglass C. North, *Institutions, Institutional Change, and Economic Performance*. The bibliographies appended to these works together constitute a most up-to-date and complete listing of the scholarly works that have contributed to the emergence of the field.

3. Alt and Shepsle, *Perspectives on Positive Political Economy*, p. 1.

4. Chalmers Johnson, *MITI and the Japanese Miracle: The Growth of Industrial Policy, 1925–1975* (Stanford: Stanford University Press, 1982); Edward Lincoln, *Japan's Industrial Policies* (Washington, D.C.: Japan Economic Institute of America, 1984); Takafusa Nakamura, *Nihon keizai: Sono seichō to kōzō* (The Japanese economy: Its growth and structure) (Tokyo: Tokyo

Daigaku Shuppankai, 1978); Daniel I. Okimoto, *Between MITI and the Market: Japanese Industrial Policy and High Technology* (Stanford: Stanford University Press, 1989); T. J. Pempel, *Policy and Politics in Japan: Creative Conservatism* (Philadelphia: Temple University Press, 1982); and Yasusuke Murakami, "The Japanese Model of Political Economy," Michio Muramatsu and Ellis S. Krauss, "The Conservative Policy Line and the Development of Patterned Pluralism," and Yutaka Kosai, "The Politics of Economic Management," in Kozo Yamamura and Yasukichi Yasuba, eds., *The Political Economy of Japan*, vol. 1, *The Domestic Transformation* (Stanford: Stanford University Press, 1987).

5. In this context, those who hold power adopt policies and create or maintain institutions to distribute income/wealth as would a profit-maximizing monopolist, that is, the strongest supporters of the party in power receive the most wealth/income while weaker supporters receive less. See Douglass C. North, "A Framework for Analyzing the State in Economic History," *Explorations in Economic History* 16 (1979): 249–59.

6. See Kozo Yamamura, "Success That Soured: Administrative Guidance and Cartels in Japan," and Yasusuke Murakami and Kozo Yamamura, "A Technical Note on Japanese Firm Behavior and Economic Policy," in Kozo Yamamura, ed., *Policy and Trade Issues of the Japanese Economy: American and Japanese Perspectives* (Seattle: University of Washington Press, 1982). Also see Chalmers Johnson, Laura D'Andrea Tyson, and John Zysman, eds., *Politics and Productivity: The Real Story of Why Japan Works* (Cambridge, Mass.: Ballinger Publishing Co., 1989), and John Zysman and Laura Tyson, *American Industry in International Competition: Government Policies and Corporate Strategies* (Ithaca, N.Y.: Cornell University Press, 1983).

7. George C. Eads and Kozo Yamamura, "The Future of Industrial Policy," in Yamamura and Yasuba, *The Political Economy of Japan*, vol. 1, and Kozo Yamamura and Jan Vandenberg, "Japan's Rapid-Growth Policy on Trial: The Television Case," in Kozo Yamamura and Gary Saxonhouse, eds., *Law and Trade Issues of the Japanese Economy: American and Japanese Perspectives* (Seattle: University of Washington Press, 1986).

8. Masahiko Aoki, ed., *The Economic Analysis of the Japanese Firm* (Amsterdam: North-Holland, 1984).

9. Michael Gerlach, "Keiretsu Organization in the Japanese Economy: Analysis and Trade Implications," in Johnson, Tyson, and Zysman, *Politics and Productivity*; Michael Gerlach, "Twilight of the *Keiretsu*? A Critical Assessment," *Journal of Japanese Studies* 18 (1992); Masu Uekusa, "Industrial Organization: The 1970s to the Present," in Yamamura and Yasuba, *The Political Economy of Japan*, vol. 1; Paul Sheard, "The Economics of Interlocking Shareholding in Japan," *Ricerche Economiche* 45 (1991); Iwao Nakatani, "The Economic Role of Financial Corporate Grouping," in Aoki, *The Economic Analysis of the Japanese Firm*; and Paul Sheard, "The Main Bank System and Corporate Monitoring and Control in Japan," *Journal of Economic Behavior and Organization* 11 (1989).

10. Yamamura, *Policy and Trade Issues*; Yamamura and Saxonhouse, *Law and Trade Issues*; Hideto Ishida, "Anticompetitive Practices in the Distribution of Goods and Services in Japan: The Problem of Distribution Keiretsu," *Journal of Japanese Studies* 9 (1983); and Kozo Yamamura, "Joint Research and Antitrust: Japanese vs. American Strategies," in Hugh Patrick, ed., *Japan's High Technology Industries: Lessons and Limitations of Industrial Policy* (Seattle: University of Washington Press, 1986).

11. Paul R. Krugman, "Introduction: New Thinking about Trade Policy," in Paul Krugman, ed., *Strategic Trade Policy and the New International Economics* (Cambridge, Mass.: MIT Press, 1986); James Brander and Barbara Spencer, "Export Subsidies and International Market Share Rivalry," *Journal of International Economics* 18 (1985).

12. See Thomas P. Rohlen and Yasusuke Murakami, "Social Exchange Aspects of the Japanese Political Economy: Culture, Efficiency, and Change," in Yasusuke Murakami and

Hugh T. Patrick, eds., *The Political Economy of Japan*, vol. 3, *Cultural and Social Dynamics*, ed. Henry Rosovsky and Shumpei Kumon (Stanford: Stanford University Press, 1992).

13. The proportion of total votes cast for the LDP declined steadily from 57.76 percent in 1960 to 47.63 percent by 1969 and continued to decline to 41.32 percent in 1976 when the party lost its majority in the Diet and was forced to seek support of conservative "independents" and a small conservative party (the New Liberal Club, formed by those who had left the LDP a few years earlier). The LDP share of the total vote rebounded to 44.80 percent in 1979 and 47.91 percent in 1980. This is why the decade between the late 1960s and the late 1970s is referred to as the period of *hokaku hakuchū*.

14. Yasusuke Murakami, "The Age of New Middle Mass Politics: The Case of Japan," *Journal of Japanese Studies* 8 (1982); Takashi Inoguchi, "Explaining and Predicting Japanese General Elections, 1960–1980," *Journal of Japanese Studies* 7 (1981).

15. On *zoku*, see Muramatsu and Krauss, "The Conservative Policy Line," pp. 540–43. Also see Takashi Inoguchi and Yasunobu Iwai, *Zoku no kenkyū* (A study of *zoku*) (Tokyo: Nihon Keizai Shinbunsha, 1987).

16. See Kozo Yamamura, ed., *Japan's Economic Structure: Should It Change?* (Seattle: Society for Japanese Studies, 1990).

17. See Daniel I. Okimoto, "Regime Characteristics of Japanese Industrial Policy," and Yamamura, "Joint Research and Antitrust," in Patrick, *Japan's High Technology Industries*. Also see Laura D'Andrea Tyson, "Comment," in Paul Krugman, ed., *Trade with Japan: Has the Door Opened Wider?* (Chicago: University of Chicago Press, 1991), pp. 297–301, for current MITI projects promoting high-tech industries, and *Asahi Shimbun*, April 17, 1992, p. 5, for industry opposition to strengthening the enforcement of the Antimonopoly Act and increasing the amount of fines against cartels.

18. Kenneth B. Pyle, ed., *The Trade Crisis: How Will Japan Respond?* (Seattle: Society for Japanese Studies, 1987); Yamamura, *Japan's Economic Structure*. Also see sources cited in note 8.

19. Murakami, "The Age of New Middle Mass Politics."

20. For the best analytic discussion of "correct model," see North, "A Framework for Analyzing the State in Economic History."

21. See Masaaki Homma, "Tenkan-ki o mukaeta Nihon-gata kigyō shisutemu" (Japanese-type enterprise system in a period of transformation), *Asuteion* 23 (Winter 1992): 24–51. This was a special issue on the pathology of Japanese-type economy.

22. See Thomas F. Cargill and Shōichi Royama, *The Transition of Finance in Japan and the United States* (Stanford: Hoover Institution, Stanford University Press, 1988).

23. See sources cited in note 7 above.

24. See Homma, "Tenkan-ki o mukaeta Nihon-gata kigyō shisutemu"; Iwao Nakatani, *Japan problem no genten* (The origin of the Japan problem) (Tokyo: Kdansha, 1990); and Yukihiro Asami, "Sangyō-kaiwa katakunana taido o aratameru bekida" (The industries must change their unrelenting attitude [against the proposed product liability law]), *Ekonomisuto*, December 17, 1991, pp. 18–20.

25. *Asahi Shimbun*, January 14, 1992, p. 4; "Commentary," *U.S. News & World Report*, October 21, 1991, p. 55.

26. Norio Okazawa, *Seitō* (Political parties) (Tokyo: University of Tokyo Press, 1988), p. 194. Yukio Matsuyama of *Asahi Shimbun*, who was a discussant of my paper at the Woodrow Wilson Center conference, provided me with the proportion of *nisei giin* today.

27. *Asahi Shimbun*, November 30, 1991, p. 9.

28. Masahiro Okuno-Fujiwara, "Industrial Policy in Japan: A Political Economy View," in Krugman, *Trade with Japan*, p. 290.

29. The best-known among those holding this view is Karel van Wolferen, *The Enigma of Japanese Power: People and Politics in a Stateless Nation* (New York: Alfred A. Knopf, 1989).

30. See Kozo Yamamura, "Will Japan's Economic Structure Change? Confessions of a Former Optimist," in Yamamura, *Japan's Economic Structure*, for further discussion of this view.

31. On the debate concerning reasons for the limited intra-industry trade of Japan, see Edward J. Lincoln, *Japan's Unequal Trade* (Washington, D.C.: Brookings Institution, 1990), pp. 39–60, and Robert Z. Lawrence, "How Open Is Japan?" and Gary R. Saxonhouse, "Comments," in Krugman, *Trade with Japan*.

32. Akio Morita, "Nihon-gata keizai ga abunai" (Japanese-type management in peril), *Bungei Shunjū* (February 1992), p. 102.

33. Ibid., pp. 94–103. For analyses offered in support of Morita's call to change the Japanese economic system, see Chikashi Moriguchi, "Morita hatsugen no keizaigakuteki imi" (The meaning in economics of Morita's proposal), and Isamu Miyazaki, "Keiei kaikaku ni shohishano shiten o" (Adopt the consumer's viewpoint in reforming business practices), in *Weekly Economist*, April 4, 1992, pp. 24–33.

34. Homma, "Tenkan-ki o mukaeta Nihon-gata kigyō shisutemu." For no less explicit criticisms of, and a call for fundamental changes in, Japanese business practices and the economic system, also see Nakatani, *Japan problem no genten*.

35. Competitiveness Policy Council, *First Annual Report to the President and Congress: Building a Competitive America* (Washington, D.C.: Competitiveness Policy Council, 1992), p. 30.

Chapter 3

Japanese Security Issues

PETER J. KATZENSTEIN and NOBUO OKAWARA

IN THE 1980s, Japanese discussions of national security were cast in terms of the concept of comprehensive security (*sogo anzen hosho*). In the minds of many people this language provided a plausible political stance that both countered and reinforced some of the arguments of the new military "realists." Predated by systematic thinking about Japan's economic security as developed by the Ministry of International Trade and Industry (MITI) in the 1970s, this language was partly influenced by a Nomura Research Institute study that focused on comprehensive security.[1] The term *comprehensive security* subsequently appeared in the 1980 report of the Comprehensive National Security Study Group convened by Prime Minister Masayoshi Ohira.[2] The report was not formally adopted as national policy, but it had a significant impact on the domestic debate on security policy.[3] The term *comprehensive security* implied that Japan should be concerned about more than the military dimension of security. In comparison with the 1960s and 1970s, politics and economics were no longer as separate (thus denying the possibility of better relations with the Soviet Union); and Japan was moving into the Western camp rather than following an omnidirectional foreign policy.

At the same time the concept of comprehensive security was also useful for those who wanted a rationale to keep defense spending under control, a useful shield, that is, against growing American pressure for increased military spending.[4] It was, in a way, a concept congenial to politicians who were wary to confront issues of defense viewed with suspicion or hostility by Japanese voters. It remains today the guiding idea with which Japan is, for example, trying to further its security arrangements with the United States, seeking to engage Russia in East Asia, and hoping to strengthen its relations with its Asian neighbors as well as the Third World more generally. In short, the doctrine of comprehensive security has become the mechanism by which Japan has partly redefined its posture in the international system. "All Japanese policies with international dimensions—particularly defense, resources, energy, food security, and foreign aid—are placed in a security context. Comprehensive security provides a politically acceptable framework for maintaining a strong emphasis on self-defense capabilities by making security a national concern and not simply a military one."[5]

The concept of comprehensive security conveys a deeper truth about Japan's security policy. National security is deeply embedded in political and economic considerations. "The Japanese notion of 'comprehensive security,' with its explicitly economic component and with its postwar de-emphasis on the military component, is the reciprocal of U.S. emphases on military strength and defense technology. It is only a slight exaggeration to say that the Japanese will accept higher factor costs for essentially the same reason that the United States will overpay for its defense systems. It makes each feel more secure."[6] Comprehensive security thus revolves around the social stability and national autonomy that derive from a productive and technologically dynamic national economy. Such an economy is seeking to establish itself firmly in global markets, backed by a diplomacy aimed at strengthening close political relations with the United States and Japan's Asian neighbors.

This chapter's main message is simple. On questions of national security, Japan's policy is creating new national options through extending international links. The success that Japan has enjoyed in economic matters is drawing it inexorably into a world that is making increasing demands on its growing resources. Exposed to these new global pulls and constantly threatened by a domestic opposition, both from the Left and from the Right, the Liberal Democratic Party (LDP) tried to follow a policy of incremental expansion in its defense policy, accompanied by numerous political restraints to allay the fears of its opponents at home and abroad.

This chapter discusses three important areas of Japan's security policy. First, the security links between Japan and the United States deepened so much in the 1980s that the U.S.-Japan relationship now approaches a de facto military alliance. As a result Japan's military capabilities and options have increased. Second, responding initially to American pressure during the Gulf crisis, Japan's participation in some forms of U.N. peacekeeping operations is slowly preparing the ground for the assumption of a larger political role in the international system. Finally, the erosion of MITI's informal regulation of the export of dual-use technologies underscores the potential military prominence of Japan in the coming decades. The domestic and international political structures and norms that are conditioning Japan's security policy all militate against Japan's moving on its own, in the foreseeable future, to an independent military posture in world politics. But in an era of rapid change, the gradual establishment of a national option has moved Japan's security policy from weakness to strength.

Growing Military Links with the United States

In Japan's relations with the United States, the traditional American definition of security in narrow military terms has often clashed with the Japanese view of comprehensive security. From the perspective of Washington, the security arrangements with Japan constitute a defense alliance against the forces of the former Soviet Union. From the perspective of Tokyo, the full title of the treaty that was renegotiated in 1960 remains essential. It is a treaty about mutual security and cooperation. The term *alliance* was in fact until the 1980s highly problematic for describing the relations between the two countries. When Prime Minister Zenko Suzuki referred to Japan's relation with the United States as an "alliance" during his May 1981 visit to Washington, he created a political uproar in Tokyo.[7] The term connoted a degree of risk sharing and a mutuality of interest that were constricted by Articles 5 and 6 of the security treaty. In short, Prime Minister Suzuki's statement appeared to contradict the general thrust of Japan's postwar security policy, which had aimed at avoiding being drawn into the global military affairs of the United States. Apart from the use of military bases in Japan, the security arrangements with the United States were designed only to protect Japan rather than to offer the United States any military support in its regional defense of the Western Pacific. Japan's constitution and past policies have denied the Self Defense Forces (SDF) any substantial offensive military capabilities apart from the nuclear and conventional deterrence provided by the United States. A substantial decrease of the U.S. military presence in Asia thus puts strong pressure on Japan to compensate in military terms.[8]

Within the security framework that links Japan and the United States, the economic aspects have always figured prominently.[9] The Mutual Defense Assistance Program of 1954, for example, explicitly refers to the fact that "economic stability will be an essential element for consideration in the development of its defense capacities . . . Japan can contribute only to the extent permitted by its general economic conditions and capacities."[10] The American nuclear umbrella provided military conditions that were extremely favorable to the economic expansion of Japan.

Yet from the perspective of the United States, "Japan is ideally suited as a base for forward deployment of U.S. forces."[11] Japan is a very important link in America's Asian system of nuclear deterrence. It is also part of America's global network of command, control, communication, and intelligence. Numerous Japanese facilities are linked with both the North American Aerospace Defense Command and the Strategic Air Command (SAC), and they form an integral component of the World-Wide Military Command and Control System operated by the U.S. Department of Defense.[12] The high-frequency radio systems that make possible the work of both the Pacific Command and SAC are stationed at Kadena, Iruma, Owada, and Tokorozawa. The U.S. Navy's low-frequency transmitter is stationed at Yosami, one of six in the world that relays firing orders to the Trident submarines as well as attack submarines equipped with nuclear-tipped cruise missiles. Finally, Japan is fully integrated into the network of supplies for all U.S. forces in the Western Pacific. U.S. bases in Japan currently provide 80 percent of the oil storage facilities west of Hawaii, and American ammunition depots in Japan account for over 50 percent of the total land-based capacity in the Western Pacific.[13] These facts confirm that "the U.S. military's Japan-based communications, planning, targeting, and refueling infrastructure . . . make Japan an indispensable component of U.S. nuclear warfighting plans."[14]

Japan's financial support for American bases is only a small part of the growing defense links between the United States and Japan. In November 1978 the Guidelines for Japan-U.S. Defense Cooperation were issued. They ratified in diplomatic language the basic conception that had informed the National Defense Program Outline (NDPO) about the importance of U.S. forces in Japan's defense. The Guidelines spelled out a division of labor and provided for increasing levels of cooperation in operation, logistics, and intelligence. This was the first step toward reaching higher levels of interoperability of the two militaries. Japan's defense buildup during the 1980s provided for the planes and ships supposedly necessary to accomplish these new missions.[15] Critics of Japanese security policy have charged that "the intensification of cooperation between the two militaries, pursued under the Guidelines, has in fact led to Japan's further subordination. In this sense, the Guidelines can be regarded as an informal revision of the security treaty meant to lock Japanese forces into an overarching U.S. strategy."[16] As a follow-up to the Guidelines, a number of top-secret war contingency planning documents have been drawn up.[17] Joint defense planning and exercises, the possible creation of a Japan-U.S. Defense Coordination Center, intelligence exchange, joint operational preparations, growing interoperability of military equipment, and the promise of Japanese assistance, under certain conditions, to U.S. forces outside of Japan in times of emergency all point to significant changes in Japan's defensive military posture and growing links with the U.S. military.[18]

Important changes in the defense links between Japan and the United States were illustrated by the decision of the Japanese government, taken in full accord with the United States, to extend its sea-lane defenses to one thousand miles and to deploy Japan's Maritime Self Defense Force (MSDF) in the mining or blocking of the straits of Soya, Tsugaru, and Tsushima around Japan to bottle up the Soviet Pacific fleet in times of war. This policy went far beyond any commitments Japan made in the NDPO or the Guidelines, both of which mandated a strictly defensive posture for the SDF.[19] Shortly after taking office, Prime Minister Yasuhiro Nakasone decided to undertake, jointly with the United States, a study of how to make operational the extension of Japan's sea-lane protection across a one-thousand-mile stretch of the Pacific Ocean to the south and west of Japan. This measure was intended to provide support for the operations of the U.S. Navy in the area as well as to free American naval forces for deployment closer to the Mideast.[20] The sea-lane defense concept was not covered by the NDPO and thus represents a gradual change in the mission of the SDF without an explicit change in Japan's defense policy.[21]

The growing gap between an unchanging official policy and the reality of a growing regional security role for the Japanese SDF created some domestic controversy. As was true in controlling the straits, the Japanese government was in fact participating in "collective defense" measures, together with the United States, in apparent violation, in the eyes of the government's critics, of the Japanese constitution. Japan's defense cooperation with the United States thus is evidently weakening the policy constraints under which the SDF had operated before the 1980s.

Furthermore, Japan also agreed to construct an air-defense screen across Japan to interdict long-range Soviet bombers, fighter bombers, and tactical aircraft. And since 1985, the Japanese government has permitted the deployment of two squadrons of F-16 fighter aircraft in Misawa in northern Japan, with the cost to be borne equally by Japan and the United States. Opposition to this deployment was in fact quite strong because these bombers could reach the Russian Far East and thus were inherently "offensive." Similar problems were raised with the stationing of three hundred Green Berets at Okinawa in September 1983 and the deployment of SH-3H Sea King helicopters on the Yokosuka-based aircraft carrier *Midway*, since these helicopters can carry nuclear depth charges for antisubmarine warfare.

In sum the 1980s witnessed a far-reaching integration of the American and Japanese military. Increasing physical integration and interoperability of the two military forces created a system essentially of American making, with Japan playing the role of junior partner. Despite its growth in size and capabilities, especially during the 1980s, in the words of political scientist Takashi Inoguchi, the SDF remains basically dependent and subordinate to the U.S. military.[22] The mission of the Ground Self Defense Force (GSDF) to defend Hokkaido is closely linked to broader U.S. operations. The MSDF is specializing in antisubmarine surveillance in the Western Pacific as well as preparing for a potential blockade of the Japanese straits through which the Russian fleet would have to move to gain access to the Pacific. And the enhanced role of the Air Self Defense Force (ASDF) in aerial surveillance and intelligence, as well as the interdiction of long-range bombers, is auxiliary to the mission of the U.S. air force. A critic of Japan's defense policy, Glenn Hook, thus goes as far as to speak of a " 'denationalization' of the Japanese military."[23]

Sending the SDF Overseas

Japan's steadfast refusal, until the 1990s, to send members of the SDF abroad, even as members of U.N. peacekeeping missions, resulted from a deliberate policy of caution and restraint rooted in the traumatic experience of losing a disastrous war. During the Korean War, Japan was actually much more fully involved on the Korean peninsula than was being publicly revealed at the time.[24] Although no Japanese soldiers fought in Korea, Japanese shipping and railroad experts and crews worked in Korea under American or U.N. command. Their number ran into the thousands. Between October and December 1950, Japan deployed forty-six minesweepers manned by twelve hundred men; two boats were sunk, one man was killed, and eight men were injured.[25] Almost one-third of the support ships of the Inchon amphibious landing were manned by Japanese crews.[26] But this involvement occurred under the Occupation.

Although the issue of Japan's possible participation in U.N. peacekeeping operations had been discussed and analyzed inside the Ministry of Foreign Affairs (MOFA), throughout the postwar era strong public opposition had always lent such bureaucratic discussions an air of unreality. The United Nations requested the Japanese government to send SDF officers to Lebanon in 1958, but the request was denied. In response to the U.N. Security Council's passing of a resolution to impose economic sanctions against Rhodesia, the MOFA drafted the U.N. Resolutions Cooperation Bill in 1965. But with the opposition parties and parts of the government firmly resisting, the bill was not submitted to the Diet. In 1969 Prime Minister Eisaku Sato stated that Japan would participate in "any international peacekeeping machinery" that might be set up in Vietnam after a cease-fire had been negotiated.[27] In 1983 a MOFA advisory group suggested Japanese participation in peacekeeping operations, but again because of stiff domestic opposition, the government decided against making such a commitment to the United Nations.[28] When the U.S.-Japan Advisory Commission recommended in 1984 that the SDF participate in U.N. peacekeeping operations, public sentiment backed, at most, Japan's participation in international disaster relief operations.[29]

In mid-1987 the United States asked its NATO allies as well as Japan to assist the U.S. Navy by sending destroyers and minesweepers for the protection of international shipping in the Gulf against potential attacks from Iran and Iraq. Although the Security Division of the Foreign Ministry and the prime minister were leaning toward complying with the request, Cabinet Chief Secretary Masaharu Gotoda was adamantly opposed. Gotoda argued that compliance with the U.S. request would violate Japan's postwar policy of not allowing Japanese military personnel to be part of an exercise of force overseas. Such a move might endanger Japanese ships and involve Japan in hostilities.[30]

In response to the crisis following Iraq's invasion of Kuwait, the United States again suggested, in August 1990, that Japan send minesweepers and tankers to the Gulf.[31] The Japanese government again refused to comply, on the grounds that minesweepers might get drawn into hostilities. SDF ships were finally sent to the Gulf in April 1991—after the end of the war. The MSDF had carefully prepared for this eventuality since August 1990. And after the end of the war, MOFA's Security Division also had begun serious consideration of this policy option. Various factors worked in favor of deployment. Germany's decision to send minesweepers prodded the MOFA into a stronger advocacy role for Japan's taking a similar stance. And MITI recognized the need for sending minesweepers so that the Japanese-owned Arabian Oil Company could again begin exporting oil from Saudi Arabian ports. Yet MITI apparently refrained from taking a public stance, preferring instead that business organizations press for the dispatch of SDF ships. Public opinion supported this move. According to one poll conducted in March 1991, 63 percent of the respondents backed the policy while 29 percent were opposed. Some of the opposition parties were not strongly opposed either. Komeito did not formally approve the dispatch of the minesweepers, but the government's decision enjoyed the support of a substantial number of Komeito's Diet members.[32] This episode clearly indicated that the categorical opposition to the overseas deployment of the SDF had lost some of its persuasiveness in Japanese domestic politics.[33] It is unlikely, however, that Japan will quickly move to extend its participation in multinational military action authorized by the United Nations, despite the dramatic changes in the international system— changes that many observers, especially in the United States, believe warrant such a corresponding change in policy as a necessary adjustment in the post–cold war era.

The U.N. Peace Cooperation Bill, which Prime Minister Toshiki Kaifu introduced in the Diet in October 1990, revealed the political constraints under which the government was operating. The U.N. Peace Cooperation Corps that the government was proposing to institute was to be composed of volunteers on loan from government agencies including the SDF and the Maritime Safety Agency, which is part of the Ministry of Transportation. Its task was to include a variety of noncombatant functions, including monitoring a truce, holding administrative consultations with governments after the cessation of hostilities, monitoring elections, providing medical, transportation, and communication services, and rendering assistance to refugees and reconstruction activities. Under no circumstances was the corps to be allowed to engage in the "use of force" or the "threat of the use of force." Like a police force, members of the corps would carry only small weapons to be used exclusively for self-protection. But according to the bill, the corps would be permitted to cooperate with nations acting to put U.N. resolutions into effect. Diet deliberations made clear that the government intended to have the SDF operate in the area of logistics and support for multinational forces deployed in the Gulf at the time. Critics contended that cooperation with the multinational forces, even if restricted to logistics and support, would constitute a use of force. Thus only 20 to 30 percent of the public backed the bill.[34] All opposition parties were against it, and even inside the LDP less than half of the lower house members supported the bill.[35] The bill died in November 1990 in the Diet without having been put to a vote.

In September 1991, the government submitted the U.N. Peacekeeping Operations Cooperation Bill to the Diet. According to one public opinion poll in June 1991, 50 percent of the public were for and 40 percent were against the SDF's participation in peacekeeping operations of the United Nations.[36] The writing of the new bill evidently took into account the low level of support the 1990 version had generated. The new bill restricted itself to authorizing the SDF's participation in U.N. peacekeeping operations and humanitarian international rescue operations.

The government stressed the importance of making international contributions, in particular the need for Japanese support for peacekeeping operations in Cambodia, as a way to garner public approval. The 1980 cabinet decision that interpreted Article 9 of the constitution as prohibiting sending the SDF overseas with any mission involving the use of force remained a major obstacle for the government in preparing the 1991 bill. Whether the use of arms, in the face of organized attack, by the dispatched SDF personnel constituted legitimate self-defense or exemplified a use of force banned by the constitution was a major issue debated inside the government.[37] The final version of the government bill apparently decided in favor of the latter interpretation. It made overseas deployment of the SDF as part of a peacekeeping operation conditional on the opposing sides' agreement to a cease-fire, their acceptance of the deployment of the peacekeeping force, and the neutrality of that force.[38] Furthermore, to prevent the use of force by Japanese personnel abroad, the government claimed that the SDF would not be placed under the operational command of the United Nations. SDF personnel would be permitted to use arms only for individual self-defense, not as part of any organized military action.[39] This attenuated version of the original legislation passed the lower house in 1991 and was sent to the upper house.

The government's interpretation of Article 9 appears to have made compliance with Japan's constitution incompatible with U.N. norms on peacekeeping operations. Whether it would be feasible to maintain a national command over SDF personnel deployed abroad on peacekeeping operations was one of the major points of contention in the Diet debates.[40] Placement of SDF personnel under U.N. command would require a major change in the government's interpretation of Article 9. Thus the government faced a difficult dilemma. The bill was amended in the upper house, and it passed both houses in June 1992. The final version of the bill did not resolve the dilemma. But it froze, until authorization by a future law, SDF participation in peacekeeping operations that might involve a combat role. Furthermore, the three-party coalition supporting the final bill informally agreed not to implement SDF participation in logistical operations such as the transporting of weapons.[41] SDF units sent abroad under the new law would "stay far from the sound of gunfire."[42] The final compromise was consistent with the public's response to the bill. In a public opinion poll taken in November 1991, 33 percent of the respondents were in favor of and 58 percent were against SDF participation in lightly armed peacekeeping forces whose mission was to separate combatants.[43]

Under the new law, the government sent SDF personnel to Cambodia in the fall of 1992; and in March 1993 it decided to send SDF personnel to Mozambique. Ironically, as domestic agreement on the SDF's limited participation in traditional U.N. peacekeeping operations was finally being reached in the summer of 1992, the United Nations was developing a new approach that widened the scope of its operations. Its new policy authorized the deployment of heavily armored forces even in areas where cease-fire agreements did not exist. Thus, after the passing of the 1992 law, the problem of the gap between Japanese and U.N. norms became even more acute for the government. The dilemma was well illustrated by Japan's responses to the issue of Somalia. Though endorsing the U.N. Security Council decision in March 1993 to deploy a peacekeeping force in Somalia, the government took the position that the 1992 law ruled out any SDF participation in such a force because no comprehensive cease-fire agreement existed in that country. The striking contrast between the success in Cambodia and the perceived failure in Somalia has strengthened resistance to a larger or more active role for the SDF. At the same time, the SDF's performance in Cambodia somewhat allayed the fears of Japan's Asian neighbors, opening the door to higher-profile activities. Cabinet ministers have voiced opposing views on whether to revise the law to relax the conditions imposed on SDF participation in peacekeeping operations.[44] Thus SDF participation in such operations is likely to continue to be a very controversial issue in Japanese politics.

Participation in U.N. peacekeeping operations is not the only option for dispatching the SDF overseas. In the public's perception the most valuable part of the SDF is not the protection it provides for Japan but its emergency relief operations. According to a public opinion poll taken in September 1992, 73 percent of the respondents perceived providing disaster relief to be the most important role of the SDF, compared with 13 percent who thought that the SDF's major role was to defend Japan.[45] This predilection for the fight against nature over the fight against man provides a supportive public climate for Japan's participation in international relief efforts. After the 1987 earthquake in Mexico, Japan was severely criticized for its refusal to participate in the ensuing international relief effort. Legislation subsequently adopted in 1987 explicitly excluded SDF personnel from participation and provided for sending volunteer experts in various fields. When Bangladesh was hit by a typhoon in the summer of 1991 that caused more than one hundred thousand fatalities, Japan dispatched two helicopters and a rescue team of firemen.[46] In 1991 the government submitted to the Diet a bill amending the disaster relief legislation of 1987 to permit sending SDF personnel abroad.[47] The bill passed the Diet in June 1992.[48]

With the number of Japanese living overseas increasing from three hundred thousand to six hundred thousand between 1980 and 1990, an advisory committee to the MOFA recommended in the summer of 1991 that the government should increase its capability, including transport planes and telecommunications, to get in touch with potential crisis points around the globe to protect Japanese living overseas.[49] In 1992 the government submitted an amendment of the SDF law to the Diet. It would permit SDF aircraft to rescue Japanese citizens overseas in case of emergency. Although the government maintained at the same time that the SDF would not be dispatched overseas in cases that might require the use of force, the amendment met strong opposition in the Diet. Failing to get passed, it was carried over to the regular Diet session of 1993.[50] In the 1990s Japan will also confront the issue of how to secure the shipment of plutonium from France to Japan. A decision was made to have members of the Maritime Safety Agency (MSA), rather than of the MSDF, accompany such transports. This decision was implemented when plutonium was shipped from France to Japan over a two-month period starting in November 1992.

But the fear of a possible "seajacking" by terrorists could reopen the discussion.[51] Overseas police-style protection operations and the dispatch of relief teams thus are plausible political options for the deployment of Japanese military personnel overseas.

In this entire controversy, the Japan Defense Agency (JDA) has taken a strong interest. But it has been cautious in its attitude toward the possible overseas deployment of the SDF. In June 1991 the JDA announced that it favored sending SDF personnel abroad, but only for the purpose of helping in disaster relief operations and for overseeing elections and cease-fires in U.N. peacekeeping operations. The JDA remained skeptical about having the SDF participate in peacekeeping operations that involved a combat role. The reason for this hesitancy was quite clear. The JDA did not want to subject the SDF to political controversy while public suspicion against it remained strong. In contrast, the MOFA, possibly with an eye toward Japan's involvement in the Cambodian peace process, became an avid advocate of the participation of the SDF in peacekeeping operations.[52] A second reason for the caution of the JDA was its overriding interest in defining a new role for the SDF in coping with regional conflicts, in cooperation with the United States, as the Russian threat in East Asia declined. Compared with this task, Japan's involvement in peacekeeping operations was less important for the JDA. The JDA is not in principle opposed to the SDF's participation in such operations. But in contrast to establishing a new regional mission for the SDF, it deems peacekeeping operations at this time to be of secondary importance.[53] The prospect of committing perhaps several thousand men to peacekeeping at a time of severe personnel shortage has also been a deterrent. And the SDF has been acutely aware of the negative effects that a difficult peacekeeping mission might have on the morale of the SDF, as well as on the prospects for successful recruitment.[54] In 1993, the Minister of Foreign Affairs advocated legislation that the director of the JDA opposed, authorizing SDF participation in peacekeeping operations that involved a combat role.[55] In sum, the issue of sending military personnel abroad illustrates with great clarity the rigidity of Japan's security policy in the face of pressure from the United States and rapidly changing conditions in the international system.

The Prohibition of Arms Exports

Japanese business made the 1967 ban on the export of military equipment a political issue when it had to cope with a serious slump in profits in the wake of the first oil price shock of 1973. But business pressure backfired. A change in the policy, although viewed favorably by MITI, was strongly resisted by the opposition parties, and the government chose to strengthen the ban instead. In 1976 Prime Minister Takeo Miki announced that the ban would be extended to all areas of the world and to the exports of all equipment necessary for arms production.[56] In April 1978, MITI Minister Toshio Komoto affirmed before the Diet that, in addition, the export of technologies relevant for weapons production would be prohibited.[57] A Diet resolution passed by both houses of the Diet in March 1981 reaffirmed the ban.[58] According to data provided by the U.S. Arms Control and Disarmament Agency (ACDA), Japan exported $320 million worth of arms in 1983, $280 million in 1984, $100 million in 1985, $130 million in 1986, and $80 million in 1987, with virtually all of these sales presumably falling under the "dual-use" category.[59] By international standards, these are negligible sums.

According to the established government definition, "weapons" are "objects that are used by militaries and directly employed in battle."[60] "Japanese firms have been able to export some military items because the Japanese define 'military' in a much narrower sense than Americans do. . . . A naval base in Vladivostok, for example, boasts a state-of-the-art floating dock made in Japan ostensibly for commercial use. In addition, Japanese corporations are important suppliers of components to the U.S. Department of Defense and to other NATO allies as well."[61] Dual-use products and subassembly products are not covered by Japan's export ban, but their export is regulated by MITI. During the Gulf War in 1991, for example, domestic political considerations counseling restraint were overridden by the pressure from the United States for a substantial shipment of Japanese communications equipment. MITI had to ascertain very quickly what stockpiles of material existed in Japan and then help organize transshipments. Weapons like the Patriot missile most likely have Japanese parts and components. It is unclear whether shipments of critical parts and possibly components were made to the United States or directly to the Gulf. Had there been substantial domestic opposition, which there was not, a ready loophole existed under Article 12 of the U.S.-Japan Status of Forces Agreement for supplying the United States with war-related equipment in times of need.[62] The article exempts from the export ban American military forces stationed in Japan when it orders equipment for use in Japan. However, the Japanese government has no means for monitoring whether the U.S. Department of Defense is using the material in Japan or is shipping it elsewhere in the world. Weapons containing critically important components, or the components themselves, could thus have been moved out of Japan in the past or may be moved in this manner in the future.[63]

This growing dependence of the United States on Japan in some defense-related areas reflects a shifting balance of technological strength between the two countries. Traditionally, much of the defense technology that Japanese firms relied on was American. Technology transfers have been a fundamental aspect of Japan's defense procurement policy, with the added benefit that they have "offered the greatest technological benefits to domestic industry."[64] But the growth of a new form of technological nationalism, particularly in the United States, has made this form of technology import increasingly problematic. With Japan making deep inroads into the traditional strongholds of American industry, especially in high-tech areas, Congress has been increasingly hesitant to permit Japanese corporations to share in the defense technologies in which the United States has invested enormous resources—the United States currently spends 140 times more on military research and development than does Japan.[65] Protectionism in Congress was strong throughout the 1980s, but has since acquired an ominous undertone, particularly when it touches on defense-related companies or industries, as evidenced by the congressional responses to Fujitsu's attempted takeover of Fairchild and the Toshiba sales to the Soviet Union, as well as the application of Clause 2332 of the Trade Enhancement Act, which aims at defending domestic industries for national security reasons.[66]

But with its rapid move to the frontiers of civilian high-technology industries, Japan has become, in the nontraditional sense, a major military power, mostly without a conscious plan. The U.S. Critical Technologies Plan for 1990 argued that the United States lagged the Soviet Union in only one out of twenty technologies crucial to the long-term technological superiority of American weapons systems. Japan, however, led in five areas: semiconductors, robotics, superconductivity, biotechnology, and photonics.[67] Informed American observers predict that four technologies are likely to leave a major impact on the weapons of the future: very high speed integrated circuits, digital gallium arsenide circuits, microwave monolithic integrated circuits, and mercury cadmium telluride for infrared detectors. Japanese firms are very strongly positioned in the development of these four technologies.[68] Controlling important segments of the global semiconductor market will give Japanese firms the power to cut off American defense contractors from a vital raw material for their production. Furthermore, establishing a lead in civilian product cycles becomes a major military asset because civilian product cycles are only two or three years long whereas military product cycles evolve over five to fifteen years.[69] And while Japan is becoming less dependent on American military technology, America is evidently becoming more dependent on Japanese commercial technology. The export of dual-use components is likely to be a mainstay of Japan's militarily relevant exports—without a change in the existing policy prohibiting military sales.[70]

In the 1980s the ban on the export of weapons was redefined in three important respects, all of which involved the United States. First, Japan permitted, in November 1983, the export of military technology to the United States within the context of the 1954 Mutual Defense Assistance Act.[71] Japan and the United States set up the Joint Military Technology Commission (JMTC), which was charged with reviewing both the requests of the U.S. government and the responses of the Japanese government. The Japanese government specifically committed itself to facilitate not only the flow of military technology but also the transfer of dual-use technologies, and in particular production technologies, that might have application for advanced weapons systems, such as gallium arsenide, optoelectronics, compound materials, ceramics, and heat-resistant materials, which were of great interest to the United States.[72] Although before 1983 the export of dual-use technologies had already been permitted legally, the Japanese government hoped to encourage Japanese firms to be more forthcoming by also releasing the restrictions on the export of military technologies. The fear of hostile public reaction and the anticipation of minor sales were the most important obstacles that stopped Japanese firms from following the lead of the government in this area, although it should be noted that MITI has quietly continued to regulate the export, even to the United States, of dual-use products and technologies clearly destined for military use.[73] In the view of at least one American businessman, the purpose of the 1983 agreement was very clear. "I think the best way to stay ahead of the Japanese is to get access to their technology." With fewer than 20 percent of the ten thousand scientific and technical papers annually published in Japanese available in English translation, the 1983 agreement appeared to be a good way to overcome a high linguistic and technological hurdle.[74]

The intent of the establishment of the JMTC was to increase the flow of technology from Japan to the United States. But because the agreement was drafted by bureaucrats trained in law rather than engineering and thus was much too general; because American firms lacked reliable sources of information about Japanese technology, resulting in the bureaucratic rigidity of the U.S. Defense Department; and because both American and Japanese firms hesitated to forge new technology links, the United States applied for a total of only three technology transfers in the 1980s. Between 1987 and 1990, Japan transferred technology related to SAM missiles, the construction of naval vessels, and the modification of U.S. naval vessels.[75] The result was paltry considering that in the mid-1980s, more than one hundred military coproduction agreements existed in which Japanese manufacturers were using U.S. technologies, and that in the second half of the 1980s, Japan was sending ten times more researchers to the United States than it received.[76]

When President Ronald Reagan invited Japan to join Britain, Germany, and France to participate in searching for what he described as an alternative to the system of nuclear deterrence, Prime Minister Nakasone took a long time before signing, in 1987, an agreement laying out the conditions of Japan's participation in the Strategic Defense Initiative (SDI). Though it adds to Japan's technology base, SDI participation is foremost a symbol of Japan's political commitment to the U.S.-Japan Mutual Security Treaty.[77] The delay was due not only to the slow decision making in Tokyo but also to some serious political hesitations about the ambiguity of the technological and strategic implications of the SDI program.[78] And the economic incentives that Japanese business initially saw in participating in the development of potentially revolutionary military technologies with direct implications for commercial products were soon tempered. For it quickly became apparent that German business had failed to gain substantial research funding from the SDI program. In addition, Japanese businessmen increasingly worried over a drain of their technology to the United States.[79] In the end the Japanese decision was taken not on military or economic but on political grounds. On this issue Japan simply could not afford to be seen as a disloyal ally.

The 1983 technology agreement and Japan's participation in SDI have done precious little to accelerate the flow of Japanese technology back to the United States, an increasingly urgent task if the U.S. Congress is to be mollified. The 12th Meeting of the Japan-U.S. Systems and Technology Forum agreed, therefore, on five areas of technology in which flow from Japan to the United States would be strongly encouraged: rocket engines, infrared sensors, magnetic technology, ceramics, and advanced material replacing traditional steel. The agreement was heralded as a breakthrough, especially after the intense friction over the FSX jet fighter project. On the Japanese side it represents, however, a delicate political coalition, with the

MOFA as a strong proponent and MITI, at best, a reluctant ally. MITI has firsthand experience in dealing with private firms that are hesitant to let go of proprietary technologies, especially when the intended recipient is the U.S. Department of Defense, which might subject them to detailed regulations and expose them to the risk of bad publicity in Japan.[80] But MITI is becoming increasingly aware of the military significance of the commercial technologies developed by Japanese corporations. Together with the JDA, it is likely to seek to increase the leverage it has over private corporations by relaxing the restrictions on the export of dual-use technologies and products, including perhaps the permission to export the products of joint ventures with American firms.[81]

Conclusion

One of the core tenets of the study of international relations holds that rational state actors seek to maximize relative gains in the international system and, in doing so, adjust their behavior to the dictates of a changing international situation. But Japanese policymakers, rather than following strictly the logic of realist doctrine, have responded to the domestic and transnational structures and norms that embed Japan's security policy. Since the mid-1970s, changes in the international environment have affected Japan's security. The weakening of the American position in East Asia and the growth of a Soviet military presence in the late 1970s, the second cold war in Europe in the early 1980s, the dramatic changes in Soviet defense and foreign policy in the mid-to-late 1980s, the end of the cold war, and the breakup of the Soviet Union have elicited no sharp changes in Japan's security policy. Defense expenditures have crept upward—very gradually. And the various constraints that have operated on Japanese defense policy have been loosening—very gradually. The determinants of these gradual changes were not primarily the perceived threat posed by the Soviet Union or changes in the global distribution of power but the vagaries in the structures and norms, both domestic and transnational, that have affected Japan during the past two decades. Among these, political sensitivity to the domestic opposition of the LDP on the one hand and political pressure from Washington on the other have clearly been two key factors. Japanese security policy attempted to reconcile the contradictory pressures from these two sources, even if the policy appeared to be "irrational" from the perspective of traditional theories of international relations.

By 1993, international change had facilitated a dramatic shift in Japanese politics, which may alter the structural and normative foundations of Japanese security policy. Meanwhile, incremental policy changes are gradually creating new options for Japan's military. By 1984, the SDF had over fifty destroyers, twice as many as the U.S. Seventh Fleet. Japan had as many anti-submarine warfare (ASW) aircraft as were under the entire Pacific Command of the U.S. armed forces. And Japan's four hundred fighter aircraft exceeded the combined total that the United States had stationed in Japan, the Republic of Korea, and the Philippines.[82] These options are not yet explicitly national. If Japan wanted to create a national military option, it would have to acquire the offensive systems it now shuns for political reasons or, at a minimum, develop a broad range of stealth technologies.[83] In Japan, the widespread and deeply held political consensus states that military issues cannot be separated from political and economic considerations. But the technological nature of the weapons that Japan is acquiring presents a base from which such a national military option could be pursued in the event, unlikely as it is, that political perspectives should no longer be viewed as dominating military perspectives.

Both as a complement and as a possible alternative, Japanese security policy is likely to emphasize Asian regional security structures in the coming years. Since the demise of the Southeast Asia Treaty Organization (SEATO), no regional security organization has existed in Asia. Asian security is organized by a set of bilateral security pacts revolving around the United States. But since the early 1980s, the Association of Southeast Asian Nations (ASEAN) has begun to consider some regional security issues at its meetings.[84] In the 1970s and 1980s, the Japanese government was adamantly opposed to engaging the Soviet Union in regional arms-control talks. But with the demise of the Soviet Union and a growing fear of a serious deterioration of U.S.-Japanese relations, Japan's interest in a sustained security dialogue in Asia is bound to grow, as illustrated at the 1991 ASEAN Post-Ministerial Conference. With American military presence in Asia weakening, Japan is likely to become a more vocal advocate of cooperative regional security regimes. Japanese foreign policy will need not only to guarantee the continued involvement of the United States and China in Asia but also to decide whether ASEAN should gradually develop some security functions or whether Indonesia should become Southeast

Asia's regional hegemon, tied closely to Japan and loosely to the United States.

At stake is the future political definition of Japan's international context. In contrast to the United States and Europe, the rationale for Japan's SDF was not limited to the Soviet threat. American pressure and the importance of Japan's political relationship with the United States, that is, political factors, created the main rationale for the substantial increase in Japan's military capabilities during the last two decades. The clash between America's global-military interests and Japan's national-economic concerns partly explains why Japan's most important "ally," the United States, in the 1980s was "the occasion of more foreign policy, and foreign economic policy, controversies than all of Japan's potential enemies combined."[85] In the future, countering Russia may continue to be important in the minds of some defense planners.[86] Furthermore, possible instabilities in Asia, on the Korean peninsula, and in China have convinced important segments of the government and the bureaucracy of Japan's need for a minimum defensive capability even without a clear enemy.[87] However, the strategy and equipment that the SDF has adopted during the past fifteen years may not be adequate to deal with less-defined security threats in Asia in the future. The threat posed by North Korea's development of medium-range ballistic missiles and its suspected nuclear weapons program has reemphasized the importance of Japan's military reliance on the United States, so that even after the collapse of the Soviet Union the bilateral relationship is likely to remain an essential ingredient of Japan's security policy.

Japan's growing stature in the world is only incompletely reflected in its security policy. The national option that is being created now will not necessarily be exercised. Neither outright confrontation nor political acquiescence in U.S.-Japanese relations is the likely political background for the future evolution of Japan's security policy. For Japanese leaders, "autonomy and alliance need not be and are not currently antithetical."[88] In the 1970s, the SDF and the security treaty were increasingly accepted by the Japanese public. During the 1980s, the domestic impetus for incremental changes in favor of an increased defense posture was unmistakable. In the 1990s, defense spending is likely to grow at a lower rate while the political pressure for the participation of the SDF in international peacekeeping operations will probably increase. The increase in Japan's defense capabilities and the creation of a national option, brought about by linking Japan's national security to that of the United States, will undoubtedly have an effect on how Japan, its Asian neighbors, and the United States will react politically in an era of profound international and domestic change.

Notes

We are grateful for the comments that we received at the Woodrow Wilson Center conference on "Japan and the World" (January 27–28, 1992). This paper draws on material we have published in *Japan's National Security: Structures, Norms, and Policy Responses in a Changing World*, Cornell East Asian Series no. 58 (Ithaca, N.Y.: Cornell University, East Asia Program, 1993).

1. Interview No. 16, Tokyo, June 17, 1991; transcript available from the authors.

2. Comprehensive National Security Study Group, *Report on Comprehensive National Security* (Tokyo: Office of the Prime Minister, 1980); Robert W. Barnett, *Beyond War: Japan's Concept of Comprehensive National Security* (New York: Pergamon Brassey, 1984).

3. J.W.M. Chapman, Reinhard Drifte, and I.T.M. Gow, *Japan's Quest for Comprehensive Security* (New York: St. Martin's, 1982); Davis B. Bobrow, Duc Kim, and Stephen R. Hill, "Putting Up, Not Speaking Up: Japanese Government Resource Allocations to Comprehensive Security" (paper presented at the Annual Meeting of the International Studies Association, Washington, D.C., 1985); International Institute for Strategic Studies, *East Asia, the West, and International Security: Prospects for Peace*, parts I-III, Adelphi Papers Nos. 216–18 (London: International Institute for Strategic Studies, 1987); Taketsugu Tsurutani, "The Security Debate," in James M. Roherty, ed., *Defense Policy Formation: Towards Comparative Analysis* (Durham, N.C.: Carolina Academic Press, 1980), pp. 175–94; Nobutoshi Akao, ed., *Japan's Economic Security* (New York: St. Martin's, 1983); Tetsuya Umemoto, "Comprehensive Security and the Evolution of the Japanese Security Posture," in Robert A. Scalapino, Seizaburo Sato, Jusuf Wanandi, and Sung-joo Han, eds., *Asian Security Issues: Regional and Global*, Research Papers and Policy Studies No. 26 (Berkeley: University of California, Institute of East Asian Studies, 1988), pp. 28–49; Seizaburo Sato, "Japan and Pacific-Asian Security," in Robert A. Scalapino, Seizaburo Sato, and Jusuf Wanandi, eds., *Internal and External Security in Asia*, Research Papers and Policy Studies No. 16 (Berkeley: University of California, Institute of East Asian Studies, 1986), pp. 80–91; Tsuneo Akaha, "Comprehensive Security as an Alternative to Military Security in the Post-Hegemonic World: The Japanese Model and Its Applicability in East Asia" (paper prepared for the International Studies Association Convention, Washington, D.C., April 10–14, 1990); Tsuneo Akaha, "Japan's Comprehensive Security Policy: A New East Asian Environment," *Asian Survey* 31 (April 1991): 324–40; Alan Rix, "Japan's Comprehensive Security and Australia," *Australian Outlook* 41 (August 1987): 79–86; Michael G. L'Estrange, *The Internationalization of Japan's Security Policy: Challenges and Dilemmas for a Reluctant Power* (Berkeley: University of California, Institute of International Studies, 1990), pp. 16–17; Yukio Satoh, *The Evolution of Japanese Security Policy*, Adelphi Paper No. 178 (London: International Institute for Strategic Studies, 1982), p. 6; and Javed S. Maswood, *Japanese Defence: The Search for Political Power* (Singapore: Institute of Southeast Asian Studies, 1990), pp. 38–39.

4. Interviews Nos. 2 and 9, Tokyo, June 11 and 13, 1991.

5. L'Estrange, *The Internationalization of Japan's Security Policy*, p. 17.

6. Richard J. Samuels, "Consuming for Production: Japanese National Security, Nuclear Fuel Procurement, and the Domestic Economy," *International Organization* 43 (Autumn 1989): 628.

7. Atsushi Tokinoya, *The Japan-US Alliance: A Japanese Perspective* (London: International Institute for Strategic Studies, 1986), pp. 4–9; Tetsuya Umemoto, "Arms and Alliance in Japanese Public Opinion" (Ph.D. diss., Princeton University, 1985), pp. 55–57.

8. Interviews Nos. 2, 5, 15, 22, Tokyo, June 11, 12, 17, 19, 1991.

9. Masataka Kosaka, *Options for Japan's Foreign Policy*, Adelphi Paper, No. 97 (London: International Institute for Strategic Studies, 1973).

10. Daniel I. Okimoto, "The Economics of National Defense," in Daniel Okimoto, ed., *Japan's Economy: Coping with Change in the International Environment* (Boulder, Colorado: Westview, 1982), p. 239.

11. Hisahiko Okazaki, "Japanese Security Policy: A Time for Strategy," *International Security* 7, 2 (1982): 191.

12. Toshiyuki Toyoda, "Japan's Policies since 1945," *Bulletin of the Atomic Scientists* 41 (August 1985): 62. SAC was absorbed into STRATCOM in 1992.

13. William M. Arkin and David Chappell, "Forward Offensive Strategy: Raising the Stakes in the Pacific," *World Policy Journal* 2 (Summer 1985): 487.

14. Ibid.

15. Defense Agency, *Defense of Japan 1990* (Tokyo: Japan Times, 1990), pp. 213–16.

16. Glenn D. Hook, "The Erosion of Anti-Militaristic Principles in Contemporary Japan," *Journal of Peace Research* 25 (December 1988): 384.

17. Ibid., pp. 390–91.

18. Akaha, "Comprehensive Security as an Alternative," p. 17.

19. Mike M. Mochizuki, "Japan's Search for Strategy," *International Security* 8 (Winter 1983–84): 161; Arkin and Chappell, "Forward Offensive Strategy."

20. Interviews Nos. 8 and 12, Tokyo, June 13 and 14, 1991; Edward A. Olsen, *U.S.-Japan Strategic Reciprocity: A Neo-Internationalist View* (Stanford: Hoover Institution, 1985), pp. 96–97; and Reinhard Drifte, "Japan's Defense Policy: How Far Will the Changes Go?" *International Defense Review* 2 (1985): 156–57.

21. Masashi Nishihara, "The Security of East Asia: Part I," in Robert O'Neill, ed., *East Asia, the West, and International Security: Prospects for Peace*, Adelphi Paper No. 218 (London: International Institute for Strategic Studies, 1987), p. 186.

22. Takashi Inoguchi, "Japan in Context" (paper prepared for the Japan Political Economy Research Conference, Tokyo, July 23–28, 1985), p. 27.

23. Hook, "Erosion of Anti-Militaristic Principles," p. 393.

24. Theodore McNelly, "The Economic Consequences of Japan's 'Peace Constitution' " (paper prepared for the 1987 Annual Meeting of the American Political Science Association, Palmer House, Chicago, September 3–6, 1987), p. 9.

25. James E. Auer, "Japanese Militarism," *U.S. Naval Institute Proceedings* (September 1973), p. 49; James E. Auer, *The Postwar Rearmament of Japanese Maritime Forces, 1945–71* (New York: Praeger, 1973), pp. 64–66.

26. Olsen, *U.S.-Japan Strategic Reciprocity*, pp. 75–76.

27. John K. Emmerson, *Arms, Yen, and Power: The Japanese Dilemma* (New York: Dunellen, 1971), p. 130.

28. *Asahi Shimbun*, September 26, 1991, 13th ed.

29. *Mainichi Shimbun*, October 6, 1984.

30. Joseph Keddell, Jr., "Defense as a Budgetary Problem: The Minimization of Conflict in Japanese Defense Policymaking, 1976–1987" (Ph.D. diss., Political Science, University of Wisconsin, 1990), p. 230.

31. Ministry of Foreign Affairs, *Japan's Post Gulf International Initiatives* (Tokyo: Ministry of Foreign Affairs, 1991); Courtney Purrington and A. K., "Tokyo's Policy Responses during the Gulf Crisis," *Asian Survey* 31 (April 1991): 307–23; Manfred Pöhl, "Die japanischen

Streitkräfte in die Golfregion? Diskussion um den 'japanischen Ernstfall,' " in Heinz Eberhard Maul, ed., *Militärmacht Japan? Sicherheitspolitik und Streitkräfte* (Munich: Iudicium, 1991), pp. 338–62; Ian Buruma, "The Pax Axis," *New York Review of Books* 38 (April 25, 1991): 25–28, 38–39; Masaru Tamamoto, "Trial of an Ideal: Japan's Debate over the Gulf Crisis," *World Policy Journal* 8 (Winter 1990–91): 89–106; Takashi Inoguchi, "Japan's Response to the Gulf Crisis: An Analytic Overview," *Journal of Japanese Studies* 17 (1991): 257–73; and Eiichi Katahara, *Japan's Changing Political and Security Role* (Singapore: Institute of Southeast Asian Studies, 1991).

32. *Asahi Shimbun*, May 4, 6, 9, 10, 15, 16, 18, 1991, 13th ed.

33. Interviews Nos. 1, 4, 5, 18, Tokyo, June 11, 12, 18, 1991; Sadako Ogata, "Japan's United Nations Policy in the 1980s," *Asian Survey* 27 (September 1987): 957–72.

34. Akihiko Tanaka, "Japan's Security Policy in the 1990s" (paper prepared for the Eighth Shimoda Conference, November 16–17, 1990), p. 19.

35. *Asahi Shimbun*, November 9 and 10, 1990, 13th ed.

36. Ibid., June 19, 1991, 10th ed.

37. Interview No. 19, Tokyo, June 18, 1991.

38. *Asahi Shimbun*, September 19, 1991, 11th ed.

39. Tadashi Tanaka, "Kokuren Heiwa Iji Katsudo to Nihon no Sanka-Kyoryoku" (U.N. peacekeeping operations and Japan's participation and cooperation), *Hogaku Seminar* 443 (November 1991): 40–41.

40. Yoshitaka Sasaki, "Abunai Garasu Zaiku" (Dangerous glass artifact), *Sekai* (November 1991), p. 202.

41. *Asahi Shimbun*, June 16, 1992, 13th ed.

42. David E. Sanger, "Japan's Troops May Sail, and the Fear Is Mutual," *New York Times*, June 21, 1992, p. E4.

43. *Asahi Shimbun*, May 1, 1992, 13th ed.

44. Ibid., December 5, 1992, January 26, February 8, March 29, March 30, 1993, 13th eds., January 5, March 27, 1993, evening 3rd eds.

45. Ibid., September 28, 1992, 13th ed.

46. Interviews Nos. 1, 4, 16, Tokyo, June 11 and 17, 1991.

47. *Asahi Shimbun*, March 16, 1992, 13th ed.; interview No. 19, Tokyo, June 18, 1991.

48. *Asahi Shimbun*, June 16, 1992, 13th ed.

49. Interview No. 22, Tokyo, June 19, 1991.

50. *Asahi Shimbun*, March 11, 16, 19, April 5, May 8, 1992, February 4, 1993, 13th ed.

51. David E. Sanger, "Plutonium Shipment after 1992," *New York Times*, October 12, 1989; *Asahi Shimbun*, January 5, 1993, evening 3rd ed.

52. *Asahi Shimbun*, June 8 and August 16, 1991, 13th ed.

53. Ibid., September 12 and 27, 1991, 13th ed.

54. Shunji Taoka, "Igai ni Ooi Yuutsunaru Hyojo" (Unexpectedly many gloomy faces), *AERA* (December 3, 1991), p. 16.

55. *Asahi Shimbun*, January 5, 1993, evening 3rd ed.

56. Asagumo Shimbun-sha, *Boei Hando Bukku* (Defense Handbook) (Tokyo: Asagumo Shimbun-sha, 1991), p. 474; Shuji Kurokawa, "Keidanren Boei Seisan Iinkai no Seiji Kodo" (Political Behavior of Keidanren's Defense Production Committee), in Minoru Nakano, ed., *Nihon-gata Seisaku Kettei no Henyo* (Transformation of Japanese-style policymaking) (Tokyo: Toyo Keizai Shimpo-sha, 1986), p. 216.

57. Hartwig Hummel, *The Policy of Arms Export Restrictions in Japan*, International Peace Research Institute Meigaku (PRIME), Occasional Papers Series No. 4, (Yokohama: Meiji Gakuin University, 1988), p. 11.

58. John E. Endicott, "The Defense Policy of Japan," in Douglas J. Murray and Paul R. Viotti, eds., *The Defense Policies of Nations: A Comparative Study* (Baltimore: Johns Hopkins University Press, 1982), p. 454; T. J. Pempel, "From Trade to Technology: Japan's Reassessment of Military Policies," *Jerusalem Journal of International Relations* 12 (1990): 6; Drifte, "Japan's Defense Policy," pp. 155–56; and Daniel I. Okimoto, "Arms Transfers: The Japanese Calculus," in John H. Barton and Ryukichi Imai, eds., *Arms Control II: A New Approach to International Security* (Cambridge, Mass.: Oelgeschlager, Gunn, and Hain, 1981), pp. 282–85, 302–04.

59. Hartwig Hummel, *Sayonara Rüstungsexporte: Die Beschränkung des Rüstungsexports in Japan als friedenspolitisches Modell*, Tübinger Arbeitspapiere zur Internationalen Politik und Friedensforschung No. 12 (Tübingen: University of Tübingen, 1990), p. 3; Hummel, *Policy of Arms Export Restrictions*, pp. 25–36; Tanaka, "Japan's Security Policy," p. 4; and Reinhard Drifte, *Japan's Growing Arms Industry*, PSIS Occasional Papers No. 1/85 (Lausanne: Programme for Strategic and International Security Studies, 1985), pp. 79–82.

60. Asagumo Shimbun-sha, *Boei Hando Bukku*, p. 475.

61. Steven K. Vogel, "Japanese High Technology, Politics, and Power" (Berkeley Roundtable on the International Economy, Research Paper No. 2, March 1989), p. 79.

62. *Mainichi Shimbun*, February 6, 1982.

63. Interviews Nos. 3, 11, 14, 17, Tokyo, June 11, 14, 17, 1991; Drifte, *Japan's Growing Arms Industry*, p. 82.

64. Michael Chinworth, "Industry and Government in Japanese Defense Procurement: The Case of the Patriot Missile System," *Comparative Strategy* 9 (1990): 197.

65. T. J. Pempel, "From Trade to Technology: Japan's Reassessment of Military Policies," *Jerusalem Journal of International Relations* 12 (1990): 1–28.

66. Takashi Inoguchi, *Trade, Technology, and Security: Implications for East Asia and the West*, Pacific Economic Papers No. 147 (Canberra: Australian National University, Research School of Pacific Studies, Australia-Japan Research Centre, 1987), pp. 19–22.

67. Steven K. Vogel, "The United States and Japan: Technological Rivalry and Military Alliance" (paper prepared for the Institute for Global Conflict and Cooperation [IGCC] Conference, "Beyond the Cold War in the Pacific," San Diego, June 7–9, 1990), p. 3.

68. Ibid., pp. 3–4; Keddell, "Defense as a Budgetary Problem," p. 249.

69. Vogel, "United States and Japan," p. 4.

70. U.S. Congress, Office of Technology Assessment, *Global Arms Trade*, OTA-ISC-460 (Washington, D.C.: Government Printing Office, 1991), pp. 108–9.

71. Marie Söderberg, *Japan's Military Export Policy* (Stockholm: Institute of Oriental Languages, Department of Japanese and Korean Studies, 1986), pp. 126–56; Hiroo Kinoshita, "Mutual Security and Dual-Use Technology: A Consideration of Japanese-U.S. Cooperation," *Speaking of Japan* 10 (1989): 20–24; Neil Davis, "A Look at the Future of Japan's Military Industrial Complex," *Japan Times*, January 4, 1984, p. 11; Keddell, "Defense as a Budgetary Problem," pp. 163–65; Hummel, *Policy of Arms Export Restrictions*, p. 17; Drifte, "Japan's Defense Policy," pp. 155–56; Gregg A. Rubinstein, "Emerging Bonds of U.S.-Japanese Defense Technology Cooperation," *Strategic Review* 15 (Winter 1987): 43–51; and Drifte, *Japan's Growing Arms Industry*, pp. 84–87.

72. Interview No. 14, Tokyo, June 15, 1991; U.S. Congress, Office of Technology Assessment, *Arming Our Allies: Cooperation and Competition in Defense Technology*, OTA-ISC-449 (Washington, D.C.: Government Printing Office, 1990), pp. 61–62; and Rubinstein, "Emerging Bonds," p. 46.

73. Interview No. 11, Tokyo, June 14, 1991; Asahi Shimbun Keizai-bu, *Mili-tech Power: Kyukyoku no Nichibei Masatsu* (Mili-tech Power: The ultimate Japan-U.S. conflict) (Tokyo: Asahi Shimbun-sha, 1989), pp. 130–36.

76 Peter J. Katzenstein and Nobuo Okawara

74. E. S. Browning, "Japan to Share Arms Know-How with U.S.," *Asian Wall Street Journal*, August 16, 1984, p. 1.

75. Interview No. 14, Tokyo, June 17, 1991; U.S. Congress, Office of Technology Assessment, *Arming Our Allies*, p. 69.

76. Interview No. 11, Tokyo, June 14, 1991; Ellen Frost, "Realizing U.S.-Japan Defense Cooperation," *Asian Wall Street Journal*, September 1, 1985; and Jacob M. Schlesinger and Andy Pasztor, "U.S., Japan Neglect Defense-Trade Issue," *Asian Wall Street Journal*, August 7, 1990.

77. Peggy L. Falkenheim, *Japan and Arms Control: Tokyo's Response to SDI and INF*, Aurora Papers No. 6 (Ottawa: Canadian Centre for Arms Control and Disarmament, 1988); Hook, "Erosion of Anti-Militaristic Principles," p. 388; Rubinstein, "Emerging Bonds," p. 47; and Vogel, "Japanese High Technology," pp. 37–39.

78. Wayne Decker, "Japanese Decision Criteria on the Strategic Defense Initiative," in Richard B. Finn, ed., *U.S.-Japan Relations: A Surprising Relationship* (New Brunswick, N.J.: Transaction Books, 1987), pp. 163–73.

79. Ibid., p. 169.

80. U.S. Congress, Office of Technology Assessment, *Global Arms Trade*, pp. 115–20.

81. Interviews Nos. 3, 6, 8, 11, Tokyo, June 11, 12, 13, 14, 1991.

82. Keddell, "Defense as a Budgetary Problem," pp. 169–70.

83. Interview No. 23, Kyoto, June 24, 1991.

84. Yatsuhiro Nakagawa, "The WEPTO Option: Japan's New Role in East Asia/Pacific Collective Security," *Asian Survey* 26 (August 1984): 829–30.

85. T. J. Pempel, "From Exporter to Investor: Japanese Foreign Economic Policy" (paper prepared for Japanese Foreign Policy Conference, Grand Cayman, B.W.I., January 1990), p. 28.

86. Interview No. 6, Tokyo, December 10, 1991.

87. Interview No. 13, Tokyo, December 13, 1991.

88. Gerald L. Curtis, "Japanese Security Policies and the United States," *Foreign Affairs* 59 (Spring 1981): 873.

Part II

Japan in a Multipolar World

Chapter 4

Japan and E.C. '92

HENRI-CLAUDE DE BETTIGNIES

THE GLOBALIZATION of the Japanese economy—acting as the loco-motive of Pacific Basin dynamism—will remain a key feature in the chang-ing structure of comparative advantage among nations through the end of the twentieth century. Even though the growing interdependence between Japan and Europe has gained momentum, particularly since the mid-1980s,[1] the quality of the relationship has not improved at the same pace. At a time when Europeans are muddling through a painful process of building the single market, the Japanese presence in Europe is growing steadily, much faster than the European presence in the Japanese market. Though this is neither an original situation (the U.S. experience is a precedent) nor a difficult one to understand (other "globalization" pro-cesses have taken place before), it is currently creating an environment of anxiety and fear for a growing number of Europeans.

Following the acceleration of change in Eastern Europe and the former Soviet Union, U.S. politicians may turn their attention to the U.S.-Japan relationship. Europeans also are increasingly concerned with the growing Japanese presence in Europe and inevitably worry about its long-term implications. Europeans now must consider how to contend with the turbulence created by Japan's globalization.

Europeans (with nuances to be discussed later) are confronted with the Pacific challenge, with what they perceive as the insolent prosperity of Japan, with the dynamism of the Asian newly industrialized economies

(NIEs), and with the immense resources of Asia-Pacific countries (e.g., China, Indochina, and Siberia). They observe the progressive takeover of the U.S. and European electronics, automotive, and information technology sectors. They worry about Japan's progression toward assuming the leadership position in a global information society and realize also that Japanese society may be more effective in managing (and "digesting") socioeconomic and technological change. They also admire this Japanese capacity.

Europeans today, engaged in a painful if not revolutionary process to create new institutions and develop a new paradigm of society, are worried about the erosion of U.S. global leadership. They see Japan as a new champion exemplifying a radically different paradigm, a different mindscape. However, as Japan becomes a world leader—through economic success, financial might, and technological capacities—it seemingly does not know how to handle the responsibilities associated with power. For the first time, Japan may not have a model to emulate. Europeans see an adolescent Japan, still immature in the world of global affairs, watching the agony of the American father confronting the erosion of it's authority (the "Diminishing Giant Syndrome")[2] but afraid to take America's place. Can Japan assume a role of leadership when the U.S. economy is experiencing serious difficulties, an inward-looking Europe is preoccupied with attempts to build a post-1992 identity, Eastern Europe is in dire straits, the Soviet Union has passed away, Africa is in disarray, and a new distribution of power is in the offing? Japan has excelled at making quality products and selling them effectively. But can Japan play the role played by the United States in the 1960s? Has Japan a "mission," an "ideal," to promote?

Europeans are becoming aware of fundamental differences between European and Japanese societies. Europe's strong individualism, wasteful consumer habits, emphasis on leisure, and urban insecurity contrast with Japan's sense of community, in-group solidarity, frugality, cult of effort, rigor, and confidence in national leadership.

In a world rapidly growing more interdependent, in which by the year 2000 Japan will account for 16 percent of world gross national product (GNP) while the twelve European Community (E.C.) countries combined will account for 22 percent, Europeans are increasingly concerned with the globalization of the Japanese economy. Moreover, they note that Japan's GNP has grown at twice the rate of Europe's (4.2 percent versus 2.2 percent) throughout the 1980s and that this ratio is likely to continue.

Capitalizing on what they learned through their accumulated experiences in the United States, the Japanese now are developing their presence in Europe. The Japanese are growing increasingly visible, with more investment (especially in the service sectors, such as finance and insurance), more *keiretsu* manufacturing facilities [accompanied by an increasing number of subcontractors], and a widening E.C.-Japan trade deficit. Some Europeans exploit growing concerns and portray this development as a Japanese "plot." Others suggest that Japan's expansion should invite Europe to learn from the U.S. experience and resort to foreign pressures on Japan (*gaiatsu*). However, as an assistant of F. Andriessen, the E.C. Commission's vice president for external affairs, said recently after meeting Prime Minister Kiichi Miyazawa: "The United States has sticks. The E.C. doesn't."[3] And Sir Leon Brittan, E.C. commissioner for external economic affairs, noted, "A European company which assembles its products in the Far East may contribute less to the European economy than an out-and-out foreign company which produces and conducts research within Europe, using local labour."[4] He was referring to the recent Nissan plant and the ICL operation (80 percent Japanese owned), which contributes to the direct employment of 62,600 by Japanese firms in the United Kingdom. (By 1995, according to Nomura forecasts, 400,000 Britons will be employed by Japanese firms.)

Although Japanese transplants are broadly welcomed in the United Kingdom,[5] the growth of the Japanese presence in Europe continues to worry most other major European business leaders, who recently told their Japanese counterparts that the current global imbalance (in trade and investment)[6] should not be allowed to continue.

In the first part of this chapter, I will identify Japan's presence in Europe and assess its dynamics over time. I will then examine the highly differentiated reactions in France and the United Kingdom. I will conclude with a discussion of the global implications and what the future may hold.

The Japanese Presence in Europe

If one word can characterize the European-Japanese economic relationship, it is probably *imbalance*. Whether one looks at trade, investment, or people, the key feature remains disequilibrium, increasing over the years (see figures 4.1, 4.2, and 4.3).

Even though the "structural" trade deficit[7] between Japan and the E.C. was slightly reduced in 1989 and 1990 after its peak year in 1988, the gap was expected to widen again, with Europe taking over from the United States the doubtful privilege of having the largest trade deficit with Japan. Yet the trade issue with Japan is not so much one of volume as one of

Figure 4.1
E.C.-Japan Trade, 1979–89

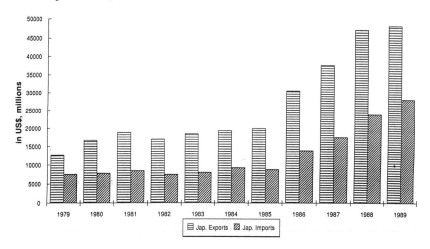

Source: Ministry of Finance, Japan.

Figure 4.2
The Investment Imbalance

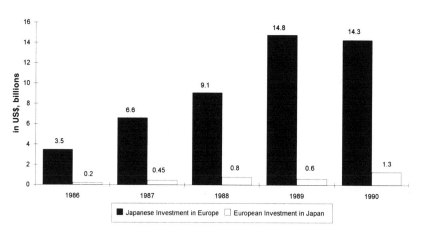

Source: Ministry of Finance, Japan.

Figure 4.3
The Human Imbalance

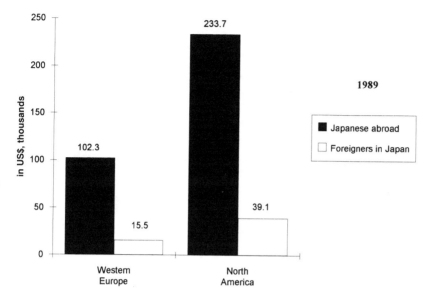

Source: Keizai Koho Center, Tokyo.

structural imbalance. From 1979 to 1990, the volume of trade between the E.C. and Japan grew from $20.2 billion to $88.6 billion, with the real growth gaining momentum after 1985. From 1980 to 1985, the E.C. deficit remained stable at around $10 billion per year, then shot up to $23 billion in 1988 before coming down slightly to $21 billion in 1989 and $18.5 billion in 1990. In only five years, the E.C. cumulated deficit amounted to $98 billion, whereas in 1991 alone it was predicted to reach an all-time record of $25 billion.

The characteristics of European-Japanese trade vary significantly according to direction of trade and to individual countries. Germany has consistently been Europe's export leader with, in 1989, an export volume of $9 billion, followed by France ($5.5 billion),[8] Britain ($4.5 billion), and Italy ($3.8 billion). The picture changes dramatically for Europe's imports with, in 1989, a German import volume of $15.9 billion, followed by Britain ($10.7 billion), Benelux ($8.6 billion), and France ($5.3 billion).

A sectoral analysis of the E.C.-Japan trade pattern makes it easier to understand the specific conditions of the trade dispute, centering on the

Table 4.1

Intraregional versus Interregional Trade, Three Blocs Compared

	% of Total Trade		
	1980	1986	1989
East Asia			
Intraregional trade	32.8	32.4	37.4
Trade with rest of world	67.3	67.6	62.6
Trade with N. America	22.1	30.8	27.5
Trade with E.C.	12.2	13.7	14.8
European Community			
Intraregional trade	50.6	56.8	58.9
Trade with rest of world	49.4	43.2	41.5
Trade with East Asia	4.9	6.3	7.4
Trade with N. America	8.7	9.6	8.9
North America			
Intraregional trade	32.3	34.7	36.3
Trade with rest of world	67.6	65.3	63.7
Trade with East Asia	18.2	27.1	27.7
Trade with E.C.	18.6	18.5	18.0

Source: F. von Kirchbach, International Trade Center, Geneva, 1991.

heavy concentration of Japanese machinery exports (particularly vehicles and heavy machinery). An analysis of the interregional versus the intraregional trade patterns helps to illustrate the logic of Japanese corporations, which are keen to be active players in the growing intraregional trade within the E.C. When three blocs (East Asia, North America, and the European Community) are compared, the fastest growth for the period 1980 through 1989 is indeed within the E.C. (see table 4.1).

As part of its globalization process,[9] Japan began to invest late in Europe—in the mid-1970s—but its investment grew rapidly after 1985, until the turning point of 1990. By March 1991 (see table 4.2), Europe had received more cumulated Japanese investment ($59.3 billion) than East Asia ($47.5 billion), though it was still well behind what the United States had received ($136.2 billion).[10] As Professor J. Gravereau has well described it, the European situation reflects the "water lily syndrome," in which Japanese cumulated investment doubled every four years (1972–84) and more recently doubled every three years (1984–90).[11] In many areas, the situation resembles David pitted against Goliath. The ratio of Japanese investment in Europe to European investment in Japan is 10 to 1; Japan

Table 4.2
Japanese Foreign Direct Investment by Region

Financial Year	1987	1988	1989	1990	1991
Total $ (billion)	33.4	47.0	67.5	56.9	310.8
To East Asia					
US$ billion	4.9	5.6	8.2	7.1	47.5
% of Total	14.7	11.9	12.1	12.5	15.3
To North America					
US$ billion	15.4	22.3	33.9	27.2	136.2
% of Total	46.1	47.4	50.2	47.8	43.8
To Europe					
US$ billion	6.6	9.1	14.8	14.3	59.3
% of Total	19.8	19.4	21.9	25.1	19.1

Sources: Ministry of Finance and Japan Economic Institute.

Table 4.3
Japanese Investment (in U.S.$, billions)

	Total Investment	Investment in Europe (%)
Cumulated 1951–1987	139.3	15.1
1988	47.0	19.4
1989	67.5	21.9
1990	56.9	25.1

Source: Ministry of Finance, Japan.

sells ten times more consumer goods in Europe than Europe sells in Japan; Japan sends eight times more businesspeople and technicians to Europe than vice versa; and Japan exports to Europe two times more than it imports from Europe.

In 1990, Europe received 25.1 percent of Japan's foreign direct investment (FDI) of that year, as indicated in table 4.3. Japanese investment in manufacturing, however, is significantly lower in Europe (18 percent of total investment) than it is in the United States (30 percent). In the manufacturing sector, Japanese investments in Europe continue to be concentrated in electrical equipment. The bulk of the nonmanufacturing investment in Europe is in finance (59.8 percent), with Japan investing a much higher proportion in that sector in Europe than worldwide (31.4 percent).

The rates of Japanese investment in Europe accelerated for a number of reasons.[12] The evolution of the U.S.-Japan relationship and the newly

Table 4.4
Japan FDI in West Germany (in U.S.$, millions)

	1988	1989	1990
Cases	67	119	134
Amount ($)	409	1,083	1,242
Share (%)*	0.9	1.6	2.2

*Share of Japan's investment abroad.
Source: Japan External Trade Organization.

accessible prospects in Eastern Europe may be two recent factors.[13] The many other factors behind the growth of Japanese investment in Europe include the following: the globalization process of the Japanese economy; efforts to alleviate trade friction with the E.C.; evaluation of the yen and recycling of the trade surplus; attractiveness of the size and features of the European consumer market; prospects of a single market in 1993; long-term orientation of Japanese firms to build market share (accepting short-term lower margins); accumulation of know-how (in some technologies, including in banking and finance); gaining knowledge of the consumer through proximity of the market; some comparative advantages (e.g., wages in South Europe); information gathering; fear of protectionism; national and local governments' incentives; pressure for local content; and encouragement from the Ministry of Foreign Affairs (MOFA), Ministry of International Trade and Industry (MITI), and Ministry of Finance (MOF).

Though the pace of Japanese FDI in Europe is unlikely to stay at the level of the late 1980s—indeed, the pace slackened slightly from $14.0 billion in 1989 to only $14.3 billion in 1990—the decrease has been less significant than in the United States. The decrease of Japanese FDI in Europe is associated with a reorientation toward, or a recent emphasis on, Germany (see table 4.4).[14]

Even though Europeans notice and talk most about Japanese manufacturing investment, such investments represent only 17.5 percent ($7.9 billion) of Japanese FDI in Europe; the bulk of the investment is in the nonmanufacturing sector ($34.5 billion, with banks and insurance companies representing 62 percent of total direct investment). Great Britain has been for many years the privileged location for Japanese investors, and today nearly one-third of all of Japan's European investments are in the United Kingdom,[15] with 135 manufacturing plants (25 percent of the total number in Europe). Today Germany and France are receiving more Japanese investment, since Japan is keen to increase its presence in the heart of the European market. This strategy accelerates an "insiderization" process already successfully under way, enhancing Japan's understanding (from the inside) of changes in consumer demand and of the mosaic of European cultures.

European Reactions in the Face of 1992's Changes

Europeans are in the process of overcoming centuries of quarrels among themselves. They are preoccupied with the "revolutionary" process of building a single market, muddling through the difficulties of harmonizing their rules, regulations, and procedures, and trying to overcome national sensitivities regarding the sharing of power over domestic policies. Europeans also are experiencing the Japanese globalization process in very differentiated ways, though the movement from "serious concern" to "fear" is becoming more visible throughout much of Europe.

In handling their relationship with Japan, due to historic, geographic, and other reasons, Europeans do not have the same influence capacity and bargaining power as do the Americans. In the face of unavoidable tensions associated with structural economic similarities, serious frictions linked to "reciprocity," and even trade wars, the road toward mutual understanding between Europe and Japan is a bumpy one. Many would question K. Ishikawa's optimism, in his thorough study of the E.C.'s international trade behavior:

> Over the past year or two there have been some positive developments in trade and economic relations between the Community and Japan. Japan has moved towards less export-dependent economic growth, reflecting precisely the kind of structural adjustments that outsiders desire, and its tariff and non-tariff barriers (NTBs) are among the lowest of the major industrialized countries. These positive trends are reflected in its external trade, including trade with the Community. Its investment in the Community has also increased substantially over the past few years. As for the Community, there has also been some movement: its attitude toward Japan has become unmistakably more friendly and constructive. However, what remains to be seen is whether it will sustain a more liberal approach towards Japan beyond 1992, since its discriminatory attitude seems to be very deep-seated.[16]

Ishikawa indeed needs optimism, since his analysis of Europe-Japan trade and investment does raise concerns about the capacity of each partner to understand the other's logic. He sees the E.C.'s tendency toward managed trade and the use of the General Agreement on Tariffs and Trade (GATT) Article 35 against Japan as an attitude that endured throughout the 1980s. He also clearly illustrates that areas of the E.C. remain strongly protectionist:

> More than thirty years after the signing of the Treaty of Rome, and although the Treaty gives the Commission extensive competence on external trade matters, *the Community still has no common trade strategy towards Japan.* . . . Member states have retained considerable powers on trade matters, especially at the behest of those with protectionist tendencies. This ambiguous approach has been a long-established characteristic of the Community and has allowed strong protectionist elements to survive.[17]

Ishikawa sees these "discriminatory tendencies" (e.g., the ACP—preferential African, Caribbean, and Pacific countries—and the EFTA—European Free Trade Association trading arrangements) as protectionist devices, promoted particularly by French and Italian policymakers, pushing the E.C. "to seek bilateral reciprocity of trade outcomes and to target those countries which have a bilateral surplus with it (not only in terms of the general balance of trade but also in terms of sectoral balances)."[18]

Ishikawa's study illustrates the dramatic absence of a common E.C. strategy toward Japan, even though trade negotiations are increasingly moving to Brussels. This does not alleviate Japan's fear of being discriminated against. The E.C. concepts of "balance of mutual benefits" and "reciprocity"—particularly as applied in individual products and service sectors (e.g., automobiles, electronics, and other high technologies as well as financial services) and implemented through "strengthening local contents" or antidumping regulatory pressures—are perceived in Japan as devices to protect noncompetitive European firms or entire industrial sectors. The difficult discussion on reciprocity has evolved somewhat as the E.C. has come to explain that reciprocity does not mean that *all* partners must make the *same* concessions.

Beyond reciprocity, antidumping, and local content issues, which tend to fuel emotions on both sides of the Europe-Japan relationship, there is a rather fundamental question in Europe, as there is in the United States, concerning the "fairness" of Japanese trade practices. Reciprocity, as it has been well analyzed in a 1991 study by J. Gravereau and C. Feuche, is a very ambiguous concept that can be interpreted in many ways. The French have been the most active in promoting the concept's use in the very sensitive case of the automotive industry, which has quasi-exclusively crystallized the French government's attention in the monitoring of French-Japanese relations. Many Europeans, observing the difficult access to the Japanese market,[19] the low level of imports of manufactured goods (not satisfactorily explained by Japan's lack of raw materials), the still large number of so-called nontariff barriers, the collusive behavior of economic and political actors in Japan, and the subtle but effective invisible hand of the "system," are convinced that Japanese capitalism is a very peculiar brand of developmental state capitalism. They perceive the invisible hand of the Japanese market to be rigged, especially through the "structural impediments" that Washington has tried to alleviate. Other components of European concern include the strong sectoral concentration of Japanese exports (e.g., semiconductors with a quasi-monopoly in the 1MB RAM), the small (and somewhat decreasing) level of intra-industry trade,[20] and what is considered now by many to be the pseudo-liberalization of the Japanese economy as "Japanese intra-industry trade with other countries reflects a structure comparable to that of 30 years ago when the country was closed and its industries protected from foreign competitors."[21] Europeans here join Americans in suggesting "there exist presumptions according to which Japan does not play the same game as its partners."[22] The E.C., in its attempt to cope with this situation, has developed a complex defense machine. The defense includes antidumping legislation and duties, in spite of great difficulty in precisely assessing "dumping margins" and clearly identifying "real" dumping cases and in spite of Japan's complaints to the European Court of Justice in Luxembourg,[23] and to the GATT. The legislation and duties also can be applied to products that undergo final assembly by Japanese transplants in Europe (cases of "screwdriver factories").

The use by the E.C. of antidumping legislation against Japanese concerns has been a thorn in the side of both partners: it antagonized Japanese companies and industries that felt victimized (even though they modified their relationship with European distributors or increased local content in transplants); it demonstrated the great technical complexity of the issues; it required tremendously time-consuming efforts; and it sometimes illustrated the ineffectiveness (or "marginal" effectiveness) of the regulations while raising questions about the conformity of some E.C. regulations to the GATT. It is likely to become an obsolete tool in an era of globalization.

At a time when the language used to describe the Europe-Japan relationship increasingly utilizes terms borrowed from the military (e.g., *war, fortress, artillery, corporate samurai, target, invasion, tariff guerrilla, conspiracy theory*), it is time to go beneath the surface to identify trends and to assess the dynamics of a complex relationship in a global perspective. I will examine two highly differentiated cases: that of France and that of the United Kingdom.

The French Case

The Japanese presence in France has been and still is very modest and is well integrated in Japan's effort to strengthen the competitive position of Japanese firms *on a European basis.*[24] Professor K. Imai explains the information-based logic of globalization:

> One of the essential characteristics of Japanese management is the desire to obtain "on the spot information" in direct contact with parts vendors, machinery suppliers, users and consumers. The formation of a dense direct contact is the key. From this standpoint, it is essential for Japanese international firms to be an insider in each country. By being a true insider in each region, embedded in the social and economic system, the firm can create dense long term contacts with people in the region. . . . Consumers' life styles in the advanced regions of Europe, America and Japan are becoming increasingly alike, but at the same time they include unique and subtle differences reflecting each country's own culture. In depth understanding of this similarity and difference in life styles and consumer tastes will be a key element in the creation of consumers' demand in the world market. Such information cannot however be obtained by simple market research. "Live" information, obtained on the basis of one's insider status within each region as mentioned above is required.[25]

If one judged the French attitude toward Japan by the headlines of the French media, one would notice a progressive deterioration of Japan's image,[26] highlighted in the summer of 1991 by the vituperation of a new French prime minister, still having to master the duty of the job, who demonstrated that her tongue was sharper than her insight, her long-term vision, or her sense of responsibility. As prime minister, by making derogatory comments about the Japanese, Edith Cresson strengthened Japan's image of France as an arrogant, protectionist country, living on its past glory and using Japan as a scapegoat for its own industrial policy failures. To the outraged Japanese, French diplomats explained that it was just a "cultural" misunderstanding: "ants" in France are lovely creatures, diligent and hardworking, managing their life with foresight and frugality, as in the French Aesop fable.

Political leaders and senior government officials are not the only ones to produce their own Gallic brand of "Japan bashing"; some business leaders in the electronics and automobile sectors are joining in with enthusiasm. In the automotive industry, Jacques Calvet, the outspoken chairman of the Peugeot-Citroën Group, has assumed a strongly "protective" position, maintaining that Japanese cars built in the United Kingdom should not be considered European cars, for example. His references to Britain as a "Japanese aircraft carrier just off the coast of Europe" or as "Japan's fifth major island" also suggest a rather negative view of Japanese competition, a view very different from that held across the English Channel or even across the Rhine.

In reality, French perceptions of Japan are more "nuanced," as a recent survey seems to indicate. It showed that 72 percent of the French have a "rather good" or "very good" perception of the Japanese, although 53 percent agreed with the prime minister's ant analogy, perhaps with a positive stereotype of the ant. However, 71 percent of the respondents agreed that the French market had been "invaded" by Japanese products, 67 percent would be willing to pay more to buy a French car rather than its Japanese equivalent, and 68 percent noted they would be willing to work more to cope with the Japanese competition.[27] One should not place too much emphasis on these surveys, but they are important in that they affect the image of the French in Japanese society. The French (like Europeans in general) have a "love affair" with Japanese products, but regarding values and customs, they consider Japan bizarre and somewhat exotic. This perception tends to be cultivated by the media, which repeat stereotypes and build on differences, emphasize the unusual and often marginal facets of Japanese society, and present Japan as a monolithic, conformist, group- and consensus-oriented, tradition-bound, resource-poor, and quasi-militaristically organized country determined to conquer the world. In short, images remain obsolete or caricaturist, old clichés are propagated, and change is not really perceived. Thus, the dynamics of today's Japan are not really understood, and the strangeness—if not the mystery—of Japan is exploited to enhance French fears of the Japanese (as was the case in the proposed Daimler-Mitsubishi strategic alliance and the takeover of ICL by Fujitsu).

The recent acceleration of Japanese investment in France[28] reduces the gap between the Japanese presence in the United Kingdom and the rest of the E.C., though Britain remains unique in its attractiveness to Japanese investors.

The British Hospitality

Between 1951 and 1989, Britain received the bulk (35 percent) of Japanese investment in Europe, and the dominant attitude in Britain toward the Japanese tends to be very positive. A corresponding view is evident in Japan; the Japanese ambassador in London wrote: *"For Japan, Britain is the standard-bearer of an outward looking Europe. . . .* There has been a kind of mini-economic miracle which we have brought about together. There are about 1000 Japanese companies operating in the U.K., and of these, nearly 170 are manufacturing concerns."[29]

In G. Murray's book assessing the impact of the Japanese presence in the United Kingdom,[30] and in M. Munday's book analyzing the development of the Japanese manufacturing investment in Wales,[31] one gets a sense of great satisfaction and of appreciation for the many benefits brought by the Japanese to the United Kingdom and to Europe.

> Japan is playing a significant role in revitalizing the British industry and with it the British economy. Japan is restoring the industrial image and pride of regions hard hit by Britain's postwar decline. . . . Mintel International, surveying public taste and attitudes in 1989 found that British consumers are engaged in a "love affair" with Japanese products. And because of this positive attitude, Britons with an extremely positive overall attitude towards Japan outnumber those who disapprove nine to one. . . . A company like Nissan creates not only 3,000 badly needed jobs on its own site, but hundreds, perhaps thousands, more through components manufacturers who flock to set up shop just down the road in the hope of becoming a trusted supplier. . . . Two Japanese universities have established presence, one in the Northeast of England, one in the South.
>
> Japanese companies have donated millions of pounds to help promote Japanese studies at major universities and colleges. . . . To promote further goodwill, Japanese cash has provided a vital lifeline for British arts struggling for survival.[32]

The multicausality behind the United Kingdom's attractiveness for Japanese investors, discussed widely in Europe, essentially entails a sustained positive political climate toward Japanese investment (the "welcome mat"), availability of financial incentives that significantly cut start-up costs (and the regions' strong competition to promote themselves),[33] availability of a "reasonably-priced pool of relatively well educated and skilled labour,"[34] use of the United Kingdom as a good position from which to enter the large single market of the late 1990s, the language, and perhaps some "cultural" factors.

In addition to the direct and indirect creation of jobs, transplants have produced quality products for the domestic market, foreign exchange through exports, and transfers of technology and social know-how (such as how to achieve single-union deals). Looking at benefits (albeit perhaps short-term), those who praise the Japanese presence in the United Kingdom give it credit for what may seem a quasi-revolutionary change.

> Japanese manufacturing operations in Britain are helping to transform the face of industrial relations by forcing labor unions to drop traditional but outmoded working practices. Union power was gradually restricted during the past decade by legislation brought in by the government of Prime Minister Margaret Thatcher. *However, it can be argued that an equally significant factor was the arrival of Japanese manufacturers, with their insistence on single union deals and introduction of business operating systems that ended the traditional management-labor antagonism in Britain.*[35]

As long as the Japanese have been creating jobs they have been welcome, despite opposition by critics "who distrust Japan's motives and believe the whole point of Japanese investment is to turn Britain into a low-paid, low-tech Third World backwater—a virtual colony of Japanese corporatism."[36] Even though the Trojan Horse theory is making the headlines less frequently in the eleven other E.C. members today, it could easily resurface in the event of another crisis in the European automotive industry (a highly sensitive area in the E.C., particularly in its Latin parts) or in the event of another Fujitsu ICL-like operation.

Europeans are aware of the social and economic benefits Britain has enjoyed by offering a welcome mat to Japanese corporations seeking globalization, but many feel there are undercurrents at work. As Keith Thurley, a professor at the London Schools of Economics, explained:

> *Japanese business is being used as a deliberate political device to meet the needs of retooling British industry, revitalizing industries and creating changes in the organization of labour.* In every way, Britain is using Japanese wealth for its own purpose. And the people who are doing that are not necessarily friendly towards Japan. This is, in a sense, from a Japanese viewpoint, a type of rip-off activity. . . . There is a sense that although the Japanese are very powerful in Britain and clearly are not stupid—they have their own commercial

objectives in using us to penetrate the European Community, etc.—*there is a degree of exploitation of the Japanese by the British and that bothers me.*[37]

If the British have learned how to use the Japanese presence to transform the union structure, have Europeans elsewhere in Europe learned from the Japanese, and if so, what have they learned?

Transfer of Japanese management know-how is often cited as an additional contribution brought by Japanese investment in Europe. The frequent, though not systematic, use in the transplants of Japanese management techniques and tools (e.g., on-the-job training, zero defects, total quality control, *Kamban*, and *Kaizen*) is often portrayed as enriching the capital of management experience and expertise in Europe. In fact, Japanese manufacturing investment in Europe usually relies on a careful blend of Japanese management principles with local practices rather than on the transfer of techniques and tools from the parent corporate culture. In cases where techniques are transferred, trial-and-error periods are observed, followed by fine-tuning stages during which the techniques are tailored to the local environment.[38] Recently, this stage seems to have been shortened or eliminated as the Japanese have effectively learned how to deal with the highly differentiated European sociocultural realities. The Japanese, with their capacity and diligence in learning, have been very effective in accumulating experience abroad, particularly in the United States, and in transferring this invisible asset in their management practices throughout Europe. This was well illustrated in 1987 at the annual conference in Tokyo of the Euro-Japanese Management Studies Association.[39]

If Japanese corporations have done their homework in Europe, and gained much knowledge,[40] European corporations have learned from the competition (e.g., in quality management) from Japan. However, Europeans' curiosity to learn from Japan came somewhat late, they may not have learned the most useful lessons, and they may not have used Japanese transplants as the primary source of learning.

European managers realized the potential benefits of learning from Japan in the late 1970s, somewhat later than their American colleagues, and then rushed to visit Japanese factories. Japan became the Mecca for pilgrimages by European managers in search of a new gospel or, rather, became a Club Med for senior executives keen to rejuvenate their managerial thinking. More often than not they came back surprised (or amazed) by what they had seen, with ideas for a few "quick fixes" to be implemented by a few zealots. They forgot the systemic dimension in the use of these tools and were inattentive to the paramount importance of the cultural dimension in the transfer of management know-how.

Some Implications

Europe, turning a new page in its history, finds itself confronted by a double challenge. First, it needs to create a new historical identity for itself, building "unity through diversity" and finding a way to manage in a context of global interdependence. The task is huge, but the vision exists, the will is growing widespread, and the skills are progressively developing. Second, Europe needs to cope with the emergence of a new world order, where cards are distributed differently, where countries on the Pacific rim have replaced those on the Atlantic, and where Japan is acting as a catalyst of change.

When J. J. Servan Schreiber wrote *The American Challenge* about thirty years ago, he warned Europeans that they had to learn from the champions coming from the other side of the Atlantic. The point was made, European fears dissipated somewhat, and they learned from the American giant. At the same time, U.S. corporations spread investment throughout Europe and became "insiders" and partners with local communities in a relatively smooth process. Today, Europeans are experiencing difficulty coping with the challenge from beyond the now-familiar Atlantic. Japan's physical distance from Europe does not create the difficulty, for technology today effectively reduces distance; rather, the Japanese market is more closed than others.

The challenge from the East, and from Japan in particular, is not in the region's quality products (though matching that quality remains challenging) but rather is in the *software*, the system that produces the quality products, the special structure of Japanese market capitalism, its "uniqueness." Westerners do not fully understand the Japanese paradigm. Experts have written many books on, and scholars have produced careful descriptions of, the various parts of the systems and have analyzed the subsystems in depth, but no one has been able to produce a comprehensive, integrated framework with which to understand the Japanese system. An understanding of the multicausality of Japan's behavioral pattern remains sketchy, so that Westerners have difficulty anticipating Japanese behavior. Westerners realize how "different" Japan is but may not know which differences are most important. Should the world treat the "unique" Japan differently than it treats other countries (each one also being "unique")? Should we impose on Japan the Western paradigm, with the rationale that it is already dominant (though this very paradigm does not seem to have maintained our capacity to remain competitive, nor has it been conducive to the creation of a society able to overcome the dangers of egoism and materialism)? In light of Japan's performance, questions are raised concerning the Western model. Japan's model of "state development capitalism," of "communism that works," of "communautarianism," seems at the time to be working better than the model of the West. Westerners can tell themselves that Japan's high performance may not last forever, that the Japanese model has many shortcomings (observable at the level of the individual and the organization and in the quality of life), that Japan's system is culturally bound and "unique" (henceforth untransferable)—in short, Westerners can find many excuses not to change. Meanwhile, a different world order is in the offing, and the stakes are considerable.

Europeans have learned from the well-known Motorola history in Japan,[41] and from many other European and/or American examples, how the Japanese market is "managed" by a not-so-visible hand that is elusive to catch but effective in its action. Europeans have observed the following:

1. How, in just over a decade, U.S. industry lost its competitive advantage in a number of sectors, which it does not know how to regain[42]

2. How Washington used leverage (which Europeans do not have), applied high-handed *gaiatsu*, and employed trade policies to open forcefully the Japanese market, with very mixed results (e.g., in the cases of semiconductors and FSX jet-fighter negotiations, Japan eventually became stronger)

3. How the "revisionists' approach" sheds new light on the "shadow theater" of Japan's original brand of capitalism, and in which situations the lessons learned, both implicit and explicit, can be utilized in Europe

4. The limited effectiveness of Europe's antidumping artillery (which has encouraged screwdriver operations in addition to direct investment) and the increasingly obsolete (or difficult to implement) legislation on rule of origin

5. How difficult it is for the E.C. to come up with a common analysis of the situation and a common strategy, whether it is "containing Japan" or multiplying "strategic alliances," including in strategic sectors (such as semiconductors, high-definition television, or even in the automobile sector)

Europeans have yet to find a commonly agreed-upon strategy to adjust to the profound challenge lying behind industrial competitiveness and trade issues: the challenge of cultures.

The E.C. today, confronted with the consequences of Japan's ballooning current account and trade surplus approaching $100 billion, is tempted to doubt that this is a temporary distortion due to cheaper oil prices, declining demand for gold and imported luxury goods, and an observable slowdown of Japan's domestic economy. Brussels finds Japanese explanations of the trade situation increasingly less credible. MITI is arguing that Japan's surplus is a purely "conjectural" situation, in no way a long-term trend and certainly not caused by an export drive but only by the softening domestic demand (with the Japanese purchasing fewer French paintings and European works of art) even as Japan's surplus with E.C. jumps 24 percent.[43] In this respect, Ishikawa's view is shared by many:

> Japan's trading partners have complained that it has only been prepared to take economic and trade measures slowly and only at some times and in some areas. Many observers attribute this to a "small country" or "small power" mentality and regard it as an illustration of Japan's lack of the sense of international responsibility appropriate to a strong economic power. It can hardly be denied that since the Second World War, Japanese foreign policy has been markedly passive and reactive. The Japanese government has responded to foreign pressures by piecemeal individual measures. Its decision making process is slow and based on consensus between all those involved in the negotiations. This makes an unfavorable impression on Japan's main trading partners who feel that the Japanese are at an advantage, taking more time to evaluate them and double-check their facts and figures.[44]

The "unfavorable impression" is an understatement. Some European observers of Japan, wary of communication difficulties in the E.C.-Japan dialogue, suggest that the E.C. should engage in a mature Structural Impediments Initiative (SII) negotiation with Japan. They maintain that Europe should bring into question, as the United States did, the *basic foundations of each other's society.* Europe should go beyond free-riding on the outcomes of U.S.-Japanese negotiations and should help speed up the process of changing Japanese society and the Japanese socioeconomic paradigm.

Japan bashing (and other emotional reactions) is ineffective and dangerous, and the E.C. should not try to impose its own societal vision and economic paradigm on Japan. Today, Japan is an economic champion, whether Europeans appreciate it or not. Europe, to a lesser extent than the United States, cannot afford to antagonize or isolate Japan; the risk would be tremendous, not only for Europe but for the interdependent global community. The E.C. should monitor, very carefully, the development of the trans-Pacific relationship, learn from it, and develop a more mature trilateral partnership through "global" strategic alliances (not only European ones).

Furthermore, Europeans should accelerate their efforts to put their house in order and increase their competitiveness through making the hard choices at the national and at the E.C. levels (e.g., redistributing the resources of the Common Agricultural Policy—CAP—to long-term technological areas). Several sectors urgently require a "global" strategy, and two should be on the negotiation table with Japan: electronics, and banking/financial services. The July 31, 1991, agreement for the automotive sector[45] should not be a model by its results (it left unclear several important issues and did not have coercive clauses) but rather by its purpose and premises: it aimed at settling the automotive conflict among *mature* partners, willing to negotiate their activities in both their economic and political dimensions.

Notes

1. As N. Suzuki, former MITI vice minister, wrote: "From 1985 to 1990, the EC's total trade volume increased by 240 percent, with imports from Japan growing 270 percent and exports to Japan growing 360 percent. During the same period, Japan's overseas investment recorded an increase of 470 percent worldwide, and 700 percent in Europe" ("EC Does It," *Look Japan*, January 1992, p. 12). On the E.C. side, F.H.J.J. Andriessen, vice president of the E.C. Commission, wrote: "The bilateral economic relationship between the Community and Japan has intensified remarkably. Whereas in 1985 the volume of trade between the Community and Japan was 30 percent of U.S.-Japanese trade, in 1989 this figure is expected to grow to 50 percent. This increase stems both from a satisfactory development of Community exports to Japan which in the last two and a half years have been growing at a rate of 20 percent and more, but also from a redirection of Japanese exports toward EC markets, stimulated by the higher profits offered here in comparison with the United States" (Preface to Japan Economic Research Center (JERC), *Japanese Presence in Europe* [Louvain: Catholic University of Louvain, 1990], p. 38).

2. The expression is borrowed from J. Bhagwati when he compared the United States today to the nineteenth-century United Kingdom in his book *The World Trading System at Risk* (Princeton: Princeton University Press, 1991).

3. S. Brull, "EC-Japan Talks: No Gain, No Pain," *International Herald Tribune*, November 27, 1991, p. 19.

4. J. Phelps and M. Crabbe, "Japanese Influx Helps the E.C.," *European*, November 22–24, 1991, p. 20.

5. See "Japan in the UK," *Financial Times Survey*, September 20, 1991.

6. Reference was made, as an example, to the fact that in 1990, the Japanese invested abroad $56.7 billion, compared with an inflow of $2.8 billion. Is the potential foreign investor in Japan the only one responsible?

7. As in the U.S. case, European and Japanese statistics on the trade deficit differ.

8. This includes French works of art, since Japan's trade statistics account for the nationality of the artist (not the country where the piece of art has been purchased).

9. Japanese foreign investment increased from $83.6 billion in 1985 to $310.5 billion in 1990, a 3.7-fold increase.

10. Source: Japanese Ministry of Finance.

11. J. Gravereau, "Les investissements Japonais en Europe," *Japon economie et société* 31 (1991).

12. M. Yoshitomi et al., *Japanese Direct Investment in Europe*, Royal Institute of International Affairs and the Sumitomo-Life Research Institute (Brookfield, Vt: Gower Publishing Co., 1991), p. 155; and K. Ishikawa, *Japan and the Challenge of 1992* (London: Pinter Publishers, 1990), p. 151.

13. K. Imai, "Japanese Business Strategies in Europe and in an International Framework," in JERC, *Japanese Presence in Europe* (Louvain: Catholic University of Louvain, 1990), pp. 107–16, and H. C. de Bettignies, "Applied Materials Japan," a case from Stanford Graduate School of Business, 1990, p. 34.

14. T. Masuko, "Japan Firms Expanding EC Base in Germany," *Nikkei Weekly*, December 21, 1991.

15. In 1990, 47.6 percent ($6.8 billion) of the Japanese investment in Europe went to the United Kingdom.

16. Ishikawa, *Japan and the Challenge*, p. xiv.

17. Ibid., p. 120.

18. Ibid., p. 121.

19. This is in spite of a number of American and some European success stories, now well known in Europe, chronicled in such publications as J. C. Morgan and J. J. Morgan, *Cracking the Japanese Market* (New York: Free Press, 1991), p. 287; De Bettignies, "Applied Materials Japan," p. 34; J. N. Huddleston, Jr., *Gaijin Kaisha* (Tokyo: Tuttle, 1990), p. 270; R. A. Christopher, *Second to None: American Companies in Japan* (Tokyo: Tuttle, 1987), p. 257; and the many writings on BMW's penetration of the Japanese market.

20. E. Lincoln, *Japan's Unequal Trade* (Washington, D.C.: Brookings Institution, 1990).

21. J. Gravereau and C. Feuche, *Les investissements Japonais* (Joug en Gosas, France: Euro-Asia Institute, 1991), p. 64.

22. Ibid., p. 65.

23. An example is the well-known appeal of the Nakajima All Precision Company, which was rejected on May 7, 1991.

24. C. Mercier, *Japon: Stratégies industrielles et enjeux sociaux* (Lyon: Presses Universitaires de Lyon, 1988), p. 339.

25. Imai, "Japanese Business Strategies in Europe," p. 115.

26. Recent cover stories include the following: "Japon: Le pays qui fait peur," *Le Point*, December 18–24, 1989; "Comment le Japon nous envahit," *L'Express*, June 20, 1991; "Les Japonais sont des Tueurs," *Le nouvel economiste*, January 12, 1990; and Alain Minc, "Time for Europe to Fight Arrogant Japanese," *European*, May 1991.

27. J. F. Rouge, "Les Français prets a travailler plus," *Capital* 4 (January 1992): 8–10.

28. The increase was particularly visible in manufacturing: in December 1987, there were only 33 Japanese plants in the country; by June 1990 there were 141, with one-third of them started during the previous twelve months.

29. H. Kitamura, "Light at the End of the Tunnel: Anglo-Japanese Cooperation Has Created a Mini-Miracle That Will Ultimately Benefit Europe and the Rest of the World," *Japan Update*, January 1992, pp. 14–15.

30. See G. Murray, *Synergy: Japanese Companies in Britain* (Tokyo: PHP Institute, 1991), p. 222.

31. See M. Munday, *Japanese Manufacturing Investment in Wales* (Cardiff: University of Wales Press, 1990), p. 198.

32. Murray, *Synergy*, pp. 9–12.

33. Munday, assessing Japanese corporations' very careful process of choosing industrial sites, makes clear how critical is the first investment ("pathfinder") in a region (for its "demonstration effect"), the attitude and behavior of the local administration in the initial stage, the reaction of the local community, the general economic and social conditions (availability and cost of labor, unions' attitudes), and the infrastructure. Munday, *Japanese Manufacturing Investment in Wales*, pp. 30–52.

34. Murray, *Synergy*, p. 209.

35. G. Murray, "Japanese Firms Transform British Union Structure," *Mainichi Daily News*, November 12, 1991, p. 7.

36. Murray, *Synergy*, p. 210.

37. Statement of K. Thurley, quoted in ibid., p. 212.

38. A. C. Lam, "Training and Technical Innovation: the Japanese Approach," *Manchester Business School Research Newsletter*, no. 13 (December 1991).

39. See Kudo, Itagaki, Ikeda, Sakuma, Yoshimori, Park, and Heise in K. Shibagaki, M. Trevor, and T. Abo, *Japanese and European Management* (Tokyo: University of Tokyo Press, 1991), p. 272.

40. From the first YKK manufacturing investment near Manchester in 1971 to the latest Matsushita or Sony plant (in Germany or in France) in 1991, the accumulation of experience is very significant, and very visible, thanks in particular to the management of information in Japanese organizations.

41. This was recently well explained by Laura d'Andrea Tyson in "Managing Trade by Rules and Outcomes," *California Management Review*, Fall 1991, pp. 115–43.

42. Many examples are given by a European "non–Japan basher" looking at the "go" game of Japanese corporations in the United States in D. Nora, *L'étreinte du Samourai* (Paris: Calmann Lévy, 1991), p. 356.

43. *Nikkei Weekly*, December 14, 1991, p. 27.

44. Ishikawa, *Japan and the Challenge*, p. 126.

45. This was a critical agreement indeed. Japanese transplants in the United Kingdom will be able to produce 1.83 million vehicles per year in 1999. "Although the picture is not as black as it is often painted, a complete and immediate opening of the European market to Japanese manufacturers would nevertheless have an appalling impact on the European industry. According to a study by McKinsey, European manufacturers would be obliged to eliminate between 120,000 and 140,000 jobs immediately, and the market share of the Japanese manufacturers would double by 1995, reaching sales of 2.2 million vehicles. Fiat and Renault would be the European groups most seriously affected, with their sales reduced to 30,000 and 50,000 units respectively. Thus, it is Europe's independence in the field of decision, conception, and production that is at stake, and it is for this reason that the car issue has raised so much passion" (Gravereau and Feuche, *Les investissements Japonais*, p. 105).

Chapter 5

Japan and the North American Free Trade Agreement

CARLOS J. MONETA

Economic Relations between Japan and Latin America

FOR LATIN AMERICA and the Caribbean, it is a matter of the highest importance to examine the current negotiation processes among the United States, Canada, and Mexico aimed at forming a North American free trade zone. Much significance has been ascribed to the agreement—within the context of the Enterprise for the Americas Initiative launched by the Bush administration in June 1990—for the regional integration processes and the possibilities for growth in regional trade and economic development in the new international context.

Most studies of the agreement carried out in Latin America have not yet examined the impact that the North American Free Trade Agreement (NAFTA) might have on actors outside the Americas, such as in Japan or the newly industrialized Southeast Asian countries. These countries could be affected as the NAFTA evolves and new rules of the game arise in trade as the Enterprise for the Americas Initiative takes root. Even though trade between Latin America and Japan, and the official Japanese aid for development, occupy relatively marginal roles in the overall economic relationship, loans from private banks and governmental financial entities and direct foreign investment have taken on a very relevant dimension.

Trade Relations between Latin America and Japan

Japanese trade with Latin America in 1991 accounted for 4 percent of total Japanese exports and less than 4 percent of total imports. From the Latin American point of view, in 1990 Japan accounted for 4.9 percent of total regional exports and 3.5 percent of total imports. Two problems can be clearly observed.[1]

First, even though the Japanese market has increased its imports in volume by 64 percent between 1985 and 1991, the Latin American share has declined relatively. Among developing countries, the newly industrialized Asian countries (NIACs) and Association of Southeast Asian Nations (ASEAN) countries have benefited most from Japan's increased imports.

Second, trade ties between Japan and Latin America continue to be of a vertical nature, whereas trade relations between Japan and Southeast Asian countries, which are gaining greater capacities for manufactured exports, gradually are taking on a horizontal nature. Latin America exports primary products and imports manufactured products; Latin American manufactured goods have very limited access to the Japanese market. In contrast, Japanese exports to Latin America continue to be concentrated in heavy industry, chemicals, and transportation equipment (the latter accounts for nearly half of Japan's total exports at present).

Even though Latin America generally is found to be losing ground in the Japanese market as compared with the NIACs and ASEAN, Mexico, Venezuela, Brazil, and Chile have managed some progress in their trade relationships with Japan. Chile, for example, now can claim Japan as its first market for exports.

Japan-Mexico

Japanese exports to Mexico increased more than fourfold during the 1979–91 period while imports from Mexico increased nearly fivefold (see table 5.1). Mexico is the largest Latin American exporter to Japan. The bulk of Japanese exports consists of automotive parts and accessories, electronic microcircuit equipment, television image tubes, electrical and mechanical machinery and equipment, and sound equipment. Of Japanese imports, oil, lubricants and by-products, silver, salt, concentrated minerals, fresh foodstuffs, fish, and shellfish account for 55.4 percent, and integrated digital units account for 2.2 percent.[2]

Table 5.1
Japan: Trade Balance with Mexico, 1978–91 (in U.S.$, millions)

	Exports	Imports	Balance
1978	640.01	354.28	285.73
1979	842.20	484.51	357.69
1980	1,214.58	926.71	287.87
1981	1,708.40	1,435.94	272.46
1982	957.99	1,533.78	(575.79)
1983	579.39	1,888.62	(1,309.23)
1984	887.04	2,257.83	(1,370.79)
1985	984.16	1,852.36	(868.20)
1986	1,040.51	1,479.23	(438.72)
1987	1,391.65	1,639.23	(247.58)
1988	1,772.00	1,591.00	181.00
1989	1,908.00	1,730.00	178.00
1990	2,271.00	1,931.00	340.00
1991	2,818.00	1,742.00	1,076.00

Sources: 1978–87 data: the Bank of Japan. 1988–91 data: Japan Tariff Association, *The Summary Report: Trade of Japan* (Tokyo: Keizai Koho Center, 1993).

In 1990, $16.8 billion of a total of $26.9 billion of Mexican exports pertained to energy products, illustrating the economic transformation of Mexico and the increasingly autonomous nature of its petroleum industry. Of the nonenergy products, manufactures played a leading role, at $14.1 billion.[3] In 1989, energy products constituted a 32.0 percent share of exports; automobile equipment, 16.7 percent; and chemical products, 6.8 percent, followed by textiles and leather products at 2.7 percent.[4] A substantial portion of exports in the automobile, electronics, and electric sectors is produced for the U.S. market.

Japanese Foreign Direct Investment (FDI)

Japanese Investments in Latin America

Approximately 17 percent of Japan's accumulated foreign direct investment (FDI), plus 18 percent of Japan's total private bank debt and 10 percent of Japan's public debt, is located in Latin America. Japanese official development assistance (ODA) to Latin America is relatively marginal (in fiscal year (FY) 1991, Latin America received approximately 17.3 percent of total Japanese ODA, compared with Asia, which obtained 63.6 percent).

Furthermore, Latin America has been progressively losing the privileged position it held throughout the late 1970s as one of the largest recipients of Japanese FDI flows.

Total Japanese FDI since 1951 in Latin America accounted for 12.1 percent of the total Japanese FDI in 1976, 14.4 percent in 1987, and 8.0 percent in 1992, with a declining trend.[5] Consequently, if compared with Japanese investment in other regions, Latin American involvement in Japanese FDI has decreased. Thus, whereas in 1985 it accounted for 19 percent of the total Japanese investment in the world, in March 1992, it was only 12 percent of that investment.[6]

Latin America's relative marginal situation, despite its low-cost labor and the abundance of natural resources, is mainly due to the emergence of more attractive markets in other areas, the serious external debt problems that caused a drastic decline in Latin American growth during the 1980s, and the ever-changing national profit remittance and exchange policies followed by the various Latin American governments.

The transnationalization of Japanese banks, linked to the same process occurring in the major Japanese industrial groups, has influenced the conduct of Japanese commercial banks in Latin America. Direct Japanese investment has concentrated massively in the so-called tax havens (i.e., Cayman Islands, Panama, Bermuda, the Virgin Islands, the Bahamas) in services, insurance, and flags of convenience, with only a limited portion remaining for productive investment in manufacturing, trade, and natural resources. Between fiscal years 1951 and 1992, 72 percent of the total of Japanese direct investment in Latin America was concentrated in these tax haven countries, with Panama holding 55.6 percent of the total.[7] These operations largely pertain to recycling activities.

Investment in productive sectors is concentrated, first, in Brazil and Mexico and, second, in Argentina, Chile, and Peru. In 1992, investments in tax havens and Panama accounted for 77 percent of the investment flow. Of the 8 percent of total Japanese direct investment that flowed to Latin America during this year, Brazil received only 1.4 percent, Mexico 0.2 percent, Argentina 0.1 percent, and Chile 0.8 percent.[8]

The sectors benefiting from Japanese foreign direct investment also have been changing over the years. In the early 1960s, accumulated direct investment in Latin America was concentrated in manufacturing, accounting for 65 percent of the total. In later years, this proportion declined to a low of 14.9 percent in 1992, whereas investments in finance and insurance were growing quickly (39 percent of the total that year).

Japan is a very important investor in Latin America, placing third after the United States and Germany. However, although total Japanese investments in Latin America and the Caribbean in late FY 1992 were close to $46.5 billion—a figure not too far below that of Japanese investments in Asia ($58.9 billion)—$33.5 billion was placed in the financial circuit of tax havens and Panama, with only some $13 billion remaining for investments in industry, trade, and natural resources. This fact clearly shows the essential differences between Japanese investments in Southeast Asia and Latin America. Whereas in Southeast Asia, Japanese investments are placed in productive sectors, in Latin America they pertain to recycling, insurance, and services.[9]

Japanese Investments in Mexico

Even though the cumulative share of Japanese FDI in Mexican foreign investment did not exceed 5 percent in the late 1980s and its behavior was unstable, varying from year to year, from the Mexican government's perspective, Japanese investments in Mexico are important. In 1991 accumulated FDI in Mexico totaled $32.9 billion, of which Japan's share was $1.5 billion. The total for Japanese investments from FY 1951 through FY 1992 was $2.12 billion. Within this context, if those projects that have already been identified in petrochemicals, manufacturing, and tourism are realized, it is possible that the level of Japanese investment will reach $4 billion by the end of 1994, when Carlos Salinas de Gortari's administration will leave office.[10]

It should be pointed out, however, that the pace of new Japanese investments has decreased since 1989. Investments in Mexico in 1991 amounted to $193 million, but a large part of this total pertained to swaps. The debt-swap mechanism has been widely used by the Japanese in FDI flows to Mexico. Thus, assets may be purchased from companies and investments may be made without fresh capital contribution.[11] For 1992, investments were only $60 million. Among the reasons given by Japanese businessmen for this small-scale investment, aside from their concern over the NAFTA plans, were their inadequate knowledge of the Mexican market and their persisting perception of strong Mexican state intervention in the economy, despite the profound changes introduced by the Salinas de Gortari administration.[12]

The number of Japanese companies in Mexico has been increasing in recent years; in August 1990, there were 190 such companies. Most are joint ventures with at least 50 percent Japanese ownership.[13] Japanese investments in Mexico are concentrated in the electric and electronic industry, the automobile industry, plastics, and chemicals.

Maquila

The *maquila* phenomenon, or the creation of "industrial free trade zones" for the production and assembly of manufactures for export, should be examined in this framework. Various developing countries, including Mexico, utilize such devices to spur economic growth through incorporating technology and foreign investments into an industrialization process geared toward exports. In the case of Mexico, the government's purpose was to attract new foreign resources, develop certain areas of the country, and generate employment.

In the 1970s, Japanese investments in Mexico were aimed at the local market, located in the central areas of the country, and only 10 percent of the total sales value was exported. During the 1970s, Mexico did not yet possess the conditions that led to the boom in foreign investments in *maquila* industries in the 1980s—very low salaries and, in the case of Japanese investments, a drastic reduction in the value of the dollar versus the yen.[14] The eventual increase of Japanese participation in *maquila* was part of the new internationalization strategy of Japanese companies threatened by increasing U.S. protectionism. This quickly led them to the installation of plants on U.S. territory and to the relocation abroad of part of their industrial operations to maintain competitiveness. With the *maquila*, the possibility arose of importing duty-free inputs from the United States, processing and reexporting them, and paying customs fees on Mexican value-added components and on non-U.S. inputs only.

Thus, assembly plants emerged quite independently of other investments in the country, in order to support the more significant Japanese investments in the United States aimed at the U.S. market. During the 1980s, Mexican *maquila* activity grew considerably, concentrating in areas bordering on U.S. territory, with the total number of plants increasing threefold. Although Japanese *maquila* plants rose from eight to seventy in number, this is a small number when taking into account total existing plants (2,064 in 1992, see table 5.2).

Japanese companies have concentrated in the electronic and automobile sectors—two industries in which Mexico has considerably improved its competitive edge vis-à-vis the United States in recent years. Hence, those

Table 5.2
Profile of Maquila *Plants in Mexico, 1992*

Number of *maquila*	
Total	2064
Japanese-owned	70[a]
Total Number of Employees	517,629
Total Value Added	$3.6 billion[a]
Location	
Baja California	37.3%
Chihuahua	16.9%
Tamaulipas	13.4%
Coahuila	8.5%
Other	8.0%
Distribution by Industry	
Electronics (materials and accessories)	24.6%
Transportation Equipment	23.7%
Electronic Goods	11.0%
Textiles	10.9%

[a] Data from 1990
Source: INEGI, *Estadística de la industria maquiladora de exportación 1978–88* (Mexico: 1991), and *Avance de información económica: industria maquiladora de exportación* (Mexico: Banco Nacional de México, 1992).

sectors in the United States have reacted strongly, pressing for a halt to the inflow of Japanese *maquila* products into their country.

The preceding observations illustrate that Japan is one of the most important countries for Latin America and Mexico, whether in investment, finance, or trade. From the Japanese point of view regarding trade and investment, interest in Mexico developed in the 1960s as a result of Mexico's internal market, high growth rates, and political stability. In the 1980s, despite the crisis and the decline of the Mexican economy, Japanese credit and investment activity continued in Mexico; provision of credit largely resulted from U.S. pressure, and investment activities continued because of Japanese efforts to take advantage—through *maquila* industries—of Mexico's strategic position as a neighbor of the United States. The latter is a highly significant factor, since these investments are closely tied to Japanese investments in the United States, rather than to Japanese investments in Mexico for the local market. But Japanese FDI in *maquila* in Mexico accounts for only 4 percent of total investment in this industrial activity. Main investors in 1992 were the United States (68 percent) and Mexico (25 percent).[15]

Japan and the NAFTA

Japanese Prospects in Latin America

The Japanese have advocated concerted actions by the three main centers of world economy—the United States, the European Community (E.C.), and Japan—to sustain a delicate global economic balance. To do so, the Japanese have two basic options: first, maintain a middle position between the United States and the E.C., maximizing advantages with the other two centers within the triad;[16] or second, establish a close relationship with one of the two so that Japan, in tandem with either the United States or the E.C., will be able to impose the guidelines for the general course of world affairs.

To date, the Japanese position continues to be that of maintaining and strengthening its close relations with the United States. Consequently, Japan's tasks are to contribute to achieving a structural improvement of the U.S. economy (i.e., through transferring part of Japan's corporate and management culture) and to diminish, wherever possible, all friction with this power so that both countries' economies can perform satisfactorily.[17] These goals are important for establishing concerted bilateral leadership in the international economy and for preventing the United States from developing "unilateral globalism."[18] Thus, the interaction between Japan and the United States continues to define the limits of possible Japanese action in Latin America.

Consequently, relations between Japan and Latin America must be considered within a reference framework with several decisive factors.[19] First, the United States continues to be a priority in Japanese foreign policy. Second, Latin America continues to be identified as within the U.S. sphere of influence. Third, the Asian rim of the Pacific Basin, particularly the NIACs, ASEAN, and the People's Republic of China, is the natural sphere of Japanese influence and continues to be held as a priority in Japan's Third World trade and investments.

The foregoing does not imply that certain countries in Latin America, including Mexico, cannot acquire higher importance for Japan as new actors along the other rim of the Pacific Basin. Latin America's position potentially could be enhanced, however, with the organization of a regional economic bloc under the leadership of the United States. It is precisely thus that Japan has perceived the recent NAFTA negotiations and the Enterprise for the Americas Initiative.[20] Japanese leaders and analysts view both with great concern.[21]

The Japanese perception of Latin America is that of a region in which, with the exception of Japanese financial interests, Japanese economic interests already committed are not of great significance.[22] This does not mean that Japan should not have its own initiatives in the region, nor that they cannot be realized. The important factor, however, is the order of priorities. At the present stage, it behooves Japanese interests to support regional development in the context of a "shared domain" with the United States in world economic leadership.

Regrettably, it should be stressed that this Japanese position does not take into account Latin American interests and prospects. Some countries, among them Mexico, see in Japan and the E.C. the opportunity to offset the predominant U.S. presence and to diversify economic ties, actively seeking investments, technology, and new markets. But this role of Japan as an offsetting axis will not develop if the situation remains as described.

Within this reference framework, an important problem for Mexico lies in the evolution of U.S.-Japanese relations. If those relations continue to deteriorate, how are the U.S. administration, the U.S. Congress, and the companies whose interests may be affected (e.g., the electronic and automobile industries) to perceive Mexico's efforts to increase economic ties with Japan in the context of the NAFTA? Moreover, from the point of view of Japan, how will economic policy toward Mexico be affected by the evolution of U.S.-Japanese relations? These and other more specific questions will be examined in the following section, where an attempt is made to identify elements that will contribute to the formulation of possible responses.

The Probable Impact of the NAFTA on Japanese Economic Relations

Japan's response to the NAFTA poses several questions. First, to what extent are current investment levels in the north of Mexico linked to the NAFTA? Second, how might the Free Trade Treaty affect Japanese trade and investment guidelines? Third, what would be the effect of an increase in Japanese direct investment in Mexico, the United States, and Canada? Some comments are offered below, based on these questions.

In the success of *maquila* industries, the cost of labor is not the only decisive factor. Other relevant factors are the proximity to the U.S. market and the comparative advantage of adapting rapidly to changes in demand and other local economic factors, together with an attractive fiscal system. If these conditions change and major obstacles to the U.S. market arise due to "rules of origin"[23] and other mechanisms, manufacturers will likely turn to other developing countries, and investments will diminish in the north of Mexico.

In this regard, the Bush administration indicated that strict rules of origin should be applied to the agreement among the United States, Canada, and Mexico in the creation of a North American free trade zone. The Bush administration sought to ensure that manufacturing companies from third countries, operating in Mexico, would incorporate a high percentage of U.S. components in the products sent to Canada and the United States[24] and thereby prevent Japan and other third countries from evading U.S. tariffs by introducing products through Mexico. The U.S. automobile industry, like the steel and electronics industries, is strongly opposed to allowing Mexico to become an unofficial entry gate for foreign products and parts.

In the case of foreign automobiles, the main non-U.S. plants in Mexico are Nissan of Japan, which does not have *maquila* in Mexico, and Volkswagen of Germany. U.S. corporations required higher percentages of national content than in the U.S.-Canada agreement (50 percent of the total). The NAFTA automotive provisions specify that automotive goods must contain North American content ranging between 62.5 percent (for passenger automobiles and light trucks and engines and transmissions for such vehicles) and 60 percent (for other automobiles and automotive parts) in order to qualify for NAFTA treatment.[25] In any case, major Japanese automobile makers plan to expand their plants in the United States,[26] but an increase in local content in the rules of origin applied to the NAFTA could affect the production of smaller automobiles, which would be based in Mexico for export to the U.S. market.

In the electronics field, where Japanese, Korean, and Taiwanese companies have concentrated their *maquila* industries, linking their assembly lines in Mexico with production and marketing networks in the rest of North America, the impact of stricter rules of origin varies according to subsector. If rules of origin applied are relatively lenient, a high growth rate can be expected in Japanese and Southeast Asian investments in Mexico during the next few years.

It should be kept in mind that Canada, the United States, and Mexico have agreed that the main criterion for determining whether a product is eligible for the benefit of free importation under the NAFTA is whether or not the products from third countries have experienced substantial transformation in the territory of the countries included in the agreement.[27] Furthermore, a study prepared in February 1991 by the U.S. International Trade Commission, at the request of several U.S. Congress committees, indicated that current differences between the *maquila* and other productive plants in Mexico may erode under the NAFTA.[28] Consequently, it may be expected that the *maquila*, or at least some of them, will go beyond assembly operations and become complete manufacturing plants. It should be pointed out that Mexico requested to maintain the current status of the *maquila* under the NAFTA.[29] Therefore, this system will continue in effect, at least until the NAFTA begins to operate. This circumstance would offer the *maquila* the opportunity to function for several more years.

The NAFTA and Japanese Investment and Trade Trends

In the examination of the probable behavior of investments, Japanese prospects should be considered from the Japanese point of view. The following are some of the factors that should be taken into account, aside from the obvious ones such as the results of the Uruguay Round negotiations and the evolution of U.S.-Japanese relations.

The Pace of Japanese Investment in North America

Japanese FDI in North America (the U.S. and Canada) decreased from an average of 48.1 percent of total FDI (FY 1986–90) to 45.3 percent in 1991. The share of FDI going to Europe rose to 22.5 percent, followed by Asia (14.3 percent) and Latin America (8.0 percent).[30]

The FDI statistics show that from 1986 to 1990, there was a certain boom in Japanese foreign investment. Among other traits, this boom was characterized by the dramatic appreciation of the yen and its purchasing power, a strong emphasis on investment in industrialized countries as a strategy to avoid trade friction, a change in manufacturing from labor-intensive to processing and assembly industries, and the development of global strategies by Japanese corporations.[31] Transportation and electrical machinery sectors represented an outstanding share of Japanese investment in manufacturing in both Europe and the United States. However, with regard to the electronic sector, Asia was the main target.

On the other hand, the early 1990s showed an important slowdown of Japanese foreign investment. The main factors include the completion of a cycle of large-scale projects, economic stagnation or recession in the developed countries, and increased competition and diminishing returns from affiliates abroad.[32] In those countries faced with more difficult times, a different attitude prevailed, with more care given to investment and the increased costs of raising funds. The situation was particularly adverse in the United States, where the recession was on the move and sales and earnings for Japanese affiliates were abruptly declining.

Trends in External Production and Exports in the Electrical and Automobile Sectors

If we examine the trends in Japanese overseas production ratios[33] and Japanese export ratios of electronic equipment industries (assembly and parts) and the automobile industry (assembly and parts), patterns emerge. Studies carried out in Japan on this subject point out that in the electronic assembly industry, export ratios[34] will remain at 1989 values (38.3 percent) until 1993, but overseas production ratios are likely to increase from 23.8 percent in 1989 to 27.1 percent in 1993.[35] The automobile industry, in turn, will remain steady. However, assemblers indicate that overseas production ratios will change from 17.1 percent in FY 1989 to 25.7 percent in FY 1993.[36]

The overall figures point to general trends that are not specific to the U.S. and Mexican markets. However, given the relatively minor importance of the latter, the figures suggest the predominant trends. Moreover, Japanese companies are making special efforts to increase local components in their U.S. production. By 1993, a local content level of 44.5 percent of the total could be reached in the electronics industry (except for semiconductors), and in the automobile industry the level could rise from 60.7 percent in 1989 to 71.5 percent in 1993.[37]

The foregoing is evidence that Japan will increasingly be able to satisfy the demands for local content in its U.S. plants. Assembly and parts plants located in developing countries should adapt to this trend, which has been clearly established in the automobile industry but which varies (as to percentage of local content) in the electronics industry.

Strategies Guiding Investment

Data on investment and trade trends should be accompanied by an analysis of business strategies. In the context of a general trend toward international specialization and globalization, Japanese companies seem determined to improve their position and expand their share of local markets.

This determination naturally varies according to region and sector. Thus, investments in the United States have, to a great extent, been a response to the need for counteracting "voluntary restrictions" to exports, dumping problems, and trade restrictions. For this reason, trade restrictions continue to be a major factor behind the Japanese decision to invest in developed countries. Moreover, the promotion of intrafirm specialization, diversification of production bases overseas, and the development of products adapted to this market form the core strategy of those firms that are investing in North America (and the E.C.).[38]

The Evolution of Japanese Direct Investment in Mexico, the United States, and Canada

Taking into account the slowdown and uncertain growth perspectives, it was reasonable to expect the kind of investment behavior adopted by Japanese enterprises during 1992 and 1993. The number of Japanese corporations planning to increase their overseas investments was almost equal to that of Japanese corporations planning to decrease such investments. In a broad survey carried out among companies in the automobile sector in 1991, 48.6 percent of respondents planned to increase their investments during the period, whereas 45.7 percent planned to reduce them or not invest at all. Likewise, in the electronic equipment industry, 42.3 percent would and 42.3 percent would not increase investments.[39]

Consequently, trends that were pointing to a decline in investment rates between 1990 and 1993 in leading sectors such as electronic equipment, chemicals, steel, and machinery in general were confirmed by the facts. In particular, electronics and automobile firms, two major sectors that are present in Mexico and that have generally been the elite force in Japanese manufacturing investments throughout the world, reduced their investments in the medium term.

This trend can naturally be altered by any one of many factors in the United States, Canada, and Mexico. If it can be assumed that the results of the NAFTA will not substantially hinder Japanese interests, it can be expected that investment in the three countries will increase. If the agreements seriously affect third-country access to the U.S. market through Mexico, there will probably will be a greater concentration of direct investment in U.S. territory. As it remains unclear how some of the vaguer parts of the treaty will be implemented, it is likely that the Japanese attitude toward Mexico observed during the last two years will prevail: "wait and see." It should not be forgotten that for Japanese *maquila* plants, incentives to operate in Mexico depend for the most part on whether or not they have access to NAFTA benefits.[40]

In Mexico, Japanese companies will not have problems when using input from any of the three NAFTA member countries for production purposes. However, if the input is Japanese or from any other country that is not a part of the agreement, the resulting products will have to face the rigid and high barriers placed by the rules of origin included in the NAFTA. If Japanese companies established in Mexico want to enjoy advantages in market access, they must use inputs from the United States, Canada, and Mexico or resort to subcontracting firms in any one of these three countries.

In Japan as well as in the "dragon" and "tiger" countries of the Pacific Basin, the following possible effects are feared: (1) the competitive advantages to be obtained by Mexico through the NAFTA in this new regional market of North America will generate a shift in trade due to the substitution of Asia-Pacific exports to the United States and Canada by goods produced in Mexico; and (2) Mexico's competitive advantage as a link to the NAFTA could lead to an increase in productive investment from the Asia-Pacific, Europe, and the United States (some of this investment would represent a shift away from potential investments in the Asia-Pacific, and some might be capital flight from Asia to Mexico).

An increase in investments in the United States would probably have a mixed impact on the economies of Canada and Mexico. On the one hand, a favorable stimulus to economic growth in the United States would mean increased exports from both countries to that market. On the other hand, since the available resources for investment by Japanese companies have been diminishing due to the decreasing growth rate of the Japanese economy and severe adjustments adopted by Japanese companies, this could also mean that there would be less direct investment in Canada and Mexico.

And increased Japanese investments in Mexico would contribute to economic growth and to Mexico's import capacity for both Canadian and U.S. goods.

Possible Effects on Trade on Both Sides of the Pacific Basin

Another topic that should be mentioned, though it will not be studied here, is the impact of the NAFTA on trade flows with Asia. For our purposes, it will suffice to mention that various estimates exist regarding the possible impact of the NAFTA on trade between both sides of the Pacific Basin. Some feel that the effects will be few, since current tariffs between the United States and Mexico are very low and the degree of integration of both economies is very high. Moreover, some economists point out that economic growth in Mexico would produce a significant increase in Mexican imports from third countries. Likewise, government sources have stated that the Free Trade Treaty between the United States and Canada has not had the strong impact on trade flows that Mexico expected.

However, in Southeast Asian countries, it is expected that substantial trade can be channeled to Mexico if the tariff barriers that now protect the various U.S. market sectors are broken down.[41] Businesspeople in the NIACs are seriously considering consolidation of investments in Mexico.

Probable Effects on Japanese Investment in the Rest of Latin America

The previous section examined Japanese direct investment and financial flows to the region. In principle, a first conclusion on the subject would indicate that current trends in Japanese FDI flows to the region will be reaffirmed. In this context, several parameters guide Japanese FDI.[42] First, we can expect a response, though still very cautious and limited, to the structural reform processes in Latin American economies where Japanese companies believe these changes have proceeded in the correct manner (though insufficiently). Second, we can expect maintenance, and even expansion, of a Japanese presence in countries or territories that are important centers of hemispheric marketing and shipping, especially if they are tax havens. Third, the location of the Latin American country with respect to markets considered essential for Japan will continue to be important, especially for Mexico and, to a lesser degree, parts of the Caribbean and Central America. Considering these criteria as a whole, some factors have decreased in importance (i.e., labor costs or the need to control certain inputs and natural resources).

Given the asymmetries between the North American Free Trade Area (NAFTA) and the rest of the Latin American region, the Japanese will tend to concentrate investments in the NAFTA. The other group of relatively privileged countries is composed of Venezuela, Chile, Costa Rica, Colombia, and Brazil. In view of the Japanese globalization strategy, however, this trend could be changed in the long range by the rapid and effective realization of the principal subregional integration agreement (MERCO-SUR, composed of Argentina, Brazil, Uruguay, and Paraguay), given the region's significant potential market and exporting to third-market possibilities.

Another factor that could produce significant changes in the investment policy would be the establishment of a Free Trade Treaty with all or part of South and Central America, through the Enterprise for the Americas Initiative. This, however, is a long-term scenario, for which very few elements are available for analysis.

Possible Effects for the United States in the Long Term

To the extent that Japan's strategic view of its relations with the United States in the global framework continues unchanged, it can be expected that Japanese actions in the Latin American continent will be influenced primarily by U.S. interests in the area. In this framework, the evolution of U.S.-Japanese relations with respect to Latin America will be substantially affected not only by changes occurring in the relative situation between both countries but also by the willingness of the United States increasingly to share its power and thus satisfy the legitimate requirements of Japan for concerted leadership sharing. Thus far, the United States has proved itself greatly insensitive to Japanese requirements, generating a considerable increase in ill feelings and frustration among Japan's leadership.

The impact of the NAFTA will naturally depend on whether it remains adequately open or seeks a protectionist scheme. Besides, as has been pointed out,[43] the *maquila* will gradually lose its appeal vis-à-vis other types of production facilities under the NAFTA regime. An evaluation of the effects also depends on the expectations of the parties, rather than on specific economic factors alone. How rules of origin are applied as the treaty takes effect remains a crucial issue for Japan and other East and Southeast Asian exporters.

Changes in FDI trends and in transnational corporation (TNC) strategies point to the fact that Japan is seeking a role as "internal actor" in each of the other world economic centers by establishing a network of productive enterprises, integrated at regional levels and increasingly independent of the parent companies. Although Japanese companies have taken this process further, European and U.S. TNCs are also using this strategy. Therefore, TNCs as a whole are generating integrated "local" production networks in each of the other poles' economic sectors. Several important consequences are derived from this situation.[44] First, each pole's hegemonic control over its sphere of influence is hindered. This seems to strengthen the hypothesis that economic blocs are a change in scale or market size rather than a way to become closed blocs. Second, TNCs operate in these spheres, on the road to operational globalization.

Furthermore, the many sizable mergers and joint ventures being entered into by corporations from different poles contribute to the openness and permeability of the blocs.[45] Thus, for example, the facts that U.S. trade with the Pacific area surpassed trade with Europe by the mid-1980s and that East Asia continues to receive 30 percent of U.S. exports would lead one to expect that regional trade groups will be unable to become a decisive obstacle to the free trade system, even if they are able to significantly restrict its continued development.

In the global scene, the dilemma between "mercantile-technological" and "strategic-military" power remains unchanged and would seem to offer good prospects for the former category, of which Japan and the E.C. (particularly Germany) are the leading practitioners. The current process of faltering growth and economic instability may last throughout the decade and even into the beginning of the next century. For the capitalist system to experience another period of significant and sustained growth, the more relevant instabilities must be resolved (which would require consolidation of an adequate model for division and concentration of world power and a clearer definition of the lines of accumulation of wealth that could lead to new expansion). If we exclude a scenario in which a new world order is imposed practically by military determent alone, it seems that the actor (or actors) able to become the leader(s) in science and technology and management and able to fulfill the processes of concentration of wealth will prevail.[46]

It is also necessary to consider the very likely possibility that a clear supremacy will not be established for quite some time by any of the principal actors or by alliances. Taking into account the Latin American scenario, the consequences for the United States vary according to the countries in question and the evolution of subregional integration processes. It remains uncertain whether Latin American countries will seek effective and positive ties with the United States in working toward a regional free trade zone or whether the Enterprise for the Americas Initiative will interrupt these processes in favor of closer bilateral relations with the United States. Another factor, already mentioned with respect to Japan, concerns the type of relations—conditioned requests or coordination—the United States will extend to Japan. To the extent that the NAFTA and the Enterprise for the Americas Initiative cause no harm to Japan's trade share, Japanese support can be expected to continue.

Notes

1. Carlos J. Moneta, *Japón y América Latina en los años noventa. Nuevas opciones económicas* (Buenos Aires: Edit. Planeta, 1991), cap. V, and Mikio Kuwayama, *Relaciones comerciales entre Japón y América Latina: Desafíos y Oportunidades* (Santiago: CEPAL, Doc. LC/L, 1991), Seccion: Conclusiones y Recomendaciones, p. 632.

2. United Nations Statistical Office, COMTRADE.

3. Bank of Mexico, "Merchandise Trade, 1981–89," *EXIM/REVIEW* (Special Issue, Tokyo, Fall 1991), Table 12, "Mexico." (Data for 1990 is estimated.)

4. Ibid., Table 13.

5. Ministry of Finance, *Annual Report of International Finance Bureau* (Tokyo), several years.

6. Ibid.

7. Ibid.

8. Ministry of Finance, quoted in *Nippon '92: Business Facts and Figures* (Tokyo: JETRO, 1992).

9. Ibid.

10. Ibid.

11. In 1987 a group of Japanese banks carried out a transaction in the Cayman Islands whereby they purchased Mexican debt at a discount; total purchases of Mexican debt under those conditions amounted to $600 million by year-end.

12. Interview with Leopoldo Solis (former secretary of the Mexican-Japanese Joint Commission) and with directors of the Mexican-Japanese Chamber of Commerce, Mexico, June 1991.

13. Leopoldo Solis, *Inversiones niponas en Mexico* (Mexico, D.F.: Instituto de Investigacion Economica y Social Lucas Alarcon, 1991), p. 6 (internal document).

14. "In Search of Globalization: Japanese Manufacturing in Mexico and the United States," in Gabriel Szekely, ed. *Manufacturing across Borders and Oceans: Japan, the United States, and Mexico* (San Diego: University of California, Center for U.S.-Mexican Studies, 1991), p. 17.

15. Statements by Japanese executives from *maquila* plants, surveys conducted at such plants; see G. Szekely, *Manufacturing across Borders*, p. 1. For FDI in *maquila*, see *Progresso económico y social en América Latina, informe 1992*, (Washington, D.C.: Banco Interamericano de Desarrollo, 1992), pp. 252–53.

16. The changes that the present U.S.-E.C.-Japan troyka may go through, as well as possible scenarios, are dealt with in two of my studies: "Mitos y realidades del Nuevo Orden Mundial: Escenarios posibles," *Capitulos del SELA*, no. 29 (April-June 1991); "La evolucion de los espacios economicos regionales en el contexto de los cambios mundiales," in *La Politica internacional en un mundo postmoderno*, ed. Luciano Tomassini (Buenos Aires: Grupo Editor Latinoamericano, RIAL, 1991).

17. *White Paper on International Trade, Japan 1990* (Tokyo: JETRO, 1990), p. 34.

18. Carlos J. Moneta, "Situacion y perspectivas recientes en las relaciones entre Japon y America Latina," *Coloquio internacional sobre perspectiva de la economia mundial y sus efectos sobre las economias de América Latina y el Caribe* (Santiago: ILPES, IIAP, CEPAL, 1991), Chapter 1.

19. Moneta, *Japón y América Latina*, p. 126.

20. The Enterprise for the Americas Initiative was launched by President Bush in 1990. The Initiative proposes action in three key areas for the development of the countries of the region: external debt, investment promotion, and strengthening trade relations. The Initiative's long-term objective is to move toward establishment of a hemispheric free trade zone.

21. Opinions expressed by Japanese experts participating in the seminar "Latin American and Caribbean Relations with Japan" (Caracas, SELA, 1991). See also Peter Smith, *Japan, Latin America, and the New International Economic Order* (Tokyo: Institute of Developing Economies, 1990), p. 31.

22. Moneta, *Japón y América Latina*, p. 125.

23. "The nature and enforcement of the rules of origin in the agreement will determine the degree to which third countries will be able to access the U.S. market." International Trade Commission, *The Likely Impact on the United States of a Free Trade Agreement with Mexico*, USITC Publication 2353 (Washington, D.C.: USITC, 1991), p. xi.

24. "Japan and the North American Free Trade Agreement," *Japan Economic Institute Report*, no. 39A (October 18, 1991), p. 1.

25. See NAFTA, *Chapter 3, Sectoral Provisions*, Section V, H, Automotive Sector. The rules are laid out in Article 403, as elaborated by the enumeration of automotive goods in Annex 403.2 and Annex 403.3.

26. *Nikkei Weekly*, several issues; *Far Eastern Economic Review*, (July 11, 1991); and Akihiro Koido, "The Color Television Industry: Japanese-US Competition and Mexico's Maquiladoras," in Szekely, *Manufacturing across Borders*, p. 67.

27. Conversations held with researchers from the Centro de Investigacion y Docencia Economica (CIDE), Mexico, related to NAFTA negotiations, June 1992. The matter mentioned signifies that the customs classification with which the product leaves Mexico for the United States or Canada should be different from that with which the components or parts entered Mexico.

28. International Trade Commission, *The Likely Impact on the United States*, v-5; "Japan and the North American Free Trade," p. 7.

29. Conversations held with researchers from the CIDE.

30. Monthly fiscal and financial statistics, Ministry of Finance, quoted in *JETRO White Paper on Foreign Direct Investment, 1993* (Tokyo: JETRO, 1993), p. 31.

31. *White Paper on Foreign Direct Investment*, pp. 29–30.

32. Ibid., p. 32.

33. Overseas production ratio is calculated as Overseas Productions / Domestic Production + Overseas Production.

34. Export ratio is calculated as Export Sales / Total Sales.

35. Hirobumi Takaoka and Takanori Satake, "Report on Results of FY1990 Direct Investment Survey, *EXIM/REVIEW* 11 (1991): 17.

36. Ibid., pp. 16–17.

37. Ibid., pp. 18–19.

38. Ibid., p. 15.

39. Ibid., p. 10.

40. Interview with directors of the Mexican-Japanese Chamber of Commerce, Mexico, June 1991.

41. *Far Eastern Economic Review*, September 13, 1990, pp. 50–51, and October 10, 1991, p. 10.

42. Moneta, *Japón y América Latina*, pp. 133–34.

43. International Trade Commission, *The Likely Impact on the United States*, p. v-5.

44. Carlos J. Moneta, "La evolucion de los espacios economicos regionales," p. 121.

45. Ibid.

46. Ibid., p. 145.

Chapter 6

Japan and the Asia-Pacific Region: A Southeast Asian Perspective

LEE POH-PING

DESPITE SOME RECENT WRITINGS to the contrary, let me assert at the outset of this chapter that a Japanese-dominated bloc after the fashion of the former Greater East Asia Co-Prosperity Sphere is unlikely to develop in the near future. The Japanese economy is too interdependent globally. As Jeffrey Frankel wrote in a recent essay, Japanese investment for the years 1985–88 in Europe and North America showed a rise as dramatic as, if not more than, in the Asian region.[1] And even though intra-Asian trade grew impressively from 1980 to 1989 and continues to grow, the Asian share of global trade, of which Japan constitutes a very substantial part, grew even more.[2] Such statistics suggest no trend toward an Asian autarky such as the Co-Prosperity Sphere. Nor do the present Japanese elite, and indeed the Japanese population, possess the will to effect political-military domination of the region. They realize the folly of Japan's militaristic past and are only too aware of the immense difficulties involved in such an undertaking. Moreover, the acquiescence of the Asian nations on the receiving end cannot be assumed. More politically aware and stronger than before the war, such nations would surely resist such domination.

Nevertheless, many developments could force a presently reluctant Japan to form an Asia-Pacific bloc[3] that may be something less than a modern Co-Prosperity Sphere but more integrated under Japanese leadership than at present. There is nothing irreversible about global interdependence. Since multilateral institutions that encourage such interdependence, such as the General Agreement on Tariffs and Trade (GATT), are under great strain, the present trading system could break down. Then trading blocs might ensue, with Japan likely to form an Asia-Pacific bloc.

Even more pressing on the Japanese is their changing, if not deteriorating, relations with the Americans. For much of the postwar Asia-Pacific world, the United States maintained the international order in which Japan and the Asian newly industrializing countries (NICs) prospered. The Vietnam War and the Americans' realization in the 1970s that the Japanese were one of the greatest beneficiaries of this order made the Americans believe the Japanese had a "free ride." The Americans thus encouraged Japan to play a bigger role in the region. The American attitude could be described as one of an elder brother encouraging a hesitant younger brother to assume more responsibilities.

This attitude has undergone a dramatic change lately. Japan is increasingly perceived as a threat by substantial numbers of Americans, according to recent opinion polls. And a noted political scientist, Sam Huntington, argues that the United States must meet the Japanese economic challenge if it is to remain the premier global power in the coming decades.[4] Indeed, revisionist views of Japan are increasingly popular in the United States. Consequently, the issues of the long-term viability of present U.S.-Japanese relations and of whether or not Japan should go it alone have been raised.[5]

Japan's economic involvement in the Asia-Pacific has deepened, leading to raised expectations of a greater Japanese role in the region. As stated earlier, Japanese investment increased impressively in the Asia-Pacific, rising from $2 billion in 1985 to $8.2 billion in 1988 (comparable 1985–88 figures for Japanese investment in Europe are $1.9 billion rising to $9.1 billion and in North America $5.5 billion rising to $22.3 billion; see table 6.1 and figure 6.1). The Asian figures become more significant, however, when one considers that the Asia-Pacific region's total gross national product (GNP) minus Japan's GNP is far below that of either Europe or North America. Among members of the Association of Southeast Asian Nations (ASEAN), Japan is a leading investor (despite much media attention, Japan is behind Britain in total investment in the United States), and many Asia-Pacific countries acknowledge the critical importance of Japanese investment in their development. Indeed, they make no secret of their desire for more. Concerning Japanese official development assistance, Asian countries consistently received approximately 60 percent or more of total Japanese

Table 6.1

Japan's Direct Overseas Investment in the Countries of the Asia-Pacific Region, 1985–90 (in U.S.$, millions)

	1985	1986	1987	1988	1989	1990
Thailand	48	124	250	859	1,276	1,154
Singapore	339	302	494	747	1,902	840
Malaysia	79	158	163	387	673	725
Philippines	61	21	72	134	202	258
Indonesia	408	250	545	586	631	1,105
ASEAN-5	935	855	1,524	2,713	4,684	4,082
United States	5,395	10,165	14,704	21,701	32,540	26,128
Canada	100	276	653	626	1,362	1,064
North America	5,495	10,441	15,357	22,327	33,902	27,192
Hong Kong	131	502	1,072	1,662	1,898	1,785
Taiwan	114	290	368	373	494	446
South Korea	134	435	647	483	606	284
3 Asian NIEs	379	1,227	2,087	2,518	2,998	2,515
China	100	226	1,227	296	438	349
Australia	468	881	1,222	2,413	4,256	3,669

Source: Ministry of Finance, Japan.

aid from 1980 to 1989.[6] Because of this immense impact, Japan is reminded by the region now and again of its "responsibilities."

The trade situation is similar. Intra-Asian trade has jumped from 33 percent of the total in 1980 to 37 percent in 1989,[7] quite an impressive increase (see table 6.2 and figure 6.2). What is more, Japan now trades more with Asia than with the United States.[8] Such increased trade has made Asia-Pacific nations clamor for a more open Japanese market.

Finally, some Asia-Pacific nations have called on Japan to lead them. On one level, Japan is urged to help the region develop. On another level, Japan is expected to represent the region in forums such as the Group of Seven and to bargain with other regions for better terms for the Asia-Pacific. Such calls cannot be lost on many Japanese, who may wonder if it is not their destiny to lead the region.

Since the subject of a possible Japanese-led bloc is a vast one, this chapter will focus on the following: (1) the pros and cons of the exclusion of the

Figure 6.1
Japan's Direct Overseas Investment, 1985–90

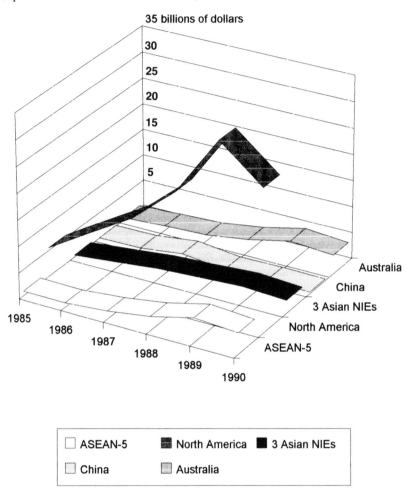

Source: Ministry of Finance, Japan.

United States from such a bloc for Japan and other Asia-Pacific Economic Cooperation forum (APEC) participants; (2) the impact of Southeast Asians' memories of Japanese aggression in World War II on current Japanese economic and security cooperation with the region; (3) possible Japanese cooperation on labor migration; and (4) the salience of the Japanese model in the region.

Figure 6.2
Japan's Total Trade, 1980–89

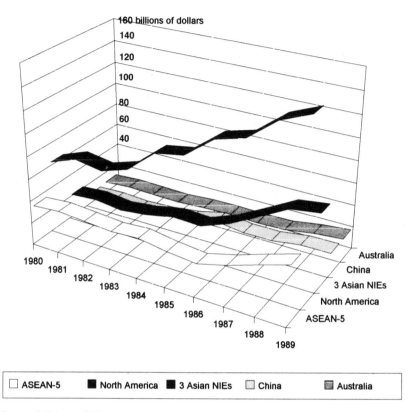

160 billions of dollars
140
120
100
80
60
40

1980
1981
1982
1983
1984
1985
1986
1987
1988
1989

Australia
China
3 Asian NIEs
North America
ASEAN-5

☐ ASEAN-5   ■ North America   ■ 3 Asian NIEs   ☐ China   ▨ Australia

Source: Ministry of Finance, Japan.

American Participation in the Asia-Pacific Region

Since the Asia-Pacific region is an ill-defined area (many not in Asia may want to claim membership in the dynamic community, and many now normally included in such a grouping do not border the Pacific Ocean),[9] this discussion focuses on APEC participants. Yet to speak of a Japanese-led APEC bloc with American participation does not make much sense. First, Japan would not be able to take many initiatives in such a bloc without looking over its shoulder to a more powerful United States. Second, such a bloc would lack character. Would it be Asian (whatever that might mean), Western, or an amalgam of both? In fact, mainly because of

Table 6.2

Japan's Trade with the Countries of the Asia-Pacific Region, 1980–89
(in U.S.$, million)

	1980 Exports	1980 Imports	1980 Total	1981 Exports	1981 Imports	1981 Total	1982 Exports	1982 Imports	1982 Total	1983 Exports	1983 Imports	1983 Total	1984 Exports	1984 Imports	1984 Total
Thailand	1,917	1,119	3,036	2,251	1,061	3,312	1,907	1,041	2,948	2,506	1,019	3,525	2,425	1,040	3,465
Singapore	3,911	1,507	5,418	4,468	1,944	6,412	4,373	1,826	6,199	4,448	1,468	5,916	4,610	1,775	6,385
Malaysia	2,061	3,471	5,532	2,424	2,927	5,351	2,502	3,010	5,512	2,771	3,131	5,902	2,875	4,412	7,287
Philippines	1,683	1,951	3,634	1,928	1,731	3,659	1,803	1,576	3,379	1,744	1,306	3,050	1,080	1,419	2,499
Indonesia	3,458	13,167	16,625	4,123	13,305	17,428	4,261	12,005	16,266	3,552	10,432	13,984	3,073	11,175	14,248
ASEAN-5	13,030	21,215	34,245	15,194	20,968	36,162	14,846	19,458	34,304	15,021	17,356	32,377	14,063	19,821	33,884
United States	31,367	24,408	55,775	38,609	25,297	63,906	36,330	24,179	60,509	42,829	24,647	67,476	59,937	26,862	86,799
Canada	2,437	4,724	7,161	3,399	4,464	7,863	2,861	4,441	7,302	3,625	4,430	8,055	4,297	4,945	9,242
North America	33,804	29,132	62,936	42,008	29,761	71,769	39,191	28,620	67,811	46,454	29,077	75,531	64,234	31,807	96,041
Hong Kong	4,761	569	5,330	5,311	669	5,980	4,718	622	5,340	5,289	670	5,959	6,559	842	7,401
Taiwan	5,146	2,293	7,439	5,405	2,523	7,928	4,255	2,443	6,698	5,086	2,622	7,708	5,986	3,204	9,190
South Korea	5,368	2,996	8,364	5,658	3,389	9,047	4,881	3,254	8,135	6,004	3,365	9,369	7,227	4,213	11,440
3 Asian NIEs	15,275	5,858	21,133	16,374	6,581	22,955	13,854	6,319	20,173	16,379	6,657	23,036	19,772	8,259	28,031
China	5,078	4,323	9,401	5,095	5,292	10,387	3,511	5,352	8,863	4,912	5,087	9,999	7,217	5,958	13,175
Australia	3,389	6,982	10,371	4,779	7,419	12,198	4,581	6,961	11,542	4,280	6,642	10,922	5,184	7,296	12,480

Source: Ministry of Finance, Japan.

Table 6.2

Japan's Trade with the Countries of the Asia-Pacific Region, 1980–89 (continued)
(in U.S.$, million)

	1985			1986			1987			1988			1989		
	Exports	Imports	Total	Exports	Imports	Total	Exports	Imports	Total	Exports	Imports	Total	Exports	Imports	Total
Thailand	2,030	1,027	3,057	2,030	1,391	3,421	2,953	1,796	4,749	5,162	2,751	7,913	6,838	3,583	10,421
Singapore	3,860	1,594	5,454	4,577	1,463	6,040	6,008	2,048	8,056	8,311	2,339	10,650	9,239	2,952	12,191
Malaysia	2,618	4,330	6,948	1,708	3,846	5,554	2,168	4,772	6,940	3,060	4,710	7,770	4,124	5,107	9,231
Philippines	937	1,243	2,180	1,088	1,221	2,309	1,514	1,353	2,867	1,740	2,044	3,784	2,381	2,059	4,440
Indonesia	2,172	10,119	12,291	2,662	7,311	9,973	2,990	8,427	11,417	3,054	9,497	12,551	3,301	11,021	14,322
ASEAN-5	11,617	18,313	29,930	12,065	15,232	27,297	15,633	18,396	34,029	21,327	21,341	42,668	25,883	24,722	50,605
United States	65,278	25,793	91,071	80,456	29,054	109,510	83,580	31,490	115,070	89,634	42,037	131,671	93,188	48,246	141,434
Canada	4,520	4,773	9,293	5,526	4,895	10,421	5,611	6,073	11,684	6,424	8,308	14,732	6,807	8,645	15,452
North America	69,798	30,566	100,364	85,982	33,949	119,931	89,191	37,563	126,754	96,058	50,345	146,403	99,995	56,891	156,886
Hong Kong	6,509	767	7,276	7,161	1,073	8,234	8,872	1,561	10,433	11,706	2,109	13,815	11,526	2,219	13,745
Taiwan	5,025	3,386	8,411	7,852	4,691	12,543	11,346	7,128	18,474	14,354	8,743	23,097	15,421	8,979	24,400
South Korea	7,097	4,092	11,189	10,475	5,292	15,767	13,229	8,075	21,304	15,441	11,811	27,252	16,561	12,994	29,555
3 Asian NIEs	18,631	8,245	26,876	25,488	11,056	36,544	33,447	16,764	50,211	41,501	22,663	64,164	43,508	24,192	67,700
China	12,477	6,483	18,960	9,856	5,652	15,508	8,250	7,401	15,651	9,476	9,859	19,335	8,516	11,146	19,662
Australia	5,379	7,452	12,831	5,227	6,980	12,207	5,146	7,869	13,015	6,680	10,285	16,965	7,805	11,605	19,410

Source: Ministry of Finance, Japan.

U.S. membership, some have called APEC a pointless organization. Third, in bloc terms, APEC would lack clarity of aim. The United States itself is part of the North American Free Trade Agreement (NAFTA), which excludes many APEC members and which might conflict with APEC. In short, APEC with U.S. membership cannot really be a bloc or Japanese-led. The fall 1993 APEC meeting, held in Seattle, confirmed the importance of U.S. leadership: Japan's role was fairly passive. Hence this discussion can more usefully be centered on the potential advantages and disadvantages for Japan and other APEC participants of a Japanese-led Asia-Pacific bloc without U.S. involvement.

Concerning the advantages of a Japanese-led bloc, Japan would be able to bargain with other areas, specifically the European Community and North America, either for the continuation of the present multilateral system, of which Japan is a great beneficiary, or for better terms for itself should the other two regions turn into trading blocs. Japan by itself has some bargaining power, but that power is greatly enhanced if Japan speaks for the rest of the Asia-Pacific region as well. The region not only has substantial economic relations with North America and Europe but also has immense potential for future economic growth.

In an Asia-Pacific bloc, Japan would have a clear field. At present, although Japan is very competitive in the Asia-Pacific region, it is not without challenge from the Europeans and Americans in high-tech industries such as telecommunications, luxury cars, and oil exploration and export. If the Europeans and Americans were excluded, Japanese economic influence would grow even greater.

For the rest of the Asia-Pacific countries, a growing identity of interest with Japan—particularly in the desire to continue the present trading system—will make them increasingly look to Japanese leadership. They know they cannot credibly bargain with Europe and North America without Japan. Also, certain quarters in Southeast Asia believe that a Japan firmly anchored in the Asia-Pacific region will mean less diversion of Japanese investment and aid elsewhere. Nor can Japan, being the only leader, resist the special demands of the region, such as a stabilization scheme for the price of certain primary commodities, by claiming it has global "responsibilities."

However, China and ASEAN, two of the more important members of the Asia-Pacific grouping, differ in their attitudes toward Japanese leadership of such a bloc. Although China may at present accept the need for Japanese economic relations, particularly in investment and aid, its pride as a big nation with a long history, together with the existence of still potent Socialist thinking, will not make it easy to accept a dominant Japanese economic presence for an extended duration.[10] Certainly in the international political arena, China considers Japan as more a rival for influence than a leader.

There is less ambivalence on the ASEAN side. All the ASEAN countries look favorably on Japanese economic relations, and some have clamored for more Japanese investment and aid. Also, the Malaysian call for an East Asian Economic Caucus (EAEC) implies a willingness on the part of at least some ASEAN nations to accept, if not Japanese economic leadership, at least a role for Japan in defending Asian economies.

Such a bloc, however, may have to contend with considerably reduced access to the American market, or with no access at all, given that an excluded United States would have no good reason to resist protectionism against Asia-Pacific goods. The impact would be severe, if not disastrous, for many Asia-Pacific economies. Japan and Taiwan each export about a third of their total to the United States, and many of the others export not much less. Even the People's Republic of China needs the U.S. market for its economic development. Japan would have to be able to overcome the loss of the U.S. market, and then serve as an alternate market for the Asia-Pacific nations, in order to alleviate the severe impact on the growth of the region's economy. For the present, and perhaps even in the long term, it is unlikely that Japan would serve as an alternate market.

Furthermore, the desirability of bloc formation is questionable. Almost everybody, at least in rhetoric, is against it, yet bloc formation could very well occur if the Asia-Pacific region excluded the United States. Because of the tremendous importance of the United States to the global economy and indeed to the global security system, the universal engagement of the United States is one of the best guarantees against a breakdown of the global economy. U.S. engagement abroad is now being questioned in the United States itself, and U.S. exclusion from the Asian region would only fuel the argument against free trade. Hence, for the interest of the Asia-Pacific region, the ambiguity of a situation in which the United States participates both in APEC and in NAFTA might have to be tolerated.

Third, a Japanese-led bloc could well lead to Japanese domination. The GNP of Japan exceeds the combined GNPs of all the other APEC participants including China, minus North America. Despite Japanese good intentions, many believe that such overwhelming Japanese economic weight may not be good for the Asia-Pacific region. Unlike some of the previously mentioned Southeast Asians, others are less sanguine about the unalloyed benefits of a Japan anchored firmly in Asia. These critics note, for example, that the Japanese have not been very forthcoming with technology transfer (a perennial Korean complaint), nor with putting more locals in high managerial positions in Japanese firms (a complaint of many Southeast Asians as well as Americans).[11] At the very least, they argue, the United States is needed in the Asia-Pacific region as a counterweight to Japan.

War Memories and Security Cooperation

Are fears of Japanese dominance also influenced by the memories of Japanese aggression in the Second World War? Despite what is often believed by both Japanese and Asians alike, such memories now matter little in economic relations. It has been almost half a century since the end of the Second World War. The generation that experienced Japanese atrocities either has passed away or is increasingly giving way to a younger generation, whose knowledge of such atrocities is only secondhand. The younger generation is more impressed with Japan's dazzling economic success and what can be gained from it. For example, the Malaysian finance minister, Anwar Ibrahim, a man in his forties, was quoted as saying that he was more sanguine about Japanese influence in Southeast Asia than Lee Kuan Yew, known for his reservations about the Japanese, since he, unlike Lee, was from the younger generation.[12]

Second, it must be said that in Southeast Asia, unlike in Korea and China, there is some ambivalence toward the Japanese role in the war. Although all Southeast Asians agree that the Japanese were harsh conquerors, nevertheless some countries, such as Indonesia and Burma, acknowledge that Japan gave a boost to their nationalist movements against the European colonialists. Their independence struggles would have been much more difficult without the destruction of the white man's might and prestige by the Japanese advance and without the Japanese promises of independence for them. Thailand, on the other hand, did not experience that harsh an occupation and was allied to Japan at one stage. Only in the Philippines, where the Americans had promised independence before the Japanese conquest, and in Singapore, where a majority are of Chinese descent, did the Japanese occupation have no redeeming political value. It is no accident that Emperor Akihito's visit to the ASEAN countries in

1991 involved only Thailand, Malaysia, and Indonesia and did not include the Philippines or Singapore.

Third, economic interaction often overcomes antagonism. Since the war, Japan has greatly expanded its economic relations and aid throughout Southeast Asia. Japan also has taken efforts to improve its image, so that the perception of Japanese as "*samurai* in business suits" is weaker.

In security cooperation, however, war memories do have an impact. First, any mention of Japanese troops in Southeast Asia conjures up the image of cruel conquerors. Southeast Asians have known of Japanese troops in no other capacity in their history. Unlike Japan's experience with American troops—who, although seen as conquerors by the Japanese after the war, were subsequently perceived as enlightened occupiers and defenders of Japan against the Communist bloc—Southeast Asia has not experienced the better side of Japanese troops. They fear a repeat of the Second World War experience.

Second, war memories also affect how Southeast Asians perceive potential Japanese attempts to assume a larger security role—such as through dispatching troops overseas or through amending Article 9 of the Japanese constitution—inclining them to interpret pessimistically the effects on Japanese democracy. Many are readily persuaded by the argument that Japan has not come to terms with its past—an argument reinforced by the Japanese Ministry of Education's attempt to "sanitize" Japan's role in the war in school textbooks, by Japan's denial of what almost all Asians consider a historical fact such as the Nanking Massacre, and by the refusal on the part of Japan to offer an outright apology to the Asians for Japan's war record. In this school is Lee Kuan Yew, who believes Japan has yet to undergo a catharsis regarding its war role, a cleansing he believes the Germans have gone through.[13] Lee thinks that the Japanese, once unrestrained, would prove to be equally as good generals and admirals as they have been businessmen, given their commitment to excel in anything they do. The result would be a military power of fearsome consequence, Lee suggests.

War memories are only one factor, however. A deeper concern is the impact of a rearmed Japan on the strategic situation in Southeast Asia and indeed Northeast Asia. Japan is no military pygmy (even with its military expenditure of about 1 percent of its GNP, Japan ranks alongside the nations that have the largest military expenditures in the world). Such a rearmed Japan could free itself of the U.S.-Japan security agreement and become a free-floating agent of immense strength, creating a profound strategic uncertainty in Southeast Asia. Despite some criticism of the

United States in Southeast Asia, most Asians prefer the stability afforded by U.S. strategic involvement to the uncertainty created by a rearmed Japan.[14]

Still, the perception of American retreat and the growing importance of Japan to Southeast Asia, economically and otherwise, is convincing many Southeast Asian nations of the inevitability of some Japanese security role in the future. For the moment, some consensus exists among ASEAN nations on the acceptability of some "software" involvement, such as Japanese aid in the electronic surveillance of aircraft and ships moving in the two-hundred-mile exclusive economic zone (the ASEAN states adopted the Law of the Sea two-hundred-mile exclusive economic zone in 1982). Some ASEAN nations would appreciate the transfer of defense technology (prohibited in Japan unless such technology is going to the United States), which could enhance each ASEAN member's ability to develop its own regional security role. Some Indonesians would welcome the concessional sale of equipment and ships to help patrol those straits vital to the flow of Japanese oil, a sale unlikely under present Japanese policy.[15]

As to "hardware," the ASEAN nations basically agree that Japan should not play a unilateral security role in Southeast Asia. Other than that, there is not much agreement. In 1990, the government of Thailand under Prime Minister Chatichai Choonhavan suggested holding joint military exercises between Japan and Thailand. This provoked criticisms in Singapore, where some critics argue that there should be no Japanese troops in Southeast Asia, whether jointly with an ASEAN state, as part of a multinational group, or as part of a U.N. peacekeeping force. Lee Kuan Yew is the most forthright exponent of this view, likening the effect of dispatching such troops to that of giving liquor chocolates to reformed alcoholics.[16] This, however, may be an extreme view, for it is likely that if Japan handles the issue of Japanese peacekeeping troops under U.N. auspices with sensitivity toward the ASEAN nations, ASEAN would eventually accept it.[17]

The Flow of Labor

Japan until recent times did not experience a large influx of foreigners seeking unskilled labor (those that came were mainly from the former colonies of Korea and Taiwan and posed no greater problem to the Japanese than the resident Koreans and Taiwanese who had come before the war). Japan traditionally exported capital to the Asia-Pacific region, thus helping solve unemployment there and preventing an influx to Japan. More fundamentally, Japan did not have a great demand for labor; there were enough Japanese to fill jobs at wages industry considered acceptable. This changed with the tremendous growth of the Japanese economy and especially with the revaluation of the yen in 1985, which sent the cost of labor soaring. Added to this was a growing disinclination on the part of many Japanese to work in less-than-satisfactory occupations, such as those involving dirty and dangerous work. Thus the availability of such jobs in Japan, and the vast pay differential between what could be earned in Japan and in other countries, acted as a magnet for those from the Asia-Pacific and indeed from as far away as Bangladesh and Iran.

Though such labor was not legal, syndicates sprang up, and the Japanese government for some time turned a blind eye to the labor flows. It was easy for illegal immigrants to contact recruiters from such syndicates. But the increasing crime committed by such labor, much publicized in the media, and the ever-growing numbers of immigrants are forcing the Japanese government seriously to consider regularizing it.

Japan may legalize such labor, for a number of reasons. First, Japan has a need for such labor. Second, although such labor remains illegal, the government has difficulty controlling it and sometimes resorts to the use of deportations. Unless Japan is willing totally to prohibit tourists from the source countries—which would involve diplomatic costs with ASEAN countries and with countries, such as Iran, that supply substantial amounts of oil to Japan—illegal labor will continue to come. Japan also fears the adverse international opinion that would be created with the deportation of all foreign unskilled labor, especially if Japan could cite only its need to maintain homogeneity. Japan would be vulnerable to accusations of carrying out "racist" policies.

On the other hand, many Japanese associate Japan's rising crime rates, rightly or wrongly, with the increasing presence of foreign labor. This fear is potent, since the Japanese pride themselves on the safety of their streets. In addition, many Japanese fear the possible loss of Japan's work ethic and would prefer that Japanese nationals continue to perform all levels of labor. Furthermore, many Japanese have a deep-rooted fear that the homogeneous character of Japanese society will dissipate with the admittance of foreigners. The invidious example of Europe, with a large underclass of such unassimilated foreigners, is not far from their minds.

All things considered, if the Japanese economy continues to grow, Japan is likely to consider admitting some of this labor,[18] but it will not allow the number of foreigners in Japan to reach ratios comparable to those in either Germany or France.

Japan as a Model

Japan, unlike the United States, which enthusiastically pushed the democratic model during the high period of American influence in Asia, possessed no such mission in postwar Asia. In fact Japan, after the disaster of the Co-Prosperity Sphere, was wary of, and sought studiously to avoid, spreading any ideology of its own. "Economism," not "evangelism," was Japan's goal. But that did not prevent other nations from imitating Japan, especially when its success in development became evident, if not dazzling.

South Korea, even though an ex-colony of Japan with reservations concerning continuing Japanese cultural influence, made some conscious efforts to imitate certain aspects of the Japanese political economic system. The ruling Korean party recently attempted to merge with other similar parties to form a coalition after the fashion of the Liberal Democratic Party of Japan, and the Korean conglomerates, the *chaebol*, did learn a thing or two from the big Japanese companies.

If Korea showed some ambivalence, some Southeast Asian nations were unabashed in their admiration of the Japanese model. Singapore adopted as an official policy a "Learn from Japan" campaign in 1978, and Malaysia launched a "Look East" (basically a "Look Japan") policy in 1982. In 1987, a Filipino cabinet minister stated he wanted the Philippines to be like "Japan Incorporated."

Southeast Asian interest, however, predated the 1970s, though at a much lower level of intensity and spread across a smaller group of people. In Malaysia in the 1960s, some politically articulate people urged the government to help create an indigenous entrepreneur class (the government then was practicing a *laissez-faire* model, thus leaving the economy to be dominated by the minority Chinese population and foreign interests) by more forceful intervention in the economy. These people cited what was thought to be the successful Meiji Japanese experience of the government nurturing such entrepreneurs. In general, however, Japan did not impinge much on Southeast Asian consciousness until a later date.

If there was any one salient alternative model to the Western one, it was that offered by Chinese communism. Many Southeast Asians were impressed by the Chinese Communist party's liberation of Chinese energies toward revolutionary goals and by China's ability to fight the mightiest Western nation, the United States, to a standstill on the Korean peninsula. But by the late 1970s the international situation had changed. The Chinese model had lost much of its luster as a result of the excesses of the Cultural Revolution and the inability of the Chinese Communist party to modernize China. Even more striking was China's attempt to emulate Japan and the East Asian NICs.

Japan, in contrast, had emerged as a powerful force in the international arena, particularly in the economic sphere. After the destruction of the Second World War, Japan had rebuilt its economy to one of the largest in the world. In the process, Japan had made a great impact on the Western economy itself. News abounded of Japanese prowess in the export of cars, computers, and videocassettes. Coincident with this, many Southeast Asians perceived a decline in the work ethic of the West, particularly in Western Europe. The apparently lackluster Western economic performance and the stories of innumerable strikes added to this perception. Finally, Japan had become increasingly important to the Southeast Asian economy. Thus, many Southeast Asian countries emulated, to greater or lesser degrees, aspects of the Japanese political economy.

Southeast Asians first justified their emulation of postwar Japan by pointing out their perceived similarities of condition and attitude with Japan. Singapore saw itself as a nation without any natural resources, even fewer than those of Japan, and hence dependent on its human capital to succeed. Some Singaporeans also believed that Japan and Singapore shared a Confucian cultural tradition. Malaysians perceived some similarity between Malaysia and the Japan of the not-too-distant past. The prime minister, Mahathir Mohamad, believed that both were characterized by "a small economy dependent on international trade, with a young but rapidly growing work force." The two shared "high levels of national investment and savings and [had] enjoyed relatively low levels of inflation." More important, Mahathir continued, they shared "a common belief in monetary stability and financial discipline as preconditions to growth."[19]

Industrializing Asian countries singled out various aspects of Japanese society for emulation. Some Koreans looked to the stability and continuity of Japan's one-party dominant system. Singaporeans and Malaysians, however, did not emphasize this aspect, probably believing the benefits to be self-evident. The political systems of both Singapore and Malaysia, after they became independent states, have been dominated by one party, the Peoples Action Party (PAP) and the National Front, respectively.

These industrializing Asian countries placed the greatest stress, however, on the feature of "Japan Incorporated" (Malaysia coined its own epithet, "Malaysia Incorporated"), in which government cooperated with, rather than confronted, business. Such cooperation included government encouragement of business growth. Increasingly in the Malaysian case, this has been manifested in an emphasis on a more economic-oriented civil service, if not the actual creation of an elite group resembling the Japanese Ministry of International Trade and Industry. Exports also were given priority. Malaysia at one stage created its own general trading company, consciously modeled on the *sogo shosha* of Japan. Also singled out was the manner in which Japanese firms were able to instill the work ethic and loyalty in their employees, though the imitators seemed to show more fascination with the "control" aspects (such as preferring in-house unions over trade unions) than with the "benefit" aspects (such as life employment and paid vacations).

Critics, however, questioned whether or not Southeast Asia and Japan had much basic similarity, given their different religions, cultures, and histories. Even if "Japan Incorporated" actually existed and worked, critics pointed to the heterogeneous nature of many Southeast Asian societies. Malaysia, for example, had a bureaucracy dominated by the indigenous population, whereas business was greatly controlled by the minority Chinese and foreigners. Compared with Japan, where both sectors were dominated by Japanese and where many leaders graduated from the same university, heterogeneous Malaysia could not easily engender the critical element of mutual trust.

Critics also questioned the much-idealized image of the Japanese private sector, particularly pertaining to what was called "company welfarism." Not all Japanese employees were entitled to life employment in Japan, they pointed out. Female employees were considered temporary and were expected to leave when they got married. Other low-status employees, such as janitors, were not considered full-time, and many older employees were encouraged to retire in times of recession. Only key employees were entitled to job security, and they probably did not constitute a majority of the total employees in a particular firm. The situation was even less rosy for the employees of small- and medium-size companies, a large portion of total Japanese industry, where employees enjoyed few of the benefits big companies offered.

About a decade has elapsed since Malaysia and Singapore adopted policies emulating the Japanese model. The initial enthusiasm for the model as a whole has waned somewhat, though fascination with other aspects of Japan continues. The concrete benefits of these policies are difficult to gauge. The only thing that can be said with some certainty is that the existence of a third model—the Japanese one rather than the Western or Socialist ones—has been firmly planted in the minds of many of the Southeast Asian elite and public.

Conclusion

The Asia-Pacific region is in a state of flux. During this transition, the Asia-Pacific region, and indeed the world, will benefit from continued U.S. engagement in the region. The strategic presence of the United States, despite what some Asians may say to the contrary, is the best guarantee of regional stability.[20] Without such stability, economic development will be jeopardized. Furthermore, a United States fully engaged in the economic activities of the region gives greater freedom of maneuver to the non-Japanese Asia-Pacific nations. But a more profound reason for continued U.S. engagement lies with what American participation represents. Although historians may judge the cold war to be a wasteful era in world history, a period in which so many resources were devoted to military expenditures and to fighting a perhaps unnecessary ideological battle (it should be evident that the "natural" condition of the free market would triumph over an "artificial" command economy), the cold war nevertheless had merit in that it transcended race and nation. Many Europeans, Asians, and Africans were joined in the fight for a world where only one's economic condition counted, not one's racial or national origins. By the same token, the non-Communist bloc kept in check any national or racial antagonisms that might arise within it. With the end of the cold war and the demise of this ideological restraint, ethnic, religious, and national passions have sprung up, with the greatest intensity in the ex-Soviet bloc but in the non-Communist bloc as well. Racism is on the rise within Europe and in Europe's attitude toward other nations. The European Community, for example, seems more willing to consider the membership of countries such as Sweden and Austria than that of Turkey. Thus, there is a danger that blocs will evolve based on race, such as a European bloc, a North American bloc, and a culturally diverse Asia-Pacific bloc led by Japan. This is a consummation devoutly to be avoided. The United States, with its influence in both the Atlantic and the Pacific areas, is best poised to prevent this. Thus, as far as Asia-Pacific is concerned, continued U.S. participation and temperance in rhetoric and action will prevent such a breakup into racially based Asia-Pacific and North American blocs.

Notes

1. See Jeffrey Frankel, "Unblocking the Yen," *Economist*, November 16, 1991, p. 81. Unless otherwise stated, the terms *Asia*, the *Asia-Pacific region*, and APEC (minus North America) will be used interchangeably. *Asian region* here means ASEAN 5, Hong Kong, Taiwan, China, South Korea, New Zealand, and Australia.

2. Ibid. *Asian region* here refers to Hong Kong, South Korea, ASEAN 5, New Zealand, and Australia.

3. The word *bloc* is used somewhat loosely here.

4. Samuel Huntington, "America's Changing Strategic Interests," *Survival*, January/February 1991, p. 8.

5. On Japanese questioning of this bilateral relationship, particularly the U.S.-Japan Security Pact, see "US-Japan Security Pact: Time of Doubt," *International Herald Tribune* (Singapore), June 21, 1990.

6. Figures taken from *Japan's ODA 1990* (Japan's Ministry of Foreign Affairs), p. 42. *Asia* here refers primarily to three areas: Northeast Asia, Southeast Asia (including ASEAN), and Southwest Asia.

7. Asia's share of world trade also rose from 15 percent in 1980 to 20 percent in 1989. See Frankel, "Unblocking the Yen." The Asian economies included here are Hong Kong, South Korea, ASEAN 5, New Zealand, and Australia.

8. See "Half-full, Half-empty," *Far Eastern Economic Review*, December 19, 1991, p. 69.

9. The former group includes some Latin American countries bordering the Pacific, such as Chile, and the latter includes some ASEAN countries, such as Thailand.

10. For Chinese reservations about an Asian-Pacific bloc, presumably under Japanese leadership, see "Is Asia Ready for a New Order?" *Asiaweek*, January 11, 1991, p. 28.

11. One of the latest expressions of this complaint is found in "Time to Go for Key Posts," *Business Times* (Kuala Lumpur), August 18, 1992, p. 4.

12. However, he also warned against overdependence on Japan. See "Malaysian Finance Chief: When Neighbour Is Giant," *International Herald Tribune*, May 6, 1991.

13. See "A Contrite Kaifu Forswears Japan Military Ambition in Asia" *International Herald Tribune*, May 4–5, 1991.

14. A leading Indonesian authority on regional security has stated this point of view. See "Japan, Changing Image, Moves into Role as Asia's Advocate," *International Herald Tribune*, June 27, 1988.

15. David I. Hitchcock, "Asian Perceptions and the U.S. Response," *Washington Quarterly*, Autumn 1989, p. 129.

16. *International Herald Tribune*, May 4–5, 1991.

17. See Michael J. Green, "Japan in Asia: The American Connection," *Global Affairs*, Summer 1991. Green claims that Singapore Prime Minister Goh Chok Tong, Malaysian Prime Minister Mahathir Mohamad, and Indonesian President Suharto all told Michio Watanable, foreign minister of Japan, that their countries could accept a Japanese Self Defense Forces (SDF) role in U.N. peacekeeping operations, though they have not expressed this position officially. See note 19. For its part, ASEAN accepted the dispatch of minesweepers from Japan

to the Persian Gulf in April 1991; it was persuaded by the argument that a cease-fire was already in place there and that the removal of mines would aid navigation to Kuwaiti ports, thus helping in Kuwaiti reconstruction. ASEAN also had accepted security issues in the agenda of the postministerial conference of foreign ministers between ASEAN and its dialogue partners, which include Japan. It was a bit cautious, though, of the Japanese proposal to deepen such a security dialogue by preceding it with meetings of senior officials from Japan and ASEAN. For the present moment, ASEAN fears such an arrangement will become too institutionalized.

18. For some perspective, many prosperous Asia-Pacific nations are also the destinations of foreign labor. In Taiwan, Malaysians and Filipinos form a major portion of this labor; in Singapore, this labor consists of Thais, Malaysians, and Indian subcontinentals. Even a less prosperous nation like Malaysia is a magnet to Indonesia labor. All such recipient countries have taken steps to regularize labor flow.

19. Mahathir Mohamad, "The Japanese Model: Its Relevance for Malaysia," in M. Pathmanathan and David Lazarus, eds., Winds of Change (Eastern Productions Sendirian Berhad, Kuala Lumpur, 1984).

20. I do not subscribe to the argument that American troops should remain to "contain" Japan, to be the cap in the bottle, as an American general was reported to have said. Such carries the seed of long-term instability. American troops will eventually be seen as occupiers rather than defenders. It is far better that new positive functions be found for the U.S.-Japan mutual security agreement if the old rationale is no longer valid.

Part III

Japan in Multilateral Settings

Chapter 7

Japan's Prospective Role in the International Monetary Regime

KOICHI HAMADA

MORE THAN FORTY years ago Japan was admitted to the International Monetary Fund (IMF). At that time, Japan ranked only ninth in terms of the share of its quota in the IMF, but since 1990 it has ranked second. This may be of little practical importance, since the United States dominates voting rights, but it illustrates the increasingly important role Japan plays in international monetary relations. The main messages of this chapter are as follows: first, despite its quantitative significance in the world economy, the Japanese financial market still needs to mature qualitatively in terms of managerial skills and transparency of market rules; and second, if Japan is to play a leadership role in world affairs, it must also develop a more effective capacity in international communication by implementing various measures, including educational reforms.

During the past four decades, the yen has become nearly three and a half times stronger in its relationship to the dollar. According to the sixty-first report of the Bank for International Settlements (BIS), Japanese banks accounted for about 35 percent of the total assets owned by the BIS member banks and about 34 percent of their total liabilities at the end of 1990. Tokyo, along with its offshore banking facilities, has become one of the three largest stock and currency markets. Japan is a major surplus country in the balance-of-payments current account, thanks to its high savings rate. The high surplus has enabled Japanese businesses to buy ostentatious buildings, real estate, and movie industries all over the world. It is a potential source of funds to finance developing economies and the former Socialist countries as well. Thus, the quantitative scale of economic and financial activities of Japan is remarkable.

On the other hand, issues of quality or maturity in the Japanese financial market present a substantially different picture. First, the Japanese financial market was under the protection and "guidance," a euphemism for "control" in Japan, of the Ministry of Finance (MOF), and even though deregulation is taking place at a considerable pace, it is not yet a market completely open to and contestable by domestic and new foreign entrants. As recent infamous developments in the security and banking sectors have revealed, implicit rules abound among insiders as well as between government bureaus and private banks or security firms. Rules for attaining fairness in the financial market are not at all clear to others. Recent downfalls of Japanese stocks, in particular those of banks, seem to indicate that the financial skills of Japanese banks are not as impeccable as the technical skills of Japanese manufacturing firms. Japan has yet to undergo "labor pains" in order to realize a qualitatively mature financial market in which price mechanisms work under a set of rules that are well understood by market participants and without unnecessary interventions from the government.

Second, Japan's current-account surplus does not necessarily circulate to the part of the world where the need for investment funds is most acute, such as developing countries or former Socialist countries. Because of uncertainty in those parts of the world, a large portion of the money Japan invests goes directly, or indirectly through Europe, to advanced economies. The most notable destination is the United States, where the government "dissaves" (deficit spending) and the private savings rate is low.

Finally, Japan is not yet assuming an active leadership in international economic relations. The Gulf War proceeded as if it had been predicted by Paul Kennedy in *The Rise and Fall of the Great Powers*.[1] The "great power" had to spend more than it could afford to police the world. Accordingly, the United States looks like *samurai* (warriors) in the late feudal Tokugawa period who, although allowed to bear arms, were poor. Japan looks like *chonin* (merchants) who, although without formal political authority, were rich—even though recent turmoil in the banking and security market in Japan shows that these *chonin* have yet to settle their domestic problems. Incidentally, modern government after the Meiji restoration is believed to have been built by lower-class *samurai*. *Chonin* surely supplied financial resources but did not assume strong leadership.

Japan is now expected to take more initiatives in the world economic order. It is quite a difficult task for Japan because any careless leadership move may remind Japan's Asian neighbors of the Greater East Asia Co-Prosperity Sphere, a notorious attempt during World War II to subordinate Asian nations under Japan's hegemony. .

In this chapter, I will discuss this apparently prosperous but nonetheless delicate position of Japan in the world economy and its prospective role in the international monetary regime. In the next section, I will discuss whether Japan's financial market is sufficiently deregulated and open to the international business community and what can be done if it is not. I will then discuss the current state of the use of the yen as international currency, as well as the prospects for such a use in the future. Next I will review the flow of funds from Japan to the rest of the world and suggest possible ways in which the flow might be directed to the more needy parts of the world. I will then address what kind of international monetary regime is desirable for Japan and for the world as a whole and how Japan could contribute to realizing a desirable regime. I conclude by considering the role of the International Monetary Fund in the process of groping for an ideal monetary regime.

Deregulation and the Openness of Japan's Financial Market

Is Japan's financial market well deregulated and sufficiently open to the international community? I am afraid that the answer to this question is not an unqualified affirmative. The tide is definitely flowing in the direction of deregulation and opening of the Japanese financial market, but there is still a distance to go. Every other month or so, the news of allowing a new type of financial asset as well as insurance contract, of rendering certain interest rates to the market, or of relaxing the required portfolio positions in financial institutions makes us realize that many forms of administrative guidance are still regulating Japan's financial activities. In spite of its grand financial activities, Japan has yet to establish a financial market that is completely contestable by foreign as well as new domestic entrants.

There have been continuous pressures from abroad for Japan to liberalize and internationalize its financial markets. Because of these pressures and the domestic need to develop a more efficient system, particularly in the presence of a massive issue of government debt, Japan's financial markets changed gradually at first and now have been changing quite rapidly into a more open market that exhibits more clearly defined rules. Interest rates, which were highly regulated, became liberalized one after another. Now the interest rates on savings and ordinary deposits are being liberalized. Restrictions on banking behavior that could have worked against foreign banks have been lifted gradually. In December 1980, a newly amended Foreign Exchange Control Law[2] came into effect and liberalized regulations on foreign exchange transactions. The Tokyo or Japan Offshore Market (JOM), which was separated from the domestic financial market and made free from the domestic taxation system, was established in December 1986. At the end of 1990, the scale of the JOM in terms of outstanding credit was $605 billion—short of the scale of the London City Market but more than that of New York International Banking Facilities (IBF).

Let us briefly trace the historical development of Japan's financial development and its government control. Before World War II, Japan had created a financial market that worked fairly competitively. During the interwar years, the government did not regulate interest rates extensively. As a result of the unfortunate experience of bank runs that started in 1920 and because of the need for wartime mobilization of financial resources, Japan's financial system came under the control of the MOF and, though to a much lesser degree, of the Bank of Japan. After the end of World War II in 1945, the wartime mobilization plan was transformed to the Priority Production Plan, by which funds were channeled to the industries that the government deemed important to economic reconstruction. The IMF advised the abolition of the Priority Production Plan, and the plan was discontinued when Japan joined the IMF in 1952. However, the plan left as its legacy a system of rigid interest rates, which continued at least until the middle of the 1970s. Entry into the banking industry and establishment of branches were highly controlled. Interest rates on savings deposits were fixed at very low levels that were often utterly unfair to depositors. The advertisement of interest-rate comparison was ruled out by the agreement at the Banker's Association. The system of interest rates was determined in such a way that smaller and less efficient financial institutions could survive competition.

These protective measures have been lifted one by one, and interest rates, including deposit interest rates, have been liberalized gradually. After the amendment of the Foreign Exchange Control Law of 1980, international currency transactions have been allowed as a rule and not as a privilege. Still, handling charges for banking activities, such as domestic and international wire transfers, are fixed at a high level. For example,

Japanese students who are applying to an American graduate school have to pay about twenty dollars of handling charges to obtain a cash check in dollars for paying the application fee, which may cost less than the handling charge.

In the stock market, entry to the securities industry was strictly controlled after the bailing out of the Yamaichi Securities following the market collapse of 1965. Allegedly to protect small and inefficient security firms, brokerage fees were fixed at high levels and, indeed, at extremely high levels for large traders. For example, trading one thousand stocks priced at one thousand yen required a commission of 1.15 percent, and the trade of one million stocks at the same price required a commission of 0.075 percent. As Kenichi Ohmae and Yoshihiro Maruyama convincingly argue, this implies that a single transaction of a large lot could cost about 133 times more than that of a small lot.[3] This fixed commission fee was considered to be one of the most important reasons for the loss-offset contracts or loss-compensation activities that were attacked by the media in 1991.

Behind the journalistic attacks on security companies is the hidden envy and frustration of the silent masses against the aggressive salesmanship of security companies and against their accumulated wealth. As far as pure economic logic goes, however, loss-offset contracts or loss-compensation activities are a natural consequence of the system of fixed commission fees.

The role of the Securities Division of the MOF has been mysterious during the course of the scandal. It knew of these activities and, benignly if not explicitly, allowed them to occur. Once these activities were revealed by the National Tax Bureau (the equivalent of the Internal Revenue Service in the United States), which itself is an annex of the MOF, the Securities Division imposed administrative punishment on unlawful activities, including these loss-compensation activities. It paternally protected, controlled, and punished them. Finally, the MOF succeeded in convincing members of the Administrative Reform Committee that the new institution for security market supervision—equivalent to the Security Exchange Commission (SEC)—be established as an annex (like the National Tax Bureau) inside the MOF.[4] In light of such omnipotence of the MOF, the argument by Karel van Wolferen that the Law Department of the University of Tokyo be dissolved now sounds to me quite reasonable.[5] The majority of influential high-elite bureaucrats in the MOF are from that department.[6]

Thus, Japan's financial market is not yet a market open to and contestable by new foreign as well as new domestic entrants. The MOF's policy was allegedly intended to protect small financial institutions and brokerage firms, but in effect it helped to secure profits for large institutions and firms and to retain the administrative power of the MOF. Since so many things were determined by MOF regulations and guidance, bankers, stock traders, and insurance managers had little room to develop financial innovations themselves. It was not the best environment for the cultivation of financial entrepreneurship. Moreover, the welfare and convenience of users of financial services have not been taken fully into account.

The paternalistic attitudes of the MOF extend to consumers and individual users of financial services. They are considered to be ignorant about financial matters and in need of protection. They are discouraged from participating in transactions in financial derivatives or foreign exchanges and, in turn, are encouraged to put their money into savings instruments that still yield low rates of interest. Individual investors are slow to learn that higher rates of return can be accompanied only by higher risks. To develop a sound financial market, it is important that individuals as well as institutional investors are educated about the trade-off between risks and returns.

Of course, the MOF is not occupied entirely by those who would like to keep the protectionistic and paternalistic attitudes in the financial industry. In any bureaucracy, there is always tension between those who prefer regulation and those who aim for deregulation, as well as tension between those who attempt to keep the domestic market protected and those who are inclined to make it open internationally. Behind the tension, of course, lie the conflicts between political interests expressed by representatives of various constituencies. This was also true in the case of the Ministry of International Trade and Industry (MITI) during the late 1960s when the balance between those concerned with domestic protection of manufacturing industries and those concerned with free trade turned in favor of the latter. Incidentally, it is interesting to note that the protectionistic and monopoly-preserving attitudes of MITI were counterbalanced, albeit weakly, by the Fair Trade Commission, which is composed of representatives from many ministries such as the MOF and the Ministry of Foreign Affairs.

Now it is time for the MOF to follow the same kind of path from a defensive, authoritative, and domestic-oriented attitude to a more forward-looking, imaginative, and international one.[7] The Japanese financial market should be conducted by competitive principles. The licensing system should be replaced by a free-entry system and, simultaneously, the fixed-fee system by a competitive-fee system.

The Japanese financial market should be under open and clear rules that conform to certain international standards. The BIS requires banks operating in international activities to meet an 8 percent ratio of capital to risky assets. Japanese banks were supposed to fulfill this standard by the end of March 1993. This requirement was regarded as a substantial constraint for the Japanese banks because the average ratio for the major thirteen city banks in Japan was 7.4 percent in September 1988. This requirement has become even more difficult to meet because of the recent price decline in stocks that banks hold. The full attainment of this goal, however, would be a step toward situating Japanese banks under a well-understood international standard.

The only possible reason for the MOF to proceed gradually in reforms would be to avoid such disasters as the savings and loan crisis in the United States, which was caused by the drastic, but partial, deregulation of interest rates without consideration of resulting changes in fund flow patterns and worsened by the lack of recognition of political maneuvers in bailing out particular institutions. Recently, the dominant sentiment in the MOF seems to be changing from a desire to keep vested interests in financial industries under control to an attitude fostering international entrepreneurship of Japan's financial industry in the global market. On the other hand, the public should learn how risks are to be traded with returns and should learn to be responsible for the consequence of their risk taking. As a contrast between MITI and the Federal Trade Commission, it would be amusing to see if the new SEC equivalent in Japan will house representatives from MITI and other ministries to check the market conduct of financial institutions whose management aspects are supervised or protected by the MOF.

The International Use of the Yen

Along with a process of deregulation and internationalization of Japan's financial market, international use of the yen has been developing. The pace of internationalization of the yen lags behind the pace of internationalization of Japan's financial market and behind the role of Japan as a major supplier of funds to the international economy. We can trace the degree of internationalization of the yen by checking the three major roles of money. As the unit of account and the medium of exchange, the proportion of the yen-denominated transactions was 37.5 percent for exports, and only 14.5 percent for imports in 1990. In the same year, 13 percent of all the Euromarket bond issues were denominated in yen. The majority of international transactions in finance and trade are thus conducted in U.S. dollars, Swiss francs, and Deutsche marks. As a store of value by national monetary authorities, yen-denominated assets accounted for only 7.9 percent of their foreign reserves in 1989.

The evolutionary process of choice of an international currency is a complex one. Elimination of national barriers, as well as deregulation in the domestic market, is indeed a prerequisite for more frequent international use of the yen. After the enforcement of the new Foreign Exchange Control Law, free trade, free capital movements, and resulting currency transactions are designated as normal and require in principle no special approval. The MOF now recognizes the merit of the international use of the yen and is ready to create the necessary environment for the internationalization of the yen by deregulating the domestic market further, by fostering the offshore market in Tokyo, and by lifting restrictions on the Euro-yen market.

Needless to say, a government cannot dictate the use of its own currency as an international medium of exchange. There is an intrinsic advantage with respect to economizing information in using a single currency as international money, so it is unlikely that the dollar will be replaced by another currency unless the use of another offers a definite advantage to traders and investors throughout the world. Because of this public-good nature of an international currency, it is unlikely that two currencies will be used simultaneously as equally dominant international monies. For these reasons the dollar is expected to continue as the dominant unit of account as well as the dominant medium of exchanges.

Japan's traders, however, would find it easier to hedge against exchange risks if more contracts were denominated in yen. Even the government might enjoy some seigniorage gain, but there would be an element of cost due to the fact that the domestic monetary policy would be constrained by international considerations. In any case, Japan's government can only deregulate the financial market further and explore how market forces can facilitate the internationalization of the yen.

Japan as a Source of Funds to the World Economy

In fiscal year 1986, the current-account surplus of the Japanese economy was about 4.4 percent of its GNP. In fiscal year 1990, it was reduced to

1.1 percent of the GNP. However, this trend seems to have reversed: the trade surplus was about 2.1 percent of GNP in the calendar year 1991. Since the current-account surplus implies that national savings exceeds national investment, this indicates that Japan still serves as an important capital supplier in the world market.

Many developing countries desperately need financial resources for economic development. Eastern European countries, as well as the Commonwealth of Independent States (CIS), need an increased supply of funds to reshape themselves into market-oriented economies. Unfortunately, though essential in terms of substantial needs, their demands for funds are not "effective"—that is, their investment projects are not attractive enough to lenders in the world capital market. A crucial question concerning international intermediation is how to channel surplus funds to the most needy parts of the world economy. If the world capital market functions well, then the real rate of interest will increase, and the high savings rate of Japan as well as of the newly industrialized economies (NIEs) will be even more appreciated.

Recent theoretical advances in information economics have begun to shed light on incentive problems related to financial intermediation. It is now possible to study analytically why poor individuals or poor countries have difficulty in borrowing, why the interest rate alone is not sufficient to screen uncertain projects and credit rationing is necessary, and why certain forms of credit instruments are used in different degrees of economic development. Basically, two difficulties exist. First, there is an asymmetry of information: lenders do not know (ex-ante or ex-post) what borrowers know about their projects or their financial situations. In such cases, a screening mechanism through interest rates does not work because risky borrowers throng around lenders in order to take advantage of the possibility of defection through bankruptcy. Neither does it work among nations because a borrowing nation can defect from repayment in the event of a debt crisis. To cope with this difficulty, financial intermediaries can do research and determine the safe borrowers. However, lenders sometimes do not know what intermediaries know. Hence, under such circumstances, intermediation cannot get rid of the delegation costs.

Second, lenders do not know whether borrowers make full efforts to attain efficiency if they have an option to be bankrupt or whether they report correctly when they declare bankruptcy. Lending nations do not know whether borrowing nations are taking sufficiently stringent policies aimed at the debt crisis. This is called the moral hazard problem. To cope with this difficulty, monitoring is needed. The conditionality of the IMF or the World Bank can be regarded as a method of monitoring. Monitoring involves costs, and it is not easy to know to what extent monitoring should be used. For these reasons, it is hard to channel funds to the areas where funds are most terribly needed.

According to a recent estimate on the flow of funds in the world economy from 1980 to 1987, calculated by Masaaki Kuroyanagi, Makoto Sakurai, and me, Japan recorded $254 billion of accumulated current-account surplus with respect to the United States.[8] During that period, however, the net indebtedness of the United States to Japan increased by only $82 billion. In the meantime, the United States recorded an accumulated current-account deficit of $75 billion to the European Community, but its net indebtedness to the Community increased by $323 billion. This indicates that Japan became a creditor to the United States but by financial intermediation through Europe. Europe, in particular the United Kingdom, maintains the overhead capital that allows it to serve as the major center of financial intermediation. The market of Tokyo has yet to develop as an equivalent to that of London.

We have seen that the yen does not yet play a dominant role as a store of value in the vault of central banks. However, the yen-denominated assets already play a large role in the portfolios of economic agents. Then the question arises whether the dollar-yen rate is determined to allocate properly the asset holdings of international investors. Paul Krugman doubts this and suggests that the yen was in a bubble process in the first quarter of 1985, when the yen/dollar rate was around $1 = ¥250.[9] In four years the value of the yen almost doubled. Since it is hard to believe that the fundamentals of the yen/dollar rate changed so quickly, his point is appealing.

Japan and a New International Monetary Regime

When leading economists were presenting a case for the flexible exchange rate before the breakdown of the Bretton Woods system of adjustable exchange rates, the only postwar experiment was the floating Canadian dollar/U.S. dollar exchange rate, which did not fluctuate very wildly. The flexible exchange-rate system looked like a beauty in the distance. However, after nearly two decades of experiencing flexible exchange rates, it seems to be clear that floating exchange rates fluctuate with much more volatility than would be needed to accommodate normal trade and capital flows. Prices of goods are slow to adjust, and industrial patterns move with an inertia that economists call "hysteresis." They are predetermined by history. On the other hand, exchange rates among paper currencies are prices that can jump at any instant because of news and thus are determined by people's expectations of the future.

To anchor volatile movements of exchange rates that are determined in the asset market, it is reasonable to implement some feedback mechanism in the exchange market. From this respect the attempt to stabilize exchange rates by joint interventions of the Group of Seven (G-7) countries since the Louvre Accord can be justified. So far, however, the form of the attempted coordination seems to have been limited to ad hoc joint interventions in the foreign exchange market and to ad hoc coordination of interest-rate policy. A wide gap still exists between the actual state of world affairs and recently developed, sophisticated analyses of economic coordination.[10] There are, of course, good reasons for the existence of the gap.

One can show, as an extension of the Poole's result on the relative efficacy of the money target and the interest target in the conventional IS-LM model, that worldwide monetary disturbances are most effectively coped with by the world average interest-rate target, whereas worldwide real disturbances are best coped with by the world aggregate monetary target similar to the McKinnon tripatriate aggregate monetary target.[11] Similarly, one can show that country-specific monetary disturbances are most effectively coped with by interventions aiming for stable exchange rates, whereas country-specific real demand disturbances are most effectively coped with by flexible exchange rates. Thus one can propose a desirable rule for policy coordination only if one has sufficient knowledge of the structure of national economies and of the nature of various disturbances. This would be a formidable information requirement for any finance minister who participates in the G-7 or G-10 meetings. To recommend a particular scheme of coordination, economists should provide information on the relative intensity of disturbances.

We can give only tentative empirical answers to the question of what kind of disturbances are prevalent in the current world economy. On the worldwide level, real disturbances seem to have been strong enough to justify the use of some kind of world money target. On the country-specific level, monetary disturbances are quite prevalent but not to the degree that fixed exchange rates or very intensive exchange-market interventions dominate floating rates. Some moderate form of feedback mechanism on exchange-rate intervention seems to be recommended.[12] In any case, further studies are required to recommend a concrete form of monetary coordination.

So far we have addressed the normative aspect of the exchange-rate regime, that is, the analysis of what kind of international monetary regime is desirable. Let us turn to the positive theory of political economy of international arrangements. By a "positive theory," I mean a theory to explain the process of institutional changes, as compared with "a normative theory," which discusses the ideal regime.

Logically, one can characterize the choice that countries face in international monetary negotiations as a game with two stages: the first stage is to agree on a set of rules or a reform of the existing rules, and the second stage is to play a strategic policy game under the agreed-upon set of rules.[13] The first stage consists of the joint choice of a set of rules such as the gold standard, a uniform world money, a currency union, flexible exchange rates, or a certain intervention rule in the exchange market. The second stage consists of playing a macroeconomic policy game given the agreed-upon set of rules. The structure of this second stage has been well analyzed by applications of game theory.

One can apply the principle of optimality of the dynamic programming. The principle says that if a path in a program is optimal, then any path from the middle of the path should also be optimal. Before agreeing to a set of rules, participants evaluate the outcomes of the most plausible policy interactions given a set of rules. They try to choose the set of rules that guarantees the best outcome in the policy interaction game. If one considers this two-stage game in terms of the Nash equilibrium game, then one is in fact applying the concept that game theorists call "subgame perfectness."

Policy games are played repeatedly through time, whereas the outcome from the game of agreeing on a set of rules comes into effect at a certain instant of time, which is decided by the agreement as well. Here timing itself is an important strategic variable.

In the game of agreeing on a set of rules, the existing set of rules is most likely to continue unless a new agreement is made among the participants. For example, in the current situation, unless the countries agree to adopt a gold (or special drawing rights) standard, or they agree to fix exchange rates, or a subgroup of countries such as the European Community agrees to stabilize the exchange rates among themselves, the existing regime of a highly managed float will continue. I once compared the game situation of the choice of rules to what game theorists call "the battle of the sexes." The battle of the sexes refers to a situation in which a boy and a girl choose where to go on a date. The boy prefers to go to, say, a boxing match, and the girl prefers to go to a concert. If they do not agree on the destination, they will be left solitary at home. Similarly, each country may have a different preference for the desirable exchange-rate regime, so that a reform of the international monetary regime will take place only when the reform is attractive enough for agreement by each participant. A new reform must be incentive-compatible for participating countries.

This simple comparison, however naive it may look, gives us some interesting insights into the positive theory of institutional reforms.[14] First, reforms will more likely take place when the existing regime is in crisis. In crisis, the existing situation becomes so intolerable to participants that many of them start preferring any kind of reform to the status quo. The shift to the floating regime from the Bretton Woods to the floating exchange-rate system can be interpreted in this way. An international monetary reform will more likely be realized by sheer necessity than through the implementation of a well-prepared blueprint. Second, just as alternating between a boxing match and a concert may be a desirable solution in the battle of dating, some combination of reform plans may be more palatable to participants than pure reform plans. In this regard, one may be reminded of the eclectic nature of the adjustable-peg regime, which combined characteristics of fixed exchange rates and occasionally adjustable ones.

Finally, what can political leadership do to realize a reform that is desirable for the leader as well as for the system? It can convince reluctant as well as inactive potential participants of the positive benefits of the new reform, or it can contrive a threat strategy against those participants who do not agree, or more preferably, it can devise a mechanism to change the benefit-cost structure of the new reform in such a way that it may be more agreeable to reluctant or inactive participants.

What is a desirable path for Japan to take now? First, it can calmly observe the process of monetary unification in Europe while carefully studying the economic pros and cons for some possible currency unification in Asia. If the European unification and the North American Free Trade Area turn out to be a success, Japan may proceed to cooperate with other Asian nations to create a currency area. Second, Japan may respond more independently, or strategically, by suggesting the move to create a free trade area, such as the East Asian Economic Caucus (EAEC), or a common currency area involving Japan, after assessing the consequences of the U.S. decision to create a closed free trade area with Canada and Mexico.

Conclusion

In spite of its affluence and its importance in quantitative terms in the world, Japan now faces two related questions: how can it achieve qualitative maturity in its financial market, and how can it play a proper leadership role in the world economy? I have argued that the Japanese market should be deregulated and transformed into a contestable market open to both domestic and foreign new entrants.

In terms of the IMF quota, Japan is now regarded as one of the most influential countries. The question remains whether it is influential in terms of political and, more important, intellectual leadership as well. Japan has already contributed substantially as far as Asian issues are concerned. As for general issues, it has not been very articulate. Probably the only exception was the Miyazawa Plan for resolving the issue of large-debt countries by mobilizing the funds from the IMF and the International Bank for Reconstruction and Development (IBRD, or the World Bank). This served as a basis for what is now called the Brady Plan.

A natural question arises as to whether Japan can contribute to the screening and monitoring of development projects by applying its celebrated "main bank system."[15] In this system, creditors of a firm delegate the task of monitoring a firm's projects to a certain bank, that is, the main bank. The main bank, which is close to the firm in its *keiretsu* (firm group) relationship, does research, monitors, and often sends managers to the firm. If the firm is losing profits, the main bank normally shares the burden, even though abandoning the firm to bankruptcy or even yielding the main bank position to a bank from other *keiretsu* is not ruled out. This system can be a useful way of achieving proper monitoring by a single bank without blocking the function of risk sharing.

If something similar to this system is applied to international loans, it will present an innovation in the content of conditionality. Problems remain to be solved. Is it appropriate that only the IMF and the IBRD play the role of main banks that bear the risks of project failure? Should the government of a single country play the role of a main bank instead? In either case, do monitoring and lending function properly without exefficiency problems and possible corruption related to bureaucratic or government behavior?

We have seen that Japan as well as some of the NIEs will be important lenders in the world economy. Japan will be expected to take more initiatives in terms of assuming international leadership as well as in terms of providing a supply of funds. Despite Japan's substantial contribution to the burden of the Gulf War—$9 billion, almost equal to Japan's annual oil bill to the Middle East—its position was not clearly understood by other countries. Making pecuniary contributions but not shedding any blood is difficult to defend against the charge of free-riding. And the lack of articulation by the Japanese government seemed to have deepened the misunderstanding. Japan needs to be clearer and more articulate in communicating to the rest of the world its positions, intentions, motives, and ideals.

I repeat the need for leadership by Japan in the future. In the Asian context, however, Japan should be very cautious in taking leadership because of its aggressive activities in the past. (This also explains the rather passive behavior of Germany in the political domain.) The NIEs and the countries of the Association of Southeast Asian Nations are closely related to the Japanese economy, as indices of the interrelationship of trade concentration indicate. But Japan, in addition to needing to be more articulate, needs to assess carefully the economic effects of cooperation before making proposals for regional integration in trade as well as in money.

Notes

I am indebted to Munehisa Kasuya, Shinji Takagi, and participants of the "Japan and the World" conference for their helpful comments and to Carolyn M. Beaudin for her editorial assistance. This was written when I was visiting the Department of Economics, Osaka University, whose hospitality much facilitated the completion of this chapter.

1. Paul Kennedy, *The Rise and Fall of the Great Powers* (New York: Random House, 1988).

2. It is symbolic that the title of the new law still includes the word *control*.

3. K. Ohmae and Y. Maruyama, *Shoken kinyu shijo kaikaku* (A market-oriented reform of the Japanese financial system) (Tokyo: President-sha, 1991).

4. Ibid.

5. Karel van Wolferen, *The Enigma of Japanese Power: People and Politics in a Stateless Nation* (New York: Alfred A. Knopf, 1989).

6. I hesitate to endorse his proposal, however, because I graduated from that department before I turned to economics.

7. Needless to say, I do not mean that the old element in MITI has disappeared. Adherence to the Large-Scale Retail Store Act is an example of the remainder of the old element.

8. M. Kuroyanagi, K. Hamada, and M. Sakurai, "Towards the Estimation of the World Asset and Debt Market," *Prospective International Capital Ownership Patterns across the Pacific,*

NIRA Research Output (National Institute for Research Advancement [NIRA]) 4, (1991): 6–20.

9. P. Krugman, *Exchange Rate Instability* (Cambridge, Mass.: MIT Press, 1989).

10. For example, see W. H. Buiter and R. C. Marston, eds., *International Economic Policy Coordination* (New York: Macmillan, 1987).

11. S. Fukuda and K. Hamada, "Towards the Implementation of Desirable Rules of Monetary Coordination and Interventions," in Y. Suzuki and M. Okabe, eds., *Toward a World of Economic Stability: Optimal Monetary Framework and Policy* (Tokyo: University of Tokyo Press, 1988).

12. K. Hamada, J. W. Ryou, and Y. Tsutsui, "Real and Monetary Disturbances in the G-7 Countries: Implication for the Choice of an International Monetary Regime," mimeo, 1989.

13. K. Hamada, *Political Economy of International Monetary Interdependence* (Cambridge, Mass.: MIT Press, 1985).

14. Ibid., chapter 2.

15. Masahiko Aoki, "The Motivational Effect of Quasi-debt Contracts on the Informationally Participatory Firm," CEPR Publication No. 220, Stanford University, 1990.

Chapter 8

Japanese Aid in the New World Order

SUSAN J. PHARR

JAPAN TODAY vies with the United States as the leading aid donor to the developing world. In 1989 Japan emerged as number one, only to be eclipsed the following year by America. But in 1991 and 1992 Japan reclaimed the lead. In a telling commentary on the status of bilateral relations, the United States contested that claim in an unseemly tug-of-war over what should be counted as official development assistance (ODA) in the complex world of today. But given Japan's aid commitments for the future, the key role the country played at the 1992 Rio environmental conference and elsewhere in recent years, and the current mood in America, a changing of the guard will continue to occur, making Japan's leadership in development—despite recent economic setbacks at home—an important foreign policy reality of this decade. Coming out of reparations agreements with Asian countries that suffered at Japan's hands during World War II, Japan's foreign assistance program grew out of historical circumstances quite distinct from those that gave birth to U.S. aid efforts, and there are marked differences in the two countries' approaches to Third World development and aid giving. Japan retains a strong commitment to economic infrastructure building, which represented 40.6 percent of its aid commitments in 1991,[1] but provides numerous other types of development funding, including program assistance (i.e., balance-of-payments support) and major new support for addressing global environmental concerns. Edging away from the political neutrality of the past, Japan announced in 1991 that in considering a country's aid, it would weigh arms spending levels, steps toward democratization and market reform, and human rights, and as of 1994 it had taken modest steps in implementing the new policy. The Japanese aid program continues to grapple with a number of problems today, from chronic understaffing to a continuing international perception that it is "overly commercial." Heightened trade tensions between the United States and Japan as well as a weakening American commitment to foreign assistance pose obstacles to bilateral cooperation in a world in which the need for development leadership can only grow.

The Rise of Japan as an Aid Donor: Background

Japan's commitment to establishing a leadership role in Third World development has been one of the most consistent features of its foreign policy since 1980. Behind Japan's rise as a funder of Third World initiatives lie a variety of factors: the staggering size of Japan's gross national product (GNP) and thus the country's high stakes in a stable global economy, Japan's historical experience as a former Third World nation and its view of itself as a development model, international criticism that Japan is not doing its share in world affairs coupled with popular reluctance at home to support an enlarged military role, and the never-ceasing economic friction between Japan and its major trading partners, which leads Japan to look for offsets to tensions through seeking to cooperate in other policy domains. By the late 1980s the rising threat of regional trading blocs provided a further spur to developing an integrated regional economy in Asia through aid and investment, a trend that continued after the North American Free Trade Agreement (NAFTA) was put in place in January 1994. Japan's commitments to nonmilitary international public-goods spending in the Third World persisted even in the 1980s era of administrative reform (*gyōsei kaikaku*) and tight budget constraints; aid has had a favored place in the budget over the past decade, even in the recessionary times of the mid-1990s.

Historically speaking, Japan's foreign aid program began in the 1950s out of war reparations to the Asian countries that had been victims of Japanese imperialism. Its aid program in the sixties and early seventies has been characterized, even by many of its contemporary defenders, as an extension of "Japan Inc.," aimed at promoting the export of Japanese goods and at securing access to raw materials, mainly in Asia. Indeed, 65.1 percent

Table 8.1

Geographical Distribution of Japan's Bilateral ODA, 1989–92
(Net Disbursement Basis)

	Share (%)			
	1989	1990	1991	1992
Asia	62.5	59.3	51.0	65.1
Northeast Asia	13.6	12.0	8.0	13.7
Southeast Asia	32.8	34.3	25.5	39.6
(ASEAN)	(31.5)	(33.1)	(24.2)	(35.1)
Southwest Asia	16.1	12.9	17.4	11.7
Middle East	5.4	10.2	20.4	4.3
Africa	15.3	11.4	10.3	10.1
Central and South America	8.3	8.1	9.5	9.1
Oceania	1.4	1.6	1.3	2.0
Europe	0.2	2.3	0.2	1.2
Not allocable by region	6.8	7.1	7.5	8.2
Total	100.0	100.0	100.0	100.0

Sources: Japan, Ministry of Foreign Affairs, *Basic Statistics on Japan's Economic Cooperation* (Tokyo: MOFA, 1993). 1992 figures provided by the Economic Cooperation Bureau, Ministry of Foreign Affairs, private communication, February 1994.

of Japan's aid, even today, continues to go to Asia (see table 8.1), and of the ten top recipients of Japan's official development assistance in 1992, eight were Asian countries (see table 8.2). After the "Nixon shocks" of 1971 and the oil shock of 1973–74, Japanese foreign aid, though continuing its "commercial" focus, became more overtly political as Japan sought to diversify its resources through building better bilateral relations with non-Asian resource-producing countries. By 1980, policymakers in Japan had developed the framework of "comprehensive national security" (*sōgō anzen hosho*), a concept that treated various types of global contributions as interchangeable, and thus implicitly acknowledged that foreign aid could be seen in a burden-sharing context. This set the stage for discussions in the 1980s and 1990s of ways for the United States and Japan to cooperate bilaterally and multilaterally on foreign assistance to the developing world (including aid to Russia and other post-Socialist claimants to resources) and for Japan to win points with America and other industrial countries for doing so.

While aid giving slowed in the 1980s in a number of other donor countries, Japan's aid level (boosted dramatically by yen appreciation after 1985) continued to climb, bringing Japan to the level of $9.0 billion for

Table 8.2
Top Recipients of Japan's Bilateral ODA, 1989, 1991, and 1992
(Net Disbursement Basis)

Rank 1989	(%)	Rank 1991	(%)	Rank 1992	(%)
1. Indonesia	16.9	1. Indonesia	12.0	1. Indonesia	16.0
2. China	12.3	2. India	10.9	2. China	12.4
3. Thailand	7.2	3. Egypt	7.0	3. Philippines	12.2
4. Philippines	6.0	4. China	6.6	4. India	5.0
5. Bangladesh	5.5	5. Philippines	5.2	5. Thailand	4.9
6. India	3.8	6. Jordan	4.9	6. Vietnam	3.3
7. Sri Lanka	2.7	7. Turkey	4.8	7. Pakistan	2.0
8. Pakistan	2.6	8. Thailand	4.6	8. Bangladesh	1.9
9. Nigeria	2.5	9. Peru	4.0	9. Malaysia	1.9
10. Kenya	2.2	10. Sri Lanka	2.9	10. Peru	1.8
Total	61.7	Total	62.9	Total	61.4
Japan's World Total	100.0	Japan's World Total	100.0	Japan's World Total	100.0

Sources: Japan, Ministry of Foreign Affairs, *Basic Statistics on Japan's Economic Cooperation* (Tokyo: MOFA, 1993). 1992 data provided by the Economic Cooperation Bureau, Ministry of Foreign Affairs, private communication, February 1994.

fiscal year 1989, as compared with the United States at $7.7 billion, and to widespread recognition as the number-one donor.[2] In 1990, in the official, dollar-denominated aid account-keeping of the industrial countries, the United States once again became the leading donor, due to depreciation of the yen against the dollar. The following year, the U.S.-Japan rivalry and American reluctance to cede global leadership were reflected in U.S. efforts to maintain its top position by inflating its aid figures. The official U.S. aid figure for 1991 was $11.5 billion, compared with $11 billion for Japan, but the American total included $1.85 billion of military debt forgiveness for Egypt—a Gulf War–related write-off that many donor countries were reluctant to see counted as development assistance.[3] For 1992, the United States once again swept military debt forgiveness into its total, claiming $11.66 billion to Japan's $11.15 billion in aid. Japan, rejecting this ploy, steadfastly proclaimed itself the number-one donor for both years.[4]

If we look at the total capital (ODA plus private investment) inflow to the Third World from donor countries, Japan far overshadows the United States and has done so since 1985. This represents a dramatic reversal. As late as 1983, $23 billion of U.S. capital went to developing countries in the form of either private direct investment or aid, whereas the same figure for Japanese capital was only $7.9 billion. However, for 1990, the figures had dropped to $11.1 billion for the United States but had soared to $18.7 billion for Japan.[5] At the Tokyo Summit in 1993, Japan announced the fifth in its series of "ODA doubling plans," designed to increase aid levels substantially (the first had been launched in 1977 under Prime Minister Takeo Fukuda). The plan called for raising Japan's aid level by 40 to 50 percent, for a projected total of $70 to 75 billion over the 1993–97 period.[6] Even in the recessionary climate of the early-to-mid 1990s, there was little evidence that Japan's general commitment as a force in development was likely to flag in any major way. Indeed, key politicians and officials have continued to push for higher aid levels. In June 1991, for example, Foreign Minister Tarō Nakayama was reported in the media as expressing hopes that over the next five to ten years, Japan's aid would be raised to 1–2 percent of GNP from the current level (.32 percent for 1991).[7] The figure was quickly disclaimed by his ministry as far too optimistic, but his statement reflects the general mood of support among leaders for Japan's role vis-à-vis the developing world. On the eve of the 1993 Tokyo Summit, a Japan rocked by political turmoil reaffirmed its commitment to addressing development needs, noting that it was the only Group of Seven (G-7) country prepared to increase its aid levels by substantial amounts.[8]

Japan also has taken a larger role in dealing with the Third World debt problem. The Miyazawa Plan, which later resurfaced as the Brady Plan, was a good example of the change in the Japanese approach, from a passive acceptance of the leadership of other countries to efforts to seize the initiative in international development problem-solving. At the Toronto Economic Summit in 1988, Prime Minister Noboru Takeshita promised to write off $8 billion of debt owed to Japan by the world's least developed countries.[9] A second debt-relief measure that same year wrote off $5.5 billion in yen credits.[10] Japan announced several years ago a $30-billion three-year capital recycling plan aimed at channeling Japan's private-sector capital surplus to developing countries and, at the Paris Economic Summit in 1989, announced another even larger recycling plan of $65 billion for the 1987–92 period. Beyond the Tokyo Summit in 1993, Japan pledged another $50 billion for the 1993–97 period.[11]

Beyond these initiatives, Japan has increasingly sought leadership on problems judged to be critical for the future by the industrial nations. A good example is Japan's stepped-up commitment since 1988 to addressing environmental concerns. At the Paris Summit, Japan promised to provide noninterest loans for environment-protection projects in developing countries and pledged $2.3 billion over the 1989–91 period in environmental aid. At the Earth Summit in Rio in June 1992, Japan announced that it had exceeded that target and captured headlines by pledging $7 billion or more over the five-year period ahead.[12] In 1993, Japan claimed to be on track in meeting its Rio commitments and announced additional environment initiatives.[13]

After the Persian Gulf War, the domestic context of aid giving changed significantly in national soul-searching over Japan's future international role. Public support remains relatively strong, but as the volume of funding has increased, aid-related issues have become far more politicized. Though concepts such as "global partnership" and "responsibility sharing" continue to enjoy support in official circles, public hostility to *gaiatsu* (foreign pressure)—which President George Bush's visit, automakers in tow, to Tokyo in January 1992 greatly exacerbated—makes bilateral forms of co-operation politically sensitive and helped doom Prime Minister Kiichi Miyazawa's effort in the fall of 1991 to pass a special tax to increase foreign aid. Perceptions of President Bill Clinton as a Japan basher have been widespread in Japan, contributing to a growing percentage of Japanese— 64 percent in a February 1994 survey—who saw Japan's relations with the United States as "not good."[14] In the tense and competitive climate of relations among G-7 countries in a recession-plagued world, officials in Japan braced themselves for new rounds of "aid friction" as Japan's economic presence in the developing world continued to grow.

Among the Japanese public, a perception of worsening relations leads to a sensitivity over types of Japanese foreign aid spending (such as "strategic" aid) that appear to represent appeasement of U.S. demands. Though there continues to be broad-based support in Japan for the country's leadership in development, Japanese-style political correctness requires that Japan appear to launch its initiatives independently rather than in response to pressures from the other industrial countries, especially the United States. Domestic pressure also has mounted to see Japan's economic leadership as a donor country translate into enhanced standing and visibility in international organizations. The appointment of scholar-diplomat Sadako Ogata as U.N. High Commissioner for Refugees in 1991 received much press coverage in Japan, and the major new increases in Japan's aid to refugees after her appointment appeared to signal Tokyo's willingness to assume a larger donor role when other leading nations take steps to share power. The call for greater international recognition has centered on the U.N. Security Council. Many Japanese were deeply rankled to see

Russia, an economic basket case, replace the USSR on that body alongside Britain and France, both of which are economic midgets compared with Japan in GNP terms, ODA levels, and contributions to the United Nations itself. After the collapse of Japan's ruling Liberal Democratic Party, the coalition that replaced it has slowed, at least for the present, the nation's pursuit of a seat, reflecting conflict within the coalition over Japan's role in peacekeeping—a key, from the standpoint of many member nations, to Japan's claims; but gaining a permanent seat on the Security Council is likely to remain a central Japanese foreign policy objective of the 1990s.

Looking to the Year 2000: Japan's Development Vision

Along with its major new commitments for a quantitative expansion of aid and capital to the developing world, Japan has been engaged in a significant rethinking of its aid program on a wide variety of issues, ranging from how to improve its implementation to what the goals and philosophy of its development efforts should be. On the eve of the 1990s, one leading development expert, the scholar Ryōkichi Hirono, outlined the major issues in development for the coming decades as (1) providing a steady supply of food, (2) effecting population control, (3) reducing unemployment, (4) developing appropriate technologies, (5) improving the handling of fiscal deficits in developing countries, (6) improving trade deficits, and (7) protecting the environment.[15] His projections offered an accurate forecast. When Japan announced an "ODA Charter" in 1992, all these areas figured prominently.

Hirono's work, along with that of the Keio University scholar Yasuhiko Torii, provides clues for analyzing the Japanese view of development problems and of the role that foreign assistance should play. Torii argues that international organizations have failed to rethink aid in light of the profound changes that are occurring globally, and he holds that there has not been a clear-enough distinction between economic "cooperation" and "assistance," an issue of growing importance given the increasingly wide disparities in levels of development among aid-recipient countries. The type of technology and know-how that is being transferred from the donor to the recipient, and also the relation between the donor and the recipient, vary depending on the developmental stage of each recipient country.[16]

According to Torii, economic cooperation involves four stages as countries move from being LLDCs (least among the less developed countries) to becoming (like Japan) members of the industrial club. For the donor country, the relationship to the recipient moves through (1) aid, (2) assistance, (3) cooperation, and (4) coordination. Aid giving is appropriate for LLDCs; its rationale is humanitarian, it should be grant-based, and its aim should be nation-building, meeting basic human needs, and providing emergency assistance. In LLDCs, he argues, it is fully appropriate to build basic economic and social infrastructure such as public housing, roads, or water-supply systems. It is also appropriate to provide bricks and mortar for an educational system and for medical-care delivery, as well as to supply technical assistance in those infrastructural efforts. For countries in the industrialization stage, or those countries that have severe external debt problems, "assistance" (presumably funded more by loans than grants) is more appropriate than "aid"; what is required is building high-grade infrastructure (airports, ports, highways, railroads, and telecommunication networks) and providing technical assistance in the form of education and know-how in the use of advanced technologies. A large part of ODA to the countries in the Association of Southeast Asian Nations (ASEAN) falls into this category. Such countries, in Torii's view, are at the crossroads of transformation into industrial nations. However, since the highly industrialized countries are constantly producing new technologies and know-how, it is difficult for these advanced developing countries to catch up and keep up, given the speed of change in the world economy. Developing countries need access to technological and financial assistance and with such help can benefit (as Japan once did) from being latecomers in terms of research and development. Numerous forms of technical assistance are appropriate in such nations, including technology transfer, transfer of managerial know-how, further investment to help the country respond to the competitive world market and keep up with technical innovations, and help with the international marketing of products.[17]

Torii's work, like that of Hirono, provides an intellectual justification and explanation for many features of Japan's foreign assistance efforts: the emphasis on loans over grants in all but the poorest countries; the emphasis on economic and social infrastructural support for development; and, by implication, the close relation among foreign aid, trade, and investment in moving developing countries up the ladder represented by the four stages. Such work delineates a clear development continuum. Once countries "graduate," the next stage is cooperation between old and newly developed countries to help address continuing problems. Presumably the countries of industrial East Asia would fall into this category in their relations with

Japan today. The cooperation stage is characterized by mutual encouragement of investment and trade between the new graduate and the more advanced country, industrial adjustment, codevelopment of resources, large-scale joint projects, cultural cooperation, and cooperation for national security. Torii sees this category of cooperation as vital for stimulating demand in the world market. As countries move to the most advanced level of development, the final stage is "coordination," in which countries on the highest step of the development ladder begin to participate—as Japan does today—in discussions on policy coordination issues that affect the world economy. Implicit in Torii's work of the late 1980s is a vision of the type of integrated regional economy that is taking shape in Asia, an economy in which countries at all four stages of development are becoming interlinked through patterns of aid, trade, and investment. Japan is at the top of the pyramid, extending different forms of economic cooperation depending on whether the country is Bangladesh or South Korea, but countries moving up the ladder help those below them.[18] The recent emergence of South Korea, Taiwan, and Singapore as fledgling aid donors is fully consistent with such a vision, though their rising economic activities in the region, along with China's surge in economic growth and resultant prominence, defy any effort to portray Asia in the mid-1990s as an integrated regional economy with Japan at its hub.

Japan's Development Approach: Criticisms, Responses, and New Directions

In the mid-1990s, as in the past, Japan, like all other donor countries, faces criticisms of its foreign assistance efforts. Perhaps only the United States, with its neglect of international organizations in the 1980s, its disproportionate share of aid for a small number of countries (such as Israel and Egypt, and recently, Russia), and its preoccupation with security rationales for aid, has come in for greater criticism from development professionals. In the early 1990s, the climate of international opinion regarding Japan's aid appeared to have improved, as evidenced by the tone of such books as *Yen for Development*, published by the Council on Foreign Relations in 1991.[19] There are several possible reasons for this shift: rapid economic growth in countries such as Thailand, seemingly boosted by Japanese investment and aid, and the relative dynamism of the entire Asian region, where Japan's economic leadership has been so visible; the growing recognition that Japan's role as a donor holds the key for future develop-ment initiatives; and the country's determined efforts to improve and ex-pand its aid program. Most types of criticism heard over the years from development professionals abroad have been echoed by at least some in-dividuals and groups back in Japan. Reviewing them provides an oppor-tunity to look at Japan's response and at recent initiatives and trends.

Lack of an Aid Philosophy

The Japanese development community has mounted a concerted effort since the mid-1980s to develop and articulate an aid philosophy and a view of the development process derived in part from Japan's historical experi-ence. Official statements have become clearer, but they can seem far afield of Japan's actual practices. Taking into account what Japan does, as well as what it says it does, one can name the following as key components of that philosophy:

—An emphasis on self-reliance as the goal of development aid (which dovetails with the view that loans are better development tools than grants for all but the poorest countries and that write-offs of unpaid loans are generally a mistake)

—A strong belief in stability and a reluctance to use aid money in any way that could be seen as challenging existing authority relations in a country

—A view that aid should be given for economic development purposes (rather than for strategic or other purposes, as in the case of U.S. aid to Israel, for example)

—A view that aid giving is a natural responsibility of membership in the industrial club

—"Political neutrality," that is, a belief that political litmus tests should not be applied, which during the cold war translated into a policy that Socialist countries, if they met other criteria, were eligible for Japanese aid

—A predisposition to give aid in coordination with other donors and to be responsive to their criticisms of Japan's aid initiatives

—An increasing emphasis on humanitarianism as an appropriate ratio-nale for aid giving

—A strong belief that the Japanese private sector has an important role to play in development, in conjunction with Japanese government efforts

Key elements of this view were challenged by a policy, announced by Prime Minister Toshiki Kaifu in April 1991, to weigh new types of considerations in implementing ODA for countries: (1) trends in military spending levels and in weapons imports and exports; (2) trends in the "development and production of nuclear and other weapons of mass destruction"; (3) efforts to promote democratization and market-oriented economic reforms; and (4) human rights issues.[20] The policy incorporated numerous contradictory strands in aid thinking. Initiated by the Ministry of Foreign Affairs (MOFA), it took into account, among other things, the priorities of MOFA officials who were eager to see Japan fall in step with other Western nations by supporting democracy and human rights, of Ministry of International Trade and Industry (MITI) officials who sought to push aid to Socialist and former Socialist countries undergoing market reforms in order to undergird Japanese private-sector initiatives there, and of opposition party members as well as many public officials who saw arms sales by America and other donor nations as destabilizing in the Third World and who thus wanted to provide disincentives for purchases of arms by developing nations. Few politicians or officials equally support all elements of the policy. Prodemocracy MOFA officials, for example, are leery of crossing the United States and other donors on Third World arms sales, whereas MITI officials eager to boost economic activity are apt to be skeptical about the merits of intervening in the domestic politics of recipient nations (with China as a favored example) in order to support democracy and human rights. As of early 1994, few concrete steps had been taken to limit aid increases because of arms spending, although Japan has applied pressure to India and Pakistan in the interest of curbing nuclear weapons development. There was more activity on the human rights and democracy issues. In the past, Japan seldom weighed human rights violations in deciding aid; recent exceptions were Japan's brief suspension of aid to China following the Tiananmen Square incident in 1989 and Japan's continuing suspension of aid to Myanmar because of human rights violations there. Since announcing the new policy in 1991, Japan stopped aid to Haiti after the coup in October of that year and has raised human rights, corruption, and related issues in its aid dialogues with Indonesia (over Eastern Timor). It has also suspended aid to Sudan (October 1992), Kenya (November 1991–October 1993), Malawi (June 1993), Guatemala (June 1–11, 1993), and Sierra Leone (May 1993) in the face of human rights violations.[21]

In 1992, Japan unveiled an "ODA Charter," which represented the most significant attempt to date to articulate an aid and development philosophy and to reconcile the many basic contradictions that remain.

Table 8.3

Sectorial Distribution of Japan's Bilateral ODA, 1991
(Commitment Basis)

	Amount ($ millions)			Share (%)
	Grants	Loan	Total	
1. Economic Infrastructure and Services	432.44	4,941.13	5,373.57	40.6
2. Social Infrastructure and Services	1,126.44	496.08	1,622.52	12.3
a) Education	620.16	209.61	829.77	6.3
b) Health	204.78	—	204.78	1.5
3. Production Sectors	817.72	1,479.10	2,296.82	17.4
a) Agriculture	632.13	613.46	1,245.59	9.4
b) Industry, Mining, Construction	166.76	268.32	435.08	3.3
c) Trade, Banking, Tourism	18.83	597.32	616.15	4.7
4. Multisector	121.66	—	121.66	0.9
5. Others	657.32	2,766.09	3,423.41	25.9
6. Not allocable by sector	385.41	12.70	398.11	3.0
Total	3,540.99	9,695.10	13,236.09	100.0

Source: Japan, Ministry of Foreign Affairs, *Basic Statistics on Japan's Economic Cooperation* (Tokyo: MOFA, 1993).

Overemphasis on Infrastructural Projects

Japan continues to be criticized for the large portion of its bilateral aid that goes for infrastructural projects as opposed to other types of aid. In 1991, according to the Ministry of Foreign Affairs' report on Japan's ODA, for example, aid disbursements for economic infrastructure (e.g., transport, communications, and energy) were 40.6 percent of Japan's total bilateral ODA (see table 8.3). A sense of how Japan and the United States compare is suggested by Organization for Economic Cooperation and Development (OECD) figures for 1990 on aid commitments: 32 percent of Japan's ODA commitments were for economic infrastructure, compared with only 2.8 percent for the United States.[22] In official publications today, Japan mounts a strong defense of infrastructural aid, pointing out that developing countries frequently request such projects from Japan, that Japan excels in construction and has other requisite skills for providing public utilities and other economic infrastructural projects, and that although many donor countries such as the United States do not today make major commitments of infrastructural aid, leading institutions like the World Bank obviously have long stressed the importance of economic infrastructure for development. A Ministry of Foreign Affairs report for 1988 forthrightly stated that such assistance, provided through ODA loans, was "expected to continue to be an important part of Japan's aid program . . . in the future,"[23] a prediction that has been borne out, although infra-structural aid has declined as a percentage of Japan's bilateral total from 49.2 percent in 1987 to 40.6 percent in 1991.[24] Japan thus appears to be proceeding on two fronts simultaneously. On the one hand, it has made a concerted effort (carried forward in the 1992 ODA Charter) to incorporate its traditional emphasis on this type of aid giving into its overall aid phi-losophy and framework for development, pointing out that Japan's own growth was accelerated through World Bank loans for infrastructural proj-ects as late as 1965; on the other hand, it has gradually reduced the proportion of such aid in its overall portfolio.

An "Overly Commercial" Aid Program

The criticism that Japan's aid is overly commercial, a view often voiced heatedly in international forums and particularly in Washington, has tended to focus on the issue of the de jure and de facto tying of Japan's aid to procurement from Japanese sources. Much of the debate has little to do with development per se but rather with Western concern over seeing Japan's "closed market" practices extended into the Third World, shutting out Western firms from the chance to bid successfully for lucrative Japanese aid contracts. The Japanese response has been to point out that Japanese ODA is far less tied (in a de jure sense) than are the loans of other donors, including the United States (see table 8.4). Meanwhile, Japan has taken steps to increase the share of untied aid, thus allowing Western firms to bid. In 1993, Japan announced that 95.8 percent of new ODA loans pro-vided in 1992 were completely untied.[25]

The focus today is de facto tying that results from the informal role played by the Japanese private sector abroad in lobbying Third World governments to request Japanese aid projects that are favorable to their interests. To address this issue, the Japanese government in 1988 pledged to start untying the engineering services portion of its aid contracts and to allow foreign consultants to take part in the feasibility studies that ultimately result in aid projects.[26] These measures opened the way for non-Japanese, including Western, firms to bid on aid contracts that formerly were virtually out of reach because project specifications were tailored to the competitive advantage of Japanese firms. According to the Ministry of

Table 8.4

Tying Status of ODA of Selected Countries, 1990 (Commitment Basis)
(% of ODA of each country)

	Bilateral			
	Untied	Partially Untied	Tied	Multilateral
Australia	8.5	0	45.3	46.2
Canada	25.5	11.8	28.4	34.4
France*	39.5	3.6	40.8	16.2
Germany	19.5	0	38.2	26.5
Italy	9.4	0	47.2	43.4
Japan*	69.9	2.8	12.5	15.6
Norway	36.7	0	23.2	40.5
Sweden*	53.1	0	14.5	32.9
United Kingdom*	0	0	0	44.4
United States*	58.9	6.7	19.2	12.7

*Including non-ODA debt
Source: OECD, *1992 Report on Development Co-operation: Efforts and Policies of the Members of the Development Assistance Committee* (Paris: OECD, 1992), p. A-15. "Partially untied" means that LDC firms also can bid but not firms of OECD member countries.

Foreign Affairs in 1993, the share of procurement contracts from new ODA loans that went to Japanese firms declined from around 70 percent in the mid-1980s to 35 percent for fiscal year 1992; however, other OECD member countries claimed only 13 percent of the contracts that year, suggesting that the sense of grievance among Western firms will continue.[27] No criticism of Japan's aid program has been more central than the issue of tying, for it has reflected deep-seated Western fears of Japanese industrial policy operating abroad to advance private-sector interests in the Third World under the guise of development. At the same time, recent U.S. government moves to boost American private-sector interests as part of the country's aid program suggest the degree to which Japan's approach to aid is, at least to some extent, becoming a model for America.

Overconcentration on Asia and on Middle-Income Countries

Responding to the criticism that it concentrates on Asian and middle-income countries, Japan has increased aid levels to countries outside of Asia and to LLDCs while arguing that it is appropriate for Japan, as an Asian nation, to center its aid in its region, that industrializing LLDCs are in an optimal position to utilize aid money to achieve real development, and that it is often difficult to identify viable projects in many LLDCs. Aid committed to Middle East and North African nations during the Gulf War has been disbursed rapidly and has caused a rise in allocations to that region, helping Japan keep regional balance (see table 8.1). Though aid to Africa declined in percentage terms, Japan sought to maintain a role there through providing nonproject grant aid, as part of a three-year initiative launched in 1990 to provide $600 million for structural adjustment efforts, following an earlier $500-million program for that purpose.[28] Meanwhile, assistance to Central and Eastern European countries, aid that now comes from the ODA budget, drew 1.2 percent of Japan's total bilateral ODA in 1992.[29]

Grant Element and Percentage of GNP

In the grant element, the proportion of grant-to-loan aid, and the percentage of GNP devoted to aid, Japan has repeatedly been found wanting in OECD reviews of the country's aid program. The grant element, or degree of concessionality, of Japan's aid, at 75.1 percent for 1992, remained well below the Development Assistance Committee (DAC) standard of 85.1 percent, though its aid to the least developed countries was well above the standard for such countries.[30] Japan's low grant element continues to be due not to poor terms of its loans but to the high proportion of loans as opposed to grants in its portfolio. Japan defends such policies as promoting the self-reliance of Third World countries. Despite dramatic growth in Japanese assistance levels, the nation's aid as a percentage of GNP, at .30 percent in 1992, is one of the lowest among the donor countries. The United States gave still less, at .18 percent of GNP in the same year,[31] but could make the case that its security contribution brought its overall share of global burden sharing to the highest level among the advanced industrial nations. Japan, with only 1 percent of GNP devoted to defense spending, can make no such claim. It has pledged to try to reach the DAC target of .7 percent of GNP spent on aid, but its efforts to date, despite remarkable gains, are far short of that objective. Recent achievements include the increase in support for LLDCs, an increase in grants more generally, and a relaxation of conditions on ODA loans.

Decentralization and Policies of Aid Administration

Japan's aid policies result from a four-ministry decision-making system in which each ministry (Foreign Affairs, MITI, Finance, and the Economic Planning Agency) has distinct interests and even aid philosophies. Implementation is carried out by the OECF (Overseas Economic Cooperation Fund), which handles ODA loans, and by the JICA (Japan International Cooperation Agency), which provides technical assistance, but numerous other ministries play crucial roles in carrying out projects in their domain. The lack of a central authority in the policy process makes it difficult for Japan to articulate a coherent philosophy and to set clear program directions. Pronouncements by Japan's official spokespersons from MOFA are important as expressions of intent, but they do not necessarily reflect the values and practices of officials in other ministries or agencies that become involved in aid policy and practice. The gap, however, is probably no greater than that between the aid-related pronouncements of Republican administrations in the United States and the working philosophies of American development professionals in the field during the Ronald Reagan and George Bush years.

Japan's principle of providing aid on a "request basis," together with the lack of clear central directives on what developmental strategies are desirable, opens the way for extensive involvement of the Japanese private sector in lobbying recipient governments to request aid projects it favors. There has been much discussion in Japan since the late 1980s of ways to centralize and streamline aid policy-making, but with few results to date; such efforts inevitably founder in bureaucratic infighting. However, a greater effort is being made to articulate development strategies and to develop more in the way of "country strategies" to deal with the inherent problems of a request-based system.

Understaffing of Aid Personnel

Among Japanese aid professionals themselves, lack of manpower is considered to be among the most serious problems facing Japan's aid program. As a result of the Japanese government's policies since the 1980s aimed at reducing the country's budget deficit, aid personnel staffing levels (like government staffing more generally) have increased only marginally. The shortage of aid personnel means that much of the work is done by bureaucrats or former bureaucrats seconded from relevant ministries, most of whom have little development expertise. Meanwhile, funding levels have surged precipitously, leaving aid personnel in the field woefully overworked and unable to move the large amounts of aid money now available to them. In 1991, Japan's aid staff was only 36 percent of the U.S. level, despite the fact that total ODA commitments of the two countries were at almost the same level.[32] Indeed, Japanese aid agencies are so understaffed that there is an inevitable tendency, born of necessity, to put priority on those projects that can absorb large amounts of aid money rather than on projects that consume a lot of manpower but little money. Understaffing also contributes to Japan's severe "pipeline problem," that is, its slow rate of disbursing aid money.

Training for Japan's Aid Professionals

Training is another serious problem. Most aid staff in Japan have not been specifically trained for development work, and even fewer have undertaken prior study (e.g., in languages and culture) to prepare them to work in specific regions of the developing world. No ministry has a career path for development work, reducing the incentives for officials to take on specialized training; meanwhile, retirees from the ministries roost in the top spots at agencies like JICA and OECF, discouraging young staff members, who find their promotion chances blocked. Japanese universities have been severely lacking when it comes to offering training for development professionals and experts. Amazingly enough, given Japan's history as an economic success story, remarkably few universities offer courses in economic development theory. The Japanese are now actively engaged in generating ways to address their manpower training problems, from increasing the use of foreign institutions for training aid personnel to building development studies centers in Japan.

Technology Transfer and the "Appropriate Technologies" Issue

A key criticism directed at Japan from developing countries has centered on the issue of technology transfer. Numerous countries have complained that Japan has tended to make available inappropriate technologies and to provide insufficient transmission of know-how in the use of the technologies they provide. Development professionals both inside and outside Japan argue that Japan's hardware is expensive to repair and maintain and may be beyond available skill levels. In one much-cited example, Japan donated fifteen bulldozers, fifteen trucks, and fifteen Caterpillar vehicles to the Central African Republic in 1983 to be used in main road construction; when the vehicles broke down because of improper operation, JICA dispatched an engineer (the only person available at the time), who stayed in the country for two years to repair the vehicles but not to train anyone to take up the task once he left.[33] Japan's health-care efforts provide other illustrations. It has been common, for example, for Japan to build referral hospitals with sophisticated technology to provide tertiary care in countries (such as Sri Lanka) where basic primary health care is lacking.[34] Japan has responded to such criticism by stepping up its efforts to train Third World experts and by rethinking the kind of aid provided. A recent emphasis on "participatory development" has led, for example, to a focus on providing primary rather than the more capital-intensive types of health care that involve expensive and hard-to-maintain technologies. Industrializing countries such as China and ASEAN nations, meanwhile, complain that Japan exports discarded technologies that fail to help developing countries to compete sufficiently in the global marketplace.

Lack of Japanese Aid Professionals in International Organizations

The Japanese themselves see the lack of Japanese professionals in international organizations as a significant problem leading to an underrepresentation of Japanese in the international development community. There are numerous reasons for the problem, first and foremost of which is the difficulty of lateral entry or reentry into Japanese ministries or organizations for professionals who have spent significant time abroad. The far safer route for a would-be development professional is to become a career bureaucrat in MOFA, OECF, or JICA rather than to venture abroad. Study is under way in Japan to find methods to ease the reentry problems of Japanese development professionals and to reduce the career costs of serving abroad, but the problem is deeply rooted in personnel practices that make all Japanese organizations, including firms, resistant to globalization.

Problems of Training Students and Professionals from Developing Countries in Japan

Increasingly, Japan is providing training for experts, technicians, and emerging development professionals from developing countries. As of March 1992, some 88,092 trainees had come to Japan from developing countries to acquire specialized skills.[35] But problems abound. A principal one is the difficulty of the Japanese language; many developing country trainees prefer to study in English rather than in Japanese. In the case of those who come as students, another problem is the closed nature of the university world in Japan, which may make study there less attractive for foreigners (especially non-Asians) than it is in the more ethnically and culturally diverse and open U.S. academic world. The high cost of living in Japan is another major drawback. Also, though Japan is strong in providing technical skills, it is weaker in providing the type of social science training necessary in administrative and other "soft" fields, including development planning. However, as noted, the number of trainees—and students—coming to Japan annually from the developing world is now quite high. Given Japan's growing presence throughout the developing world and its economic centrality in Asia, a working knowledge of the Japanese language is becoming a valuable asset to students and experts from developing countries, swelling the ranks of those eager to gain development skills in Japan.

Lack of Nongovernmental Organization (NGO) Involvement

As of 1990, only 1.1 percent of Japanese ODA went to voluntary organizations active in development work.[36] Indeed, the figure that year was lower than in 1987, when it was 2 percent.[37] A major reason is that Japan lacks the long tradition of volunteerism found in many Western countries, including the United States, which has led to voluntary associations, church and issue groups, and other types of NGOs. Japan's leading business organization, Keidanren, through the Japan International Development Organization, is increasingly playing a coordinating role for the private sector in providing technical assistance to developing countries, and Japan is committed to increasing NGO involvement in development efforts.

Conclusion

Japan's rise as an aid donor and as a major economic force in the Third World is one of the least noted but most significant foreign policy developments of the past two decades. The only country to make the passage from the Third World to full membership in the industrial club, Japan is now the indispensable party in development initiatives, whether they be for the "old" Third World or the "new" one, which includes Central and Eastern Europe, the former Soviet Union, the post–Gulf War Middle East, and recently, Vietnam. Estimates are that the demand for capital by the Middle East, Eastern Europe, and Latin America will exceed world supply by more than $200 billion per year for several years. The post–cold war world, with its promise of peace, arms reduction, and more attention to nonmilitary concerns (the environment, global warming, the debt crisis, and development problems), now has more rather than fewer conflicts, an accelerated arms race, and widespread economic stagnation.

In this emerging reality, Japan's role becomes crucial. The sheer size of its economic presence in the Third World gives it leverage to shape policy directions and to supply capital and know-how—derived from its own remarkable development experience—to new problems. Even if Japan supplied no development assistance, it would be a potent force in the Third World because of its power as an economic model and success story. Features of the Japanese model that are mirrored with much variation in industrial East Asia, especially South Korea and Taiwan, draw study throughout the Third World. Meanwhile a new economic growth model is emerging in countries like Thailand, where Japan, along with Hong Kong, Singapore, and Taiwan, is functioning as a crucial external variable in economic development.

For the United States, as its aid levels diminish in real terms and its economic presence in the Third World, especially in Asia, continues to decline, a key question is the degree to which it will seek to cooperate with Japan or, instead, see Japan's Third World presence in competitive terms. In the absence of a common threat, the forces binding the two countries together will continue to weaken, and it will take concerted effort to identify complementarities and redefine interests in ways that respond to Japan's initiatives noncompetitively. One illustration of Japan's independent course was its decision to normalize ties with Vietnam well in advance of the United States; in addition, Japan pursues its own relations with North Korea and at some point, assuming that North Korea's nuclear weapons development efforts are checked, could take steps to bring that country into the Asian regional economy. Another illustration is a plan, discussed several years ago in Japan, for attempting to develop an economic zone in the Far East that would include South Korea, the Russian Far East, parts of China, and western Japan. Though disdained by some in Japan as a pipe dream—as crumbs thrown by national officials to local governments and private-sector interests in Japan's western prefectures who are eager for coastal development projects—the plan holds the potential of bringing economic vitality to a region much in need of it and of helping to bring North Korea out of its isolation. In the current Japanese economic climate, the plan has been shelved, but its emergence reflects creative development thinking of a kind that, if acted on in the future, would transgress on political and economic boundaries that Americans throughout the postwar era have sought to maintain. It also could advance Japan's economic interests in the long term. Will the United States see these kinds of initiatives in competitive terms and seek to block or delay them, or will it search for accommodation and new modes of cooperation with Japan in an uncertain world? These are questions for which no one currently has answers.

Notes

I would like to thank Kim Reimann, Mark Wu, Margarita Abe, and Saori Horikawa for their able research assistance. A portion of this chapter appeared in somewhat different form in a working paper, coauthored with Margarita Abe, prepared for the Japan Committee, National Research Council, National Academy of Sciences, Washington, D.C., 1989.

1. Japan, Ministry of Foreign Affairs, *Japan's ODA: 1992 Report* (Tokyo: MOFA, 1992), p. 79.

2. Japan, Ministry of Foreign Affairs, *Outlook of Japan's Economic Cooperation* (Tokyo: MOFA, 1991).

3. Figures are from a press release issued in Paris by DAC, June 30, 1992. The U.S. moves in 1991 to include military debt write-offs as ODA (with ODA defined as money in the form of grants or concessional loans for development purposes) encountered stiff opposition from other donor countries.

4. For 1992, the United States included $895 million in debt forgiveness in its figure and was awarded official recognition from DAC as the number-one donor for that year. However, DAC pledged to exclude military debt forgiveness in its calculations for future years (*Japan Times*, July 1, 1993, p. 14).

5. OECD, *1992 Report on Development Co-operation: Efforts and Policies of the Members of the Development Assistance Committee* (Paris: OECD, 1992), p. A-33.

6. *Asahi Shimbun,* June 26, 1993, p. 3.

7. *Daily Yomiuri,* June 4, 1991. Nakayama's comments were made informally to journalists, who then reported the story.

8. *Japan Times,* June 26, 1993, p. 1.

9. *Asahi Shimbun,* June 19, 1988, p. 1.

10. *Daily Yomiuri,* December 7, 1988, p. 4.

11. The package included the following components: $35 billion in untied loans (from Japan's Ex-Im Bank), $10 billion in trade insurance (from MITI), and $5 billion for purchases of bonds issued by international organizations. See *Japan Times,* June 26, 1993, p. 1.

12. Text of speech by Prime Minister Kiichi Miyazawa at the U.N. Conference on Environment and Development at Rio, June 13, 1992. Japan pledged 900 billion to 1 trillion yen ($7 to $7.7 billion) during the 1992–97 period.

13. In April 1993, a MOFA official estimated that environmental disbursements for 1992 alone had totaled $2 billion (text of speech by Shōhei Naito, deputy director general of MOFA's Economic Cooperation Bureau at a DAC meeting, Paris, April 20, 1993, p. 30). On the eve of the 1993 summit, Japan signaled its willingness to take the lead in a proposed global project to develop new energy-conserving technologies (*Japan Times,* June 1, 1993, p. 1).

14. Results of a survey conducted February 27 and 28 after the failed economic summit between President Bill Clinton and Prime Minister Morihiro Hosokawa (*Asahi Shimbun*, March 3, 1994, p. 1). The figure was the highest since the survey was first conducted in 1982.

15. Ryōkichi Hirono, "Kokusai kikan kara no Nihon eno kitai" (International organizations' expectations of Japan), *Gaiko Forum* 3 (December 1988): 40–42.

16. Yasuhiko Torii, "Yottsuno dankai ni ōjita keizai kyōryoku no jidai" (The four stages of economic cooperation), *Gaiko Forum* 3 (December 1988): 47–50.

17. Ibid.

18. Ibid.

19. See Shafiqul Islam, ed., *Yen for Development: Japanese Foreign Aid and the Politics of Burden-Sharing* (New York: Council on Foreign Relations Press, 1991), which, according to the editor, "starts with the premise that development cooperation is the most effective avenue for a gun-shy Japan to assume global responsibilities" (p. 8).

20. OECD, DAC, *Aid Review 1990/1991* (Paris: OECD, 1992), p. 31.

21. Japan, Ministry of Foreign Affairs, *Japan's ODA: 1992 Report*, pp. 29–30, *Daily Yomiuri*, October 6, 1992, p. 1. Recent examples were provided by the Economic Cooperation Bureau, Ministry of Foreign Affairs, private communication, February 1994.

22. OECD, *1992 Report on Development Co-operation*, p. A-41. In 1992, 33.4 percent of the World Bank's commitments were for economic infrastructure (ibid.).

23. Japan, Ministry of Foreign Affairs, *Japan's ODA: 1988 Report* (Tokyo: MOFA, 1989), p. 49.

24. The figures, based on actual disbursements, are for economic infrastructure and services and are from Ministry of Foreign Affairs, *Japan's ODA: 1988*, p. 50, and Ministry of Foreign Affairs, *Japan's ODA: 1992*, p. 79.

25. Japan, Ministry of Foreign Affairs, Economic Cooperation Bureau, Loan Aid Division, "Procurement Record under ODA Loans in FY 1992," May 1993.

26. Ministry of Foreign Affairs, *Japan's ODA: 1988*, pp. 14–15.

27. Ministry of Foreign Affairs, "Procurement Record under ODA Loans in FY 1992."

28. OECD, DAC, *Aid Review 1990/1991*, p. 22.

29. Data provided by the Economic Cooperation Bureau, Ministry of Foreign Affairs, private communication, February 1994.

30. Ministry of Foreign Affairs, *Japan's ODA: 1993, Summary Report* (Tokyo: MOFA, 1994), p. 15. "Grant element" refers to the degree of concessionality of the aid given. An outright grant (as opposed to a loan) has a grant element of 100 percent, for example.

31. These figures are listed in ibid., p. 15.

32. Ministry of Foreign Affairs, *Japan's ODA: 1992*, p. 65.

33. Yoshinori Murai and Machiko Kaida, *Dare no tame no enjo* (Whom is the aid for? (Tokyo: Iwanami, 1987), pp. 18–19.

34. Michael R. Reich and Eiji Marui, eds., *International Cooperation for Health: Problems, Prospects, and Priorities* (Dover, Mass.: Auburn House Publishing, 1989), pp. 102–3.

35. Japan International Cooperation Agency, *Annual Report 1992*, (Tokyo: JICA, 1992), p. 46.

36. Ministry of Foreign Affairs, *Japan's ODA: 1992*, p. 174.

37. Ministry of Foreign Affairs, *Japan's ODA: 1988*, p. 50.

Chapter 9

Japan in the United Nations

ROBERT M. IMMERMAN

WITH THE IRAQI INVASION of Kuwait in August 1990, debate over the most appropriate role for Japan in the United Nations was suddenly transformed from an occasional item of specialized academic concern into a major international political issue garnering extensive media coverage. The issue is a twofold one: (1) Is Japan actively seeking greater responsibility within the United Nations and other international organizations for shaping the post–cold war international system? (2) If so, what U.N. mechanisms and procedures are required for Japan to exercise this new responsibility?

Mixed Signals from Japan

As received by the international community, the signals emanating from Japan regarding the United Nations have been decidedly mixed. On the one hand, Japan was the single largest financial contributor ($13 billion) to U.N.-authorized actions to enforce economic sanctions and, subsequently, to use military force against Iraq. It actively sought the appointment by Secretary General Perez de Cuellar of a distinguished international relations theorist and experienced diplomatic practitioner, Sadako Ogata, as U.N. High Commissioner for Refugees and indicated that it would assume greater financial responsibility for the management of refugee flows. It campaigned vigorously and successfully for an unprecedented seventh two-year term as a nonpermanent member representing Asia on the Security Council.

Japan participated actively in U.N. efforts to negotiate a comprehensive settlement of the Cambodian conflict by holding a conference of the Cambodian parties in Tokyo, hosting a conference on economic reconstruction of Cambodia, and financing a substantial portion of the postsettlement U.N. operation in Cambodia. It lobbied to obtain the position of U.N. Special Representative in Cambodia for the most senior Japanese national in the U.N. Secretariat, Under Secretary General Yasushi Akashi.

The enactment in June 1992 of the U.N. Peace-Keeping Participation Law, authorizing limited participation by Japan's Self Defense Forces (SDF) in noncombat rear-support activities of U.N. peacekeeping operations, means that for the first time since adopting its so-called Peace Constitution in 1946, the government of Japan (GOJ) is able to dispatch its military overseas. SDF personnel have engaged in construction and transport activities in Cambodia and have been sent to Mozambique as well. The ultimate success of the challenging Cambodian operation may allow the unfreezing of the restrictions added to the peacekeeping law, thus allowing a greater scope for future SDF participation.

Japan has taken a surprisingly strong stand against reported North Korean efforts to develop nuclear capabilities. It has linked bilateral diplomatic relations and economic assistance to acceptance by the Democratic Peoples Republic of Korea (DPRK) of challenge inspections under the safeguards agreement with the International Atomic Energy Agency. It has been conspicuously active in international efforts to dissuade the DPRK from withdrawing from the Nuclear Non-Proliferation Treaty (NPT).

In the Tokyo Declaration issued jointly by Prime Minister Kiichi Miyazawa and President George Bush on January 9, 1992, Japan and the United States recommitted "their resources and the talents of their peoples to the purposes of the United Nations Charter" and agreed to "cooperate . . . to reinvigorate the U.N. organization." In this context, the Japanese Permanent Representative to the United Nations and other senior Japanese officials publicly called for revising the U.N. Charter in order to designate Japan as a permanent member of the Security Council. In the early 1990s the GOJ launched a campaign to extract from other U.N. member states as many endorsements as possible of its claim to a permanent seat. Based on the principle of "no taxation without representation," Japan has also insisted that it cannot be expected to agree automatically to finance U.N.-

sponsored collective security operations unless it is included in the consultative process leading to Security Council establishment of these operations. At the first summit-level meeting of the Security Council on January 31, 1992, Prime Minister Miyazawa agreed with fourteen other heads of state and chiefs of government that the capacity of the United Nations for preventive diplomacy, peacemaking, and peacekeeping should be strengthened.

Yet, at the same time, Japan has adopted a much more passive posture than the other major industrialized democracies toward several important international peace and security issues on the U.N. agenda. A case in point was Japan's behavior during the early phases of the Gulf War.

Although the Security Council was in almost constant session during the first few weeks of the Gulf conflict and the leaders of the other members of the Group of Seven (G-7) were in almost daily contact, Japanese policy seemed paralyzed throughout August 1990. Prime Minister Toshiki Kaifu canceled a previously scheduled trip to Middle Eastern capitals. GOJ ministers publicly squabbled over the wisdom of implementing an embargo against Iraq. Neither the GOJ nor private organizations offered to assist in the repatriation of Asian refugees who had fled from Iraq into the Jordanian desert.

Japan initially resisted extending any financial support to the U.N.-authorized multinational coalition or to U.N. members adversely affected by economic sanctions against Iraq. When Japan finally contributed, it did so out of fear that inaction would seriously harm its bilateral relationship with the United States. Heavy and continuous American pressure to shoulder some responsibility for U.N.-backed efforts to resist Iraqi aggression, rather than any sense that Japan was obliged under the U.N. Charter to join in these efforts, proved to be decisive in persuading Japan grudgingly to accept some responsibility for paying a part of the bill.

The GOJ also mismanaged its initial effort to obtain parliamentary approval of legislation authorizing participation of the SDF in U.N. operations. In the fall of 1990, even though it controlled a majority in the lower house of the Diet, it withdrew without putting to a vote in the lower house a U.N. Peace Cooperation Bill intended to authorize SDF participation in multilateral enforcement as well as U.N. peacekeeping actions. The GOJ's lackluster performance in attempting to justify this legislation, as well as its sudden withdrawal of the bill, gave rise to the suspicion that it never intended to enact the legislation and was interested only in demonstrating to Western public opinion the lack of domestic support for any Japanese physical presence in U.N. peacekeeping operations.

The U.N. Peace-Keeping Participation Law, finally enacted in the spring of 1992, was sold to a very divided public as virtually risk free, since SDF and civilian personnel would be kept away from front lines, would not be directly involved in truce supervision, and would not have responsibility for the disarming of belligerent forces. When Japan suffered its first casualties in Cambodia in the spring of 1993, opposition parties and a large part of the Japanese media urged that the SDF as well as civilian police be withdrawn at once. To its credit, the government of Japan for once held firm.

The GOJ has appeared indifferent to regional conflicts in Yugoslavia and Somalia. Moreover, senior political levels of the GOJ not only have failed to enunciate the rationale behind Japan's bid for a permanent seat on the Security Council but also have hesitated to make clear whether Japan is committed to pursuing this goal. A striking example of Japanese ambiguity in this regard has been its lukewarm reaction to the Clinton administration's early and unequivocal endorsement of permanent membership for it as well as for Germany, contained in Ambassador Madeleine Albright's June 8, 1993, speech to the Foreign Policy Association of New York. This ambiguity was further demonstrated at the 1993 session of the U.N. General Assembly where Prime Minister Morihiro Hosokawa softened Japan's position on gaining a permanent Security Council seat.

Elements of Japan's U.N. Policy

Japan's true intentions toward the U.N. system, therefore, are difficult for the Japanese to define and even more difficult for foreigners to ascertain. The crux of the problem is that there is no clearly defined policy. Instead, there is an unwieldy amalgam of the following elements: (1) the idealized image held by the Japanese public of the United Nations as a supernational moral influence; (2) the desire of Japan's political and business elites to obtain from the international community symbolic recognition of Japan's economic success; (3) the efforts of the bureaucracy to utilize multilateral mechanisms not only to solidify Japan's relationship with the United States but also to secure incremental increases in Japan's international involvement; and (4) the campaign by members of the Liberal Democratic Party and the Foreign Ministry since the Gulf conflict to gain a permanent seat on the Security Council.

Popular Attitudes

Until recently, the vast majority of the Japanese public regarded the United Nations as the embodiment of the pacifist ideals explicitly enumerated in Japan's post–World War II constitution and major pieces of legislation. For example, both the 1952 U.S.-Japan Mutual Security Treaty and the 1960 revised version express the hope that the United Nations would eventually furnish Japan, as well as other peace-loving nations, with a secure international environment.

Japan's admission to the United Nations in 1956 was hailed across the Japanese political spectrum as evidence that the nation had reentered the international community of nations and could therefore turn the page on its World War II behavior overseas. The only major tenet of postwar Japanese foreign policy that has received the support of all segments of the domestic political spectrum—from the conservatives (Liberal Democratic Party, or LDP) to the Socialist and Communist parties constituting the left-wing opposition—has been the nation's commitment to an otherwise undefined "U.N.-centered diplomacy."

Enactment by the U.N. General Assembly (UNGA) of peace and disarmament resolutions sponsored by Japan, or adoption by a U.N. specialized agency of international social and labor standards favored by Japan, became yardsticks by which the Japanese public could measure its standing in the international community. Conversely, critical references in U.N. debate or resolutions to Japanese commercial relationships with South Africa, fishing practices in the Pacific, or treatment of women in the domestic labor market were quickly transformed by the opposition parties and media into major national setbacks. Japan's defeat at the hands of Bangladesh for a seat on the Security Council in the early 1980s was interpreted at home as a major international rebuke.

Paradoxically, this popular image of the United Nations as the embodiment of the ideals toward which postwar Japan was striving has served to reinforce strong isolationist sentiments in the Japanese political culture. To many Japanese, these ideals were formulated by an outside body, and Japan's role was merely to live up to them. Japan had no particular responsibility for shaping or implementing internationally the decisions, not to mention the goals, of the United Nations or its specialized agencies. Until recently little if any attention was paid to the enforcement provisions of the U.N. Charter or even to the evolution of the U.N.'s peacekeeping functions, and little thought was given to the possibility that someday Japan might be involved in the United Nations' use of force. It was enough for Japan to pay its bills, give lip service to the ideals of the organization, and avoid being singled out for criticism by others.

The Political and Business Communities

Japan's ruling elites have had a somewhat different conception of the U.N. system. They have put high priority on securing Japan's membership in international organizations and placing Japanese nationals in senior positions in these organizations. LDP politicians and business executives attached great importance to Japan's winning a seat on the Security Council for the first time in 1958, achieving membership in the Organization for Economic Cooperation and Development (OECD) in 1964, keeping an almost permanent grip on a seat on the Economic and Social Council (ECOSOC), and securing for a Japanese national the position of under secretary general. They were not motivated by a desire to shape political or economic agendas, alter financing or budgets, facilitate the hiring of larger numbers of Japanese as international civil servants, or promote specific national policies. Instead, they sought U.N. actions that appeared to confer greater status on Japan. Their main concern was that the United Nations treat Japan the same way it treated other major powers. These same groups opposed for nearly a decade Japan's ratification of the Nuclear Nonproliferation Treaty on the grounds that the treaty, by denying Japan the option of becoming a nuclear power, would consign it to second-class status internationally. In sum, until 1990, whenever the United Nations captured the attention of Japan's politicians and business leaders, national prestige rather than policy direction was generally at stake.

The Internationalists: MOFA and Others

A third element shaping Japan's approach to the United Nations has been a small group of Japanese bureaucrats and academics linked mainly to the Ministry of Foreign Affairs (MOFA) and the Ministry of Finance. They have tried to use Japan's membership in the United Nations and other multilateral organizations both to reinforce the nation's bilateral alliance relationship with the United States and to augment gradually its responsibility for the management—if not the solution—of international political and economic issues.

During the 1960s, MOFA dominance of Japanese multilateral diplomacy meant that Japan generally supported U.S. initiatives in the United Nations and voted as a member of the Western democratic coalition. During the late 1960s and early 1970s, Japan was in the forefront of lobbying efforts to secure passage of UNGA resolutions favorable to the Republic of Korea and to defeat those endorsed by North Korea. It joined the United States in actively opposing Communist and Third World efforts to impose a Marxist-inspired Charter of Economic Rights and Duties on the international community. Australia and Japan were the only major American allies to join in the abortive 1971 effort to preserve the Republic of China's U.N. seat. With the exception of resolutions relating to Israel and the Middle East peace process (it abstained on the "Zionism equals racism" resolution in 1975), Japan's positions on substantive issues generally coincided with those of the United States until 1981. Continuous bilateral consultations, between the two U.N. missions in New York as well in capitals, were in large part responsible for this close collaboration and Japan's steadily higher U.N. profile.

This pattern was suddenly disrupted by the advent of Ronald Reagan's administration, and particularly by Ambassador Jeane Kirkpatrick's stewardship of the U.S. mission to the United Nations in New York (USUN). Japan (like other Western allies of the United States) found it increasingly difficult to associate itself with U.S. positions on a gamut of issues, ranging from arms control to apartheid, often because it had little advance notice of where the United States stood on an issue. Lack of consultation became the order of the day. In this connection, Kirkpatrick never saw fit to visit Japan for U.N.-related talks during her four-year tenure.

By 1984, MOFA appeared to recognize that the increasing isolation of the United States in the United Nations was the result of inattention at the highest levels of the U.S. government to USUN tactics (which actively sought confrontation and defeat in order to justify a de facto termination of U.S. participation in the world body). Japan feared that differences over the United Nations, if left unattended, would become a major issue of discord between the two nations, thereby threatening the solidity of the bilateral alliance.

Matters came to a head with congressional enactment of the Kassebaum amendment, which mandated the withholding of a major portion of the assessed U.S. contribution to the U.N. budget. Ironically, this measure spurred the GOJ to launch what has been until now its most notable initiative in the United Nations—Foreign Minister Shintaro Abe's September 1985 proposal to establish a "Wisemen's Group" to recommend reform of the United Nations' administrative and budgetary process. In spite of strong initial opposition on the part of that portion of the Kirkpatrick clique that had moved from USUN to the State Department's International Organizations Bureau (Ambassador Kirkpatrick had resigned her post in early 1985), the U.S. government, at the urging of the new U.S. permanent representative, Ambassador Vernon Walters, supported the Abe proposal in the 40th UNGA. The recommendations of the Group of 18 appointed by the U.N. secretary general, a group in which Japan played an active role, were approved at the 41st UNGA session, thereby enabling the Reagan administration to gradually resume payment of its arrears. This Japanese initiative had the additional benefit of restoring the close and cooperative relationship, which had existed until 1981, between the U.N. missions of Japan and the United States.

In the late 1980s, the Japanese began to adopt a higher profile on U.N. political and economic issues as well. Joining with the Germans and Italians on the 1987 Security Council in what was facetiously referred to as the "Ex-Ax(is) Group," Japan succeeded in persuading the Western permanent members of the council to make more evenhanded the draft of what was to become Resolution 598, mandating a comprehensive settlement of the Iran/Iraq conflict. Japan contributed civilian observers to the Afghanistan and Iran/Iraq peacekeeping operations, as well as a sizable number of election monitors and supplemental financing to the United Nations Transition Assistance Group (UNTAG), the United Nations' successful implementation of independence arrangements for Namibia. By early 1990, MOFA had made clear that Japan was prepared to play a major role in implementing a U.N.-negotiated settlement of the Cambodia conflict and, in this regard, to seek Diet legislation amending the basic SDF law in order to permit Japanese military personnel to participate in U.N. peacekeeping operations.

MOFA's carefully calibrated plan for gradually and quietly expanding Japan's responsibilities for international peace and stability in a U.N. context was abruptly disrupted by the Iraqi invasion of Kuwait and the subsequent external pressure for rapid and dramatic moves by Japan to counter the invasion. MOFA, accustomed to initiating incremental changes in Japanese international behavior, was incapable of providing the political leadership necessary for a significant financial or personnel contribution by

Japan. The bureaucracy, however, did not trust the political leadership at that time to initiate delicate diplomatic policies in the United Nations, primarily because Japan was then headed by a prime minister with no previous international experience. The elites did not believe their immediate interests were threatened by the Iraqi action, since they assumed that Iraq would have to sell Kuwait's oil and they were prepared to have Japan pay whatever price was asked. American pressure, which led the Japanese to fear a serious setback in the bilateral relationship, finally persuaded these elites to agree to a series of domestically unpopular Japanese contributions to the multinational effort. From its inception, the Gulf War was widely viewed in Japan as a major complicating factor in relations with the United States, rather than as a grave threat to the post–cold war international order.

Securing Access to—and Participation in— U.N. Decision Making

MOFA became the scapegoat in Japan for both the domestic political conflict and the international criticism produced by Japan's hesitant reaction to the Gulf conflict. MOFA was charged with a multitude of sins: failure to anticipate the Iraqi invasion of Kuwait; failure to assess the nature of the American response; failure to learn every detail of the deliberations of the Security Council's five permanent members (the "Perm Five") regarding a U.N. response; and—depending on the political position of the critic—failure either to prevent any Japanese involvement in the U.N.-authorized enforcement action or, conversely, to move Japan into more positive action in cooperation with its U.S. ally and Western friends.

Under this barrage of criticism, MOFA's previous policy of gradually and inconspicuously easing Japan into a larger U.N. peacekeeping role was no longer viable. Some in MOFA believed that the best defense for MOFA was to push for rapid adoption of legislation permitting the SDF to engage in all aspects of U.N. peacekeeping activities. Others claimed MOFA's best defense could be found in the argument that had Japan been a permanent member of the Security Council, it would have been privy to all the information in the hands of the Perm Five and so would not have been caught off guard by sudden decisions of the council.

As is often the case in Japanese decision making, the arguments of both groups have prevailed. Japan adopted, after less than two years of debate, epoch-making legislation authorizing SDF participation in certain aspects of U.N. peacekeeping operations. At the same time, MOFA has become the main preacher of the doctrine that Japan is entitled to a permanent seat on the U.N. Security Council. Unfortunately, however, this doctrine remains a chant empty of content rather than a carefully devised game plan. So far MOFA has not indicated how it plans to achieve its goal. Is it seeking amendment of the U.N. Charter to provide permanent membership only for Japan? Or does it seek expansion of the council to include permanent members from several developing nations? Does Japan seek other revisions in the U.N. Charter, such as explicit provision for U.N. peacekeeping and peacemaking activities? However, with the approach of the fiftieth anniversary of the U.N. Charter and the assumption of power in the political as well as bureaucratic worlds by a younger generation of Japanese, a new Japanese road map for the United Nations may yet be drawn.

Conclusion

Since the Gulf War, symbolism has triumphed over realism in shaping Japan's behavior in the United Nations. MOFA's professionals were forced to abandon their old scenario and have yet to devise a credible new one. Japan is of two minds not only with respect to permanent membership on the Security Council; its attitude toward assuming additional responsibilities for ensuring peaceful change in the world also remains unclear. The problem has been made more complicated for Japan's close friends in the United Nations, particularly the United States, by the fact that the GOJ has not proposed any plan for achieving permanent membership on the Security Council nor has it given any indication that it's permanent presence there would inspire it to play a more active role in pursuit of international peace and security. Instead, the GOJ earlier appeared to expect that the international community's recognition of Japan's economic preeminence would automatically result in revision of the U.N. Charter in Japan's favor. With the collapse of LDP rule and the advent of coalition government, Japan now appears to be waiting, rather than pushing, for U.N. change.

The Clinton administration explicitly endorses Japan's permanent membership on the Security Council but still expects Japan to take the lead in securing support from other U.N. members. Other Western member states, though sympathetic to Japan's need for international recognition, are reluctant to open what they regard as the Pandora's box of charter revision, fearing that it would lead to a major and possibly successful Third World effort to weaken the influence of the industralized democracies over the Security Council. Complicating the issue is the growing U.S. view that it must involve Japan more actively in meeting new political, economic, and environmental threats to international stability without damaging those existing mechanisms of the United Nations, such as the Security Council, that are at last assuming an active role in coping with these threats.

Recommendations

Apart from amendment of the U.N. Charter, the United States and Japan can immediately adopt several procedural steps that would contribute to a more prominent role for Japan in defining and acting on the new international agenda.

—The two nations should immediately begin to implement the provision of the 1992 Tokyo Declaration calling on them "to work together to strengthen the United Nations' peacekeeping and peacemaking functions." They should do so by instructing their respective U.N. missions to hold bilateral consultations at least once a month.

—The New York–based U.N. ambassadors of the industrialized democracies, composing the G-7, should meet monthly to attempt to coordinate their U.N. policies and tactics.

—The representatives of the ten largest financial contributors to the United Nations should meet regularly to examine the budgetary implications of all requests for additional U.N. activities.

—The United States and Japan should jointly request periodic meetings of the political directors of the foreign ministries of the G-7 in order to prepare for discussion of multilateral issues at the annual G-7 summits.

—The secretary general of the United Nations should be invited to the annual G-7 summits.

By establishing a heavy schedule of meetings at which Japan will have to take positions, these measures should contribute to strengthening the influence of the internationally minded realists within the Japanese bureaucracy. Some of these gatherings, with their high visibility, can also serve to placate those elements of the Japanese establishment who need evidence of Japan's enhanced status.

A word of caution, however, is in order. The level of popular Japanese satisfaction with the international status quo is too high and the extent of isolationist sentiment is too widespread to permit MOFA and others conscious of Japan's need for expanding its international responsibilities to move the nation rapidly toward assuming these responsibilities. Incremental change in the direction of a more active and substantive role in international organizations, induced in large part by steady but subtle outside pressure, is the best that can be hoped for from Japan.

Conclusion

Japan: A Twenty-first-Century Power?

PAUL KENNEDY

A NUMBER OF SCHOLARS, such as Robert Reich, John Muller, Richard Rosecrance, and Kenichi Ohmae, have begun to address the growing interconnectedness of societies—in production, in software, in design, and in finance—and suggest that power is being decomposed. Whereas great powers in the old days were supposed to possess a collection of particular attributes, including military, technological, financial, and cultural strength, certain emerging nations today have decided not to pursue the entire collection. They have opted to be one-, two-, or three-dimensional rather than five- or six-dimensional powers. They prefer to be technological powers but not military powers. Although there will undoubtedly be many regional conflicts and interethnic disputes, great power wars may be a thing of the past. In light of this emerging viewpoint, going back and reflecting on Japan from a historical perspective may be less useful than marching forward and trying to look into the future. What are Japan's prospects for maintaining a steady, long-term relative advantage over its commercial and technological competitors? Will Japan enhance its relative global position over the next few decades, with the accompanying implications for future global relationships?

In the first part of this chapter, I would like to outline the broad, transnational forces for change bearing down on global society. First, let us examine the implications of the demographic explosion. In thirty years we are likely to be living in a global society of 8 to 10 billion people rather than today's 5.5 billion, and 95 percent of that population growth will have occurred in the developing world. Societies in the developed world will experience relative *and*, in some cases, absolute declines as their populations age. As a result, considerable instabilities driven by population explosion and mass illegal migrations are likely. Secondly, let us consider the dangers posed by our threatened natural environment. Threats to the environment will only increase as the global population doubles, as industrialization spreads to the developing world, particularly China and India, as we eliminate rain forests, and as we continue to emit automobile gases into the atmosphere and to assault the water, air, and land. Third, let us reflect on the long-term implications of technology-driven changes, up to the year 2020. In particular, the biotech revolution will affect global agriculture and food processing, perhaps rendering anachronistic the traditional methods of growing; food will be produced in laboratories rather than on farms. Furthermore, the robotics-automation revolution will end the two-hundred-year span in world history in which individuals were brought into factories to work with machines. Those individuals now are being systematically replaced by other machines. In Japan, sophisticated robots are assembling less-sophisticated robots, all day, all night. Finally, we need to think through the implications of the global financial and communications revolution and the rise of the truly multinational corporation: are these trends, in fact, creating a "borderless world" (as Ohmae argues) and thus undermining the traditional claims to economic sovereignty advanced by the nation-state?

While these global forces bear down on all societies, some peoples are better prepared than others to handle the biotech revolution, or the population explosion, or the consequences of global warming and sea-level rises. In the same way, certain countries are more or less equipped, in educational and infrastructure terms, to handle the robotics revolution. As in all other revolutions and significant changes in history, there will be winners and losers. Just as the industrial revolution based on the steam engine in late-eighteenth-century England meant that certain groups in that society were to become historical winners, so also did it mean that the English hand-loom weaver, as well as the Indian textile industry, was the long-term historical loser. Technology may itself be neutral, but it has different effects on societies differently positioned to deal with the changes.

In this regard, it can be argued that Japan is well positioned to deal with most of today's global, transnational changes. First, the robotics-automation revolution is coming out of Japan. Even though America was the founder of robotics, few independent American robotics manufacturers remain. At the moment, 75 to 80 percent of the world's robots are made and are working in Japan, for reasons that are clear when one looks at Japanese demography.

The biotech revolution does not appear to benefit Japan immediately, since Japan does not have the giant agrichemical and pharmaceutical companies that are involved in the genetic engineering of plants and animals. But Japan is investing enormously in new biotechnology, for what seems to be a very obvious reason: unlike the United States or Western Europe, which have large surpluses, Japan is heavily dependent on imported foodstuffs. And if Japan can get the DNA technology for foodstuffs and food processing, then it becomes less dependent on imports and less insecure in its long-term position.

Concerning the global communications and financial revolution and the rise of the multinational corporations, a Japan that in 1991 had thirty-seven or thirty-eight of the world's one hundred largest multinationals, eight of the world's ten largest banks, four of the world's largest insurance companies, and a large amount of capital is in a better position to deal with globalization than most other countries. At the least, Japan is in an equally good position as the United States and Germany, provided that the "bubble economy" of the Tokyo stock market or a too-rapid rise of the yen does not undermine the fortunes of large Japanese companies.

Even those global forces that look more troubling, such as environmental problems, rising sea levels, and changes in population structures, will probably be manageable for Japan. Societies that have highly skilled work forces, with superior response systems, and that have large numbers of scientists and engineers have recourse to more options. And Japan possesses the funds and the ability to effect long-term planning.

Scientists examining climatic change do not believe that global warming, if it occurs, will be manifested in a slight, steady percentage increase in average global temperatures; rather, temperatures will reach threshholds at which unpredictable turbulences will occur. If sea levels rise one to three feet, a country with large resources of capital and skills, such as Japan, will be better off than a Bangladesh, which could disappear beneath the oceans. A capital-rich country, with engineering, technological, and financial strengths, will simply be in a better position whatever the outcome of global warming.

Regarding the aging of the Japanese population, predictions that this demographic trend will reduce Japan's exceptionalism may be exaggerated.

Japanese manufacturing is investing much more heavily than its competitors in replacing old equipment with robots in order to deal with this demographic crunch. Outside critics have gleefully forecast that Japan will suffer because it will not admit migrant workers at the same time that Japanese women are not maintaining a 2.1 fertility rate, necessary to reproduce a work force. But that criticism misses the point that Japanese businesses are replacing existing workers as far as possible with an automated form of production, both at home and abroad.

By contrast, an analysis of the impact of these transnational forces on other countries provides mixed or even dire signals. Countries in the developing world that are in the middle of a demographic explosion, that are devouring their entire environment by a doubling of the population every twenty-two to twenty-five years, that have no chance of utilizing the new technologies, and that lack the educational infrastructure necessary to address the changes bearing down on the global society are in particularly desperate positions. Japan, by contrast, has more trump cards than most other countries.

Even the United States is going to have significant problems addressing some of these forces for global change. The biotech revolution could entirely transform American farming in the next twenty years as it introduces new methods of creating foodstuffs. America, however, may not be prepared for such a transformation because, rather than engaging in long-term planning, the country prefers laissez-faire. A free market in biotechnology consists of a small number of large pharmaceutical companies that will transform the way in which food is produced.

The United States does not invest as much as Japan in robotics, except in specialized fields such as in undersea or space exploration, because the United States has no demographic incentive to do so. Unlike Japan, which invests heavily in robotics because of a need for replacement labor, the United States receives large amounts of cheap, immigrant labor. Since the United States does not have a long-term economic incentive for the development of automation technologies, the robotics revolution faded away some fifteen years ago.

The United States also is not well poised to address certain growing environmental problems, such as the draining and salinization of the Ogallala Aquifer in the Great Plains, the northward shift in the growing zones, and the issue of energy and fuel conservation. Until the arrival of the Bill Clinton administration, the United States simply had not been taking these issues seriously.

Even with regard to population growth, the United States offers a mixed picture. The positive side is that the population is not stagnant but is growing. The negative side is that a decrease in skill levels is accompanying the change in composition of the work force. The majority of those who have been leaving the work force are white, skilled males with technical and professional training. Yet a large majority of those forecast to enter the work force are ethnic minorities who have not received the level of technical skills that the retiring white males received in their day. This is a mismatch: the work force is growing, but the skill levels of those coming in are significantly lower, and this at a time of knowledge-driven economic change.

Comparatively, of course, the United States will have fewer problems in meeting these challenges than many other nations, but it appears that Japan will have even fewer problems. The latter's advantages include its high savings ratios, its heavy research and development investment in practical, commercial, and nonmilitary fields, its cooperation between management and unions, its cooperation between industries and ministries, its skill levels of the work force, and its ability to carry out long-term planning. Japanese companies' ferocious competitiveness for market shares—whether in automobiles, cameras, or computers—drives their firms in an ever-upward spiral in quality, efficiency, design, and service as they attempt to kill off the company next door. Consequently, Japanese companies present ever-improving, moving targets. Thus, while American automobile companies are steadily improving themselves, the Japanese firms are not standing still, which leaves Tokyo in a tricky political position. In the trade disputes between the United States and Japan, what is Japan's government supposed to do? Should it welcome large-scale increases in the yen's international value? Should it tell Japanese companies not to compete so vigorously against one another? Should it tell them not to carry out global strategic planning? Should it tell Toyota not to position itself inside the European, American, and Southeast Asian markets? Can it do that? When pressuring the Japanese government, is the United States looking at the wrong cause of the trade imbalances?

Economically and technologically, therefore, one might conclude that Japan is well structured to contend with the global transnational forces and could become a—not the—twenty-first-century power. This presumes, however, that forces beyond the control of the Japanese remain constant, and that the international order remains stable. Such an order involves a reasonably open trading system allowing global capitalism to function, a systematic dismantling of the cold war, perhaps sporadic regional conflicts in which Japan is not directly involved, no resurgence of Russian imperialism, touchy but not impossible relations with the European Community, delicate relations with China, the intensification of Japan's economic penetration of Southeast Asia, and the preservation of Japanese-American relations despite trade and security differences—none of which are certainties.

What would happen if this relatively stable international order failed? If instead of ever-increasing economic integration there were financial crashes and trade wars? If the former Soviet Union dissolved into chaos? If the United States reduced its commitments in the Pacific? If China grew increasingly assertive? If India emerged as a regional superpower? If rivalries developed between the "haves" and the "have nots" of the world, with many of the latter possessing sophisticated weaponry? The Japanese would not know what to do in these scenarios. As it is now, Japan lacks strength in the world of power politics, in the world of military upsets, and in the world of managing international relations. Obviously the Japanese are considering whether or not they should increase their military power, and technologically and economically they have the "surge capacity" to do so. But they also recognize the domestic and international difficulties entailed in such a proposition.

Furthermore, Japan continues to face problems in political leadership. One school of thought holds that Japan will steadily become less exceptional. It will mature economically, age and consume more, produce less, become rich, but live on consumption rather than invest in new technologies. This is the comfortable Western view of how Japan may emerge over the next decade or two. However, another possibility is that Japan will remain different. It may make some nominal concessions or cosmetic adjustments but continue to move into sector after sector to obtain larger international market shares. And it may maintain the aspects of its society that give it a competitive advantage—its educational system, investment levels, and industry's relationships with ministries—and organize to further enhance its global economic position. In doing so, Japan may benefit, but it may also provoke increasing resentment from other nations concerned about the world order. By winning economically and technologically, it could lose in the diplomatic and political areas.

How could such difficulties be avoided? Japan needs to produce some form of enlightened political leadership—statesmen and stateswomen— who can guide the country into meeting an internal transformation and providing greater international contributions. Yet it was precisely in the quality of the political leadership, especially of the Liberal Democratic Party, that Japan suffered its greatest deficiencies. Although the new coalition government shows signs of readiness for changes, until now Japan appeared unable to transform itself. If critics such as Karel van Wolferen are correct, the "system" ensures that enlightened public servants will not emerge to lead the nation.

This, then, is the overall irony. Unlike most societies, in which political leadership is considered the key element in a nation's success, Japan appeared to have constructed a machine that operated on its own. Rigorous educational standards, elite bureaucratic guidance, a commitment to savings and investment, a fanatical attention to design and service, a team-spirit ethos determined to succeed against domestic and foreign rivals, and firm social codes regarding obedience, hierarchy, and deference have carried Japan from its 1945 nadir to where it is now. These aspects of Japan form impressive elements of strength for the future as Japan responds to the transnational global challenges. But as our increasingly complex world heads into the next century, those material and technological strengths alone may not be enough to handle the political and moral tests that lie ahead. Sophisticated robots can overcome a lot of problems, but they cannot provide a vision of how Japan itself might best operate in our global society of tomorrow. Until the Japanese come up with *sustained* political leadership that seeks to provide that vision, we are all left puzzled, troubled, and in some circles suspicious of what sort of power Japan will turn out to be in the twenty-first century.

Contributors

CRAIG GARBY, former Program Associate of the Asia Program at the Woodrow Wilson International Center for Scholars in Washington, D.C., currently is at Stanford University Law School.

MARY BROWN BULLOCK is Director of the Asia Program at the Woodrow Wilson International Center for Scholars, Washington, D.C.

HENRI-CLAUDE DE BETTIGNIES is a professor at the European Institute of Business Administration (INSEAD) in Fontainebleau and a visiting professor at Stanford University.

KOICHI HAMADA is Professor of Economics at Yale University and a visiting professor at Osaka University.

ROBERT M. IMMERMAN is Senior Research Associate of the East Asian Institute of Columbia University.

PETER J. KATZENSTEIN is the Walter S. Carpenter, Jr., Professor of International Studies at Cornell University.

PAUL KENNEDY is J. Richardson Dilworth Professor of History and Director of International Security Programs at Yale University.

LEE POH-PING is Professor of Political Science at the University of Malaya in Kuala Lumpur, Malaysia.

CARLOS J. MONETA is Director of the Asian-Pacific Center (CEAP) in Mendoza, Argentina.

NOBUO OKAWARA is an associate professor of political science at the Faculty of Law, Kyushu University.

T. J. PEMPEL is Glenn B. and Cleone Orr Hawkins Professor of Political Science at the University of Wisconsin, Madison.

SUSAN J. PHARR is Edwin O. Reischauer Professor of Japanese Politics and Director of Harvard University's Program on U.S.-Japan Relations.

KOZO YAMAMURA is the Job and Gertrude Tamaki Professor of Japanese Studies and Chair of the Japanese Studies Program at the Henry M. Jackson School of International Studies, University of Washington.

Index